# Cougars on the Cliff

# COUGARS ON THE CLIFF

*One Man's Pioneering Quest to Understand the Mythical
Mountain Lion—a Memoir*

## MAURICE HORNOCKER
### WITH
## DAVID JOHNSON

LYONS
PRESS

Essex, Connecticut

An imprint of Globe Pequot, the trade division of
The Rowman & Littlefield Publishing Group, Inc.
4501 Forbes Blvd., Ste. 200
Lanham, MD 20706
www.rowman.com

Distributed by NATIONAL BOOK NETWORK

British Library Cataloguing in Publication Information Available

**Library of Congress Cataloging-in-Publication Data**

Names: Hornocker, Maurice G., author.
Title: Cougars on the cliff : one man's pioneering quest to understand the
    mythical mountain lion—a memoir / Maurice Hornocker ; with David
    Johnson.
Description: Essex, Connecticut : Lyons Press, [2023] | Includes index. |
    Summary: "Maurice Hornocker is recognized worldwide as the first
    scientist to unravel the secrets of America's most enigmatic
    predator—the mountain lion. This is a gripping account of the
    never-before-told adventures, challenges, and controversies surrounding
    his groundbreaking study of cougars in the remote reaches of the Idaho
    Primitive Area"—Provided by publisher.
Identifiers: LCCN 2022050364 (print) | LCCN 2022050365 (ebook) | ISBN
    9781493073290 (cloth) | ISBN 9781493073306 (epub)
Subjects: LCSH: Hornocker, Maurice G. | Puma—Idaho—Idaho Primitive Area.
    | Wildlife conservation--Idaho--Idaho Primitive Area--History. |
    Wildlife conservationists—United States—Biography.
Classification: LCC QL31.H68 A3 2023  (print) | LCC QL31.H68  (ebook) | DDC
    570/.92 [B]—dc23/eng/20221221
LC record available at https://lccn.loc.gov/2022050364
LC ebook record available at https://lccn.loc.gov/2022050365

∞™ The paper used in this publication meets the minimum requirements of American National Standard for Information Sciences—Permanence of Paper for Printed Library Materials, ANSI/ NISO Z39.48-1992.

*Dedicated to my three daughters,*
*whose father's long absences in the field were*
*borne without malice and accepted with forgiveness.*
*I regret the loss of time with them in those formative years,*
*but I'm forever grateful for their understanding.*

*The lord of stealthy murder, with a heart both craven and cruel.*
—THEODORE ROOSEVELT


*Two roads diverged in a wood, and I—I took the one less traveled by,*
*And that has made all the difference.*
—ROBERT FROST


*All genuine knowledge originates in direct experience.*
—MAO TSE-TUNG

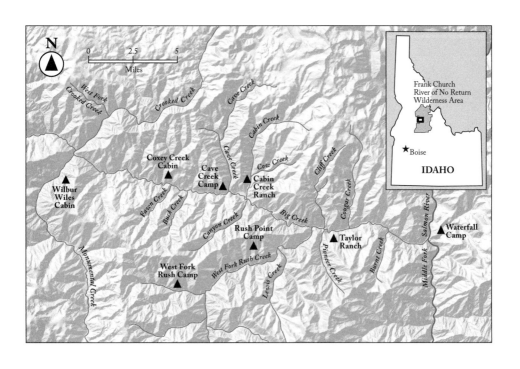

N

0    2.5    5
Miles

West Fork
Crooked Creek

Crooked Creek

Cave Creek

Cabin Creek

Coxey Creek
Cabin

Cave Creek
Camp

Cave Creek

Cow Creek

Cabin
Creek
Ranch

Cliff Creek

Wilbur
Wiles
Cabin

Fawn Creek

Back Creek

Cougar Creek

Canyon Creek

Big Creek

Salmon River

Waterfall
Camp

Rush Point
Camp

Taylor
Ranch

Monumental Creek

West Fork Rush Creek

Lewis Creek

Pioneer Creek

Burnt Creek

Middle Fork

West Fork
Rush Camp

Frank Church
River of No Return
Wilderness Area

★Boise

IDAHO

# Contents

# Preface

*When a mountain lion kills, it relies on stealth, not savagery. Instead of recklessly pursuing a fleeing elk or deer, the cat stalks until opportunity strikes, then bursts from hiding like a missile to seize the hapless prey with crushing jaws while using its forepaws to apply lethal leverage and snap the quarry's neck. That same incredibly powerful predator will also turn tail, run from a barking dog, and climb a tree to become an easy target. Human hunters have long capitalized on this behavioral incongruity to kill and ultimately push the mountain lion toward extinction. More recently, researchers began treeing the cats to save them.*

I WROTE THIS DESCRIPTION MORE THAN THREE DECADES AGO AFTER many years of cougar research in central Idaho. I'd started a book about the adventure—and stopped. Got busy with other stuff, like studying big secretive cats throughout the world.

All the while, colleagues and friends kept encouraging me to resume writing the "cougar book." But I kept setting it aside. Then I passed my ninety-first birthday and figured it was time to reboot the memoir you're about to read.

I write now as mountain lions continue to make a miraculous recovery. After decades of study by myself and many researchers who followed, wanton killing of the cats by humans has given way to science-directed management. And the cougar, an extraordinarily adaptable animal, has responded by repopulating much of its historic home range—notably without ever being officially declared threatened or endangered.

Amid this turnaround, the mountain lion's mystique lingers. So I share this never-before-told adventure story to both explore the past and lend new understanding to this great cat's aura.

Few creatures on this planet elicit the level of fascination and fear that cougars do. We hold them in awe for their embodiment of the wild. At the same time, as increasing human–cougar encounters make headlines, we dread they're out to kill us. Despite researchers' continued attempts to inform the public that these animals prefer to hunt in solitude and avoid humans, cougars remain the stuff of erroneous legend. Like a feline version of Big Foot, the mythical quality of the mountain lion lives on.

My early study of these elusive predators will always be the underpinning of the professional legacy I might leave behind and maybe the reason some people still call me "that cougar guy." In the name of science, my colleagues and I have captured, released, and followed hundreds of cougars over thousands of miles. But author Wallace Stegner, penning words I wish were mine, best captured the cougar's nimbus in his "Memo to the Mountain Lion":

> *Once, in every corner of this continent, your passing could prickle the stillness and bring every living thing to the alert. But even then you were felt more than seen. You were an imminence, a presence, a crying in the night, pug tracks in the dust of a trail. Solitary and shy, you lived beyond, always beyond. Your comings and goings defined the boundaries of the unpeopled.*

Stegner's words still prickle the now-silver hairs on the back of my neck.

Like most wildlife biologists of considerable eld (age), my name appears throughout professional journals where research findings are rendered matter-of-factually onto gray pages of print. For the most part, these are compendious narratives that include charts, graphs, data, and boiled-down conclusions. Such succinct publications are invaluable because peer-reviewed documentation is absolutely necessary to further our understanding of wild creatures that share the earth with us.

On the other hand, writing a memoir has allowed me to shed the constraints of technical writing. I've tripped my memory in this liberating exercise by poring over copious documents ranging from government agency letters and memos to newspaper articles yellowed by age. I also reexamined a decade's worth of field notes and sifted through hundreds of photographs stored in large cardboard boxes. It's been like lifting a curtain to reveal the who, what, when, where, why, and how—to borrow the journalism credo—behind scientific endeavor. It's also been a study in human behavior—not only my own and the many people who helped shed light on these enigmatic predators but also of other people who challenged the research and some who tried to sabotage it.

The Idaho cougar project, conducted between 1964 and 1973, set the stage for everything that followed in my career. The study led to my applying for and getting the position as leader of the Cooperative Wildlife Research Unit at the University of Idaho, where I served for eighteen years. Following that, I created two private nonprofit research institutes that became vehicles for continued funding and long-term studies on many wildcat species worldwide.

As a result, I've had the good fortune of laying hands on virtually all of the world's species of big cats that hunt in faraway places. I've been privileged to steal into the unpeopled environs of the world's foremost felines. And I've learned that there's little to fear about these creatures—except the fear of not learning enough to understand and save them. Healthy predator populations mean healthy ecosystems. And more work is always needed to enhance our understanding of all animals, especially those that kill for a living.

So let's rewind more than half a century to a less defined time in 1964, not necessarily to the beginning of this story but to a place where the world's first mountain lion study took root—to Idaho's wintry wilderness. It was there, in the treacherous up-and-down folds of the Payette National Forest's Big Creek drainage, that a population of mountain lions had retreated for survival and I naively set out to unravel their secrets.

# PART I
# THE FIRST SEASON

## CHAPTER ONE

# Big Country

WE HUNTED LIKE WOLVES CHURNING THROUGH HEAVY SNOW, ONE IN front of the other breaking trail, then switching off to save energy. It was late afternoon, Christmas Day 1964. A single mountain lion, the second in what would become a decade-long quest, had been captured, tagged, and released hours earlier. Our two redbone hounds, their frenzied bays echoing in the canyons below, were chasing a third cat in the bluffs above.

Late December 1964, Idaho Primitive Area: trekking with full packs toward Horse Mountain early in the study.

Then, in waning daylight, the landslide struck.

It began typically, stones skipping loose far above us, perhaps dislodged by the pursuing hounds, then slabs of rock and snow sliding downhill, followed by boulders and snapped-off trees. Within seconds, the entire top of Horse Mountain seemed bent on burying us. Up to our rumps in snow, already exhausted by the pursuit, furious that our hounds had left the tree and allowed possibly two errant mountain lions to escape, Wilbur Wiles and I were instantly faced with a force too powerful to flee. The advancing rumble built to a loud groan. Trees were now being uprooted. The earth rolled underfoot. The onslaught became a thunderous roar. It was impossible to tell from where the landslide, bolstered by tons of avalanching snow, was descending, only that it was charging down in our direction. No time to run. Frankly, no will to run. It was as if the long day of chasing mountain lions had drained us of any idea of how to escape. If the earth was about to deliver death, there seemed no way to evade it. So we stood our ground, anchored on a precarious trail that cut across the steep slope, sharing a silent wish that the hurtling onrush from above would spill ahead, behind—anywhere but on us.

Instinctively, I turned my back, looked downhill, and crouched—as if the fifty-pound pack I carried might offer some protection. Wilbur did the same. In retrospect, I suspect there is no better place for two men to consummate a lasting respect for one another than in the path of a full-blown avalanche.

And then, as quickly as it started, the landslide lunged past us some fifty yards ahead, totally erasing the sparse path we'd been following and taking a chunk of ground the size of a downtown parking lot in tow, retrieving its fury as the roar subsided to a rumble, then a groan, and finally the staccato of settling stones. Afternoon light had given way to dusk. All was silent—except for the crashing of my heart and the distant baying of Duke and Chub somewhere above, still on the trail of the cougars we'd been following.

"My . . . my god," I stammered as I turned toward Wilbur.

"Rockslide," he flatly replied. "Avalanche. Take your choice."

I gawked. There Wilbur stood in his wool clothing, his steady breaths visible in the bitter cold—this quintessential master of understatement stationed within spitting distance of what could have caused instant death, this rawhide-tough contemporary mountain man I was beginning to know as a friend and would eventually consider kin, this woods-wise oracle of precise words gradually unfolding a matter-of-fact grin that came with knowing how big country can swallow the foolhardy.

"Time to quit," he said with a deadpan expression.

Looking back on that Christmas Day nearly six decades ago, it's still hard to explain how something as harrowing as an avalanche would eventually pale in significance to what the next decade would bring. We had come to the rugged, often intimidating, sometimes sinister, always awesome backcountry of central Idaho to attempt something virtually everyone said was impossible—study mountain lions on their own turf. Too secretive. Too aloof. Too enigmatic. Too dangerous. Frankly, too challenging to collar with any real scientific understanding, said the doubters. And we were doing it in the depth of winter, with snow piling up daily, making a bad situation even worse.

But the same snow that seemed to be forever collapsing on the high country and impeding our travel was necessary. Today's telemetry technology wasn't available. And even though we'd be first to radio-collar mountain lions six years later and be able to follow them year-round, we initially worked only in winter and relied solely on snow for trailing and scent hounds to tree this mystifying animal that some people claimed to have heard "screaming like a lunatic" in the wilderness. The cats wouldn't come to us. We had to go to them. In many ways, Wilbur and I felt like pioneers trailblazing our way into a vast unknown. Or were we foolhardy dreamers?

I remember hiking in Montana, long before studying mountain lions ever crossed my mind—on the Bitterroot Divide, looking off into the seemingly endless mountains of Idaho. Around Missoula, Montana, people talked about "Idaho Country" as if legendary mountain men balked at entering. It's that intimidating. All you have to do today is park your car atop Lolo Pass on U.S. Highway 12, take a short hike, look west, and you'll understand. The country hasn't changed. It still gives me pause. In

Montana, you see the eastern slopes of the Bitterroot Range. You see valleys, gorgeous foothills, and I love it all. But Idaho lends perspective. It is so big and so vast, and you just feel those mountains go on forever—perhaps beyond imagination—or at least to the Big Creek drainage where we'd established a study area pocked with makeshift camps and stored provisions to ensure our survival.

In the 1950s and into the 1960s, very little carnivore research was being done, especially on large carnivores. Most of the wildlife investigations were on trophy game species like deer, elk, and moose. The ungulates had big recreational, monetary, and, in some cases, subsistence value. Predators, on the other hand, were dismissed as bad with no positive benefit. So my aim with mountain lions was to mark all individuals in a distinct population unit, then study the makeup of that population and its function in the environment. This had never been attempted.

We traversed the country by foot, often on snowshoes. Horses were no match for winter in the mountains. Snowmobiles, although becoming available, weren't an option because we worked within the Idaho Primitive Area, eventually to be designated by Congress under the federal Wilderness Act to remain void of internal combustion engines and mechanized travel modes. We relied on our legs, feet, and lungs, and the intake of calories necessary, to drive us beyond exhaustion in this first-ever attempt to understand mountain lion ecology.

From a logistics standpoint, the study area's many creek drainages offered both corridors of entry into the high country and a labyrinth of confusing ridges to negotiate. Big Creek tumbled from west to east for some thirty-five miles, paralleled by a U.S. Forest Service–maintained hiking trail. Tributaries flowed from north and south into Big Creek along its length like veins to the midrib of a leaf. These secondary creeks, dubbed over the years with names like Monumental, Acorn, Coxey, Cabin, Cave, Pioneer, Cliff, Cougar, Goat, and others, twisted down through steep canyons. Each stream added to a massive amount of water that for eons expelled annually into the Middle Fork of the Salmon River of No Return before gushing out of Idaho via the Snake River toward the Pacific Ocean. Amid this ragged network of peaks, valleys, ridges, and canyons, we hunted what was arguably the most ghost-like member of the world's big cats. Describing these hunts, with all their twists and turns, was as difficult then as it is now. If you feel lost, stick with us. Lots of times, Wilbur and I felt the same way.

The first month of hunting for these incredibly secretive cats left me haunted by the skeptics' predictions. We had gone four weeks without even seeing a cougar. Our early inability to get our hands on one of these magnificent predators challenged my resolve. After all, it was my big idea.

But two days before the avalanche hit, fortune took the proverbial good turn. Wilbur, who had been living and hunting alone in the Primitive Area for more than two decades, and I were working our way up Cave Creek when we made a big, broad loop around a ridge. Sure enough, we hit a cougar track in the snow. It was fairly fresh, and despite a steady rain that had been falling all morning, the dogs, yowling with excitement after being set free from their leashes, began trailing the cat. Up into steep rimrock country they disappeared, following the scent. Suddenly, Duke and Chub erupted into a barking frenzy that meant only one thing: the cat, the study's first, was treed.

In preparation for the project in Idaho, I'd done some postgraduate work on cougars while at the University of Montana, hoping to refine the capture, tranquilizing, marking, and recapture of individual lions. Questions abounded: What drug would be most effective? It had to tranquilize rather than immobilize the cat high in a tree. Falling could injure or kill the mountain lion. Would the drug's effect last long enough for us to safely handle the lion? Could we safely climb trees and lower tranquilized lions to the ground? Answers to these questions and others were crucial to the success of the Idaho project. Ultimately, my Montana mountain lion work enabled me to work with a tranquilizer gun and learn how to extract woozy cougars from trees to be examined, tagged, and released.

Wilbur had never really handled a live mountain lion. But he'd killed many of them for a bounty payment, and I hired him to work on the study not because he shared my hunch that these cats were as much misunderstood as they were maligned but because I was told that Wilbur Wiles and his dogs could do something better than anyone else—tree cougars.

During the first month of the study, I was stuck in classrooms finishing doctoral requirements at the University of British Columbia (UBC) in Vancouver. Assuming an administrative role, I tried to stay in touch with Wilbur via backcountry radiophone or through letters dropped by bush pilots. But communication was sporadic, and I often felt left in the dark. So I was thrilled to temporarily leave the academic setting; board a Cessna 180 on December 12, 1964; and bounce to a landing at Taylor Ranch, a private property within the Idaho Primitive Area. I planned to spend the university's holiday break catching mountain lions. The next day, filled with anticipation, I hiked up the Big Creek trail about eight miles to another private inholding called Cabin Creek Ranch, our initial headquarters.

The news wasn't good. Wilbur and assistant Mike Stephen had failed to capture any mountain lions. Mike and I worked together on grizzly bears in Yellowstone National Park, and he had agreed to help Wilbur when I was away at graduate school. Morale, to say the least, had ebbed by the time I got there. Just pushing yourself up, over, and around the mountains of central Idaho during winter, when snow depths could exceed fifteen feet in places and winds could whip up drifts too deep to measure, was a chore. To expend such energy and fall so far short of our goals was disheartening.

"Enough to contemplate leaving the sleeping bag zipped up around ya come morning," Mike said. "We've been pushing hard every day."

"And no luck," I lamented.

"The cats are out there," Wilbur assured us. "They're sneaky. But they don't just disappear."

And so, with no better plan than to keep fighting the odds, we mustered what enthusiasm we could. The three of us decided Mike would take a break and walk the eight miles back down Big Creek to meet the weekly mail plane and recoup at Taylor Ranch. At daybreak the next morning, Wilbur and I were off.

Nine days later, after sleeping with the hounds one night to stay warm in thirty-degrees-below-zero weather and scouring back and forth between Coxey, Garden, Lime, and Acorn creeks and finally Cave Creek, we stumbled onto the tracks that led to the study's first mountain lion.

"This is really fresh," Wilbur said as the hounds, picking up hot scent, strained into their leashes. We followed the tethered dogs as they pulled emphatically through drifts, over rock outcroppings, and into a ravine where the cougar had stalked and killed a coyote. The short story was written in the snow. Exploding from under a fir tree, the cougar bounded downhill about seventy yards and executed a devastating attack, ripping the top of the coyote's head off and disemboweling it before devouring meat from the neck and shoulders. The mountain lion then buried the carcass under a tangle of crusty snow, pine needles, and other forest debris.

"Never seen that before," Wilbur said, as if witnessing poetic justice. Like most people in those days, he was convinced that cougars were indiscriminate killers. They'd eat virtually anything they could, including other cougars and the fattest elk and deer available. They'd also eat cattle, horses, dogs, domestic cats, and probably little children given a chance—or so the thinking went back then. But by eating a varmint coyote, Wilbur figured, the mountain lion had at least registered some good.

"Interesting," I said, carefully poking through the coyote remains. Wilbur looked at me inquisitively, then turned to Duke and Chub, who showed little interest in the coyote but were eager to trail the cougar.

"I better release them now," Wilbur said, "if we want to get that cat."

The hounds blasted away, and within half an hour, they treed the cougar about twenty feet up a fir tree. Wilbur and I plodded uphill, contoured around a bluff, and arrived exhausted as the dogs were trying to climb the tree after the cat. The mountain lion—twenty feet up on a heavy limb looking down, its tawny-brown body wrapped halfway around the tree's trunk, heavy tail twitching, face seemingly etched by nature into an exquisite mask with black and white highlights, brilliant yellow-brown eyes locked on the dogs below—appeared beguiled by the building commotion. Wilbur put leashes back on the hounds and tied them aside as they bayed incessantly. Amid the cacophony, I prepared to process the cat.

"It's staying put," Wilbur confirmed, maintaining a vigil at the base of the tree.

"Judging by its size," I said, "I think it's a female."

"Probably," Wilbur agreed.

"She looks almost cooperative."

"They feel safe in trees," Wilbur said.

Tranquilizer gun loaded, I took a breath, aimed, squeezed the trigger, and managed to hit the cougar with one dart in the left hindquarter.

"Good shot," Wilbur said.

Anticipation built as we waited for the study's first mountain lion to lose its sense of place and time. Within fifteen minutes, she appeared wobbly, slipping slightly but maintaining a grip. And then suddenly, without an inkling of what was about to happen, we were astonished to see her spring from the tree, land on her feet in the snow with barely a sound, and disappear downhill in four graceful leaps.

"There she goes!" I yelled over the hounds' frantic barking. What we didn't know was that the syringe had malfunctioned and that only half the dose of drug had been injected.

Wilbur released the dogs, and they made short work of tracking the half-numb cat, catching up with her in the creek bottom. The hounds took turns nipping at the lioness. Despite being partially tranquilized, she held her own. Down the creek bottom we all ran, the cougar leaping away when it could find an opening, the dogs slashing from behind, Wilbur and I clambering to keep pace. We looked like the Keystone Cops playing animal control officers. Eventually, the cougar scrambled partway up another fir tree, only to lose her grip and tumble limply to the ground.

"Got 'em," Wilbur shouted as he intercepted the hounds and snapped leashes to their collars.

"I think she's fine," I said, easing through the snow toward the cat.

"Careful," Wilbur warned.

I crept closer and closer to the prone lioness, slipped a rope around her hindfoot, pulled it tight, and, with a syringe, reached out to inject another ten milligrams of drug into her hip. The chase was over.

"You know, I've treed a lot of cats in this exact spot," Wilbur said through shortened breaths as the dogs continued to frantically lunge for the downed prey and I began to collect myself. The lioness lay peacefully now on the ground, and I looked up from admiring her. We had come some fifteen miles on this hunt, slogging through heavy, wet snow. The East Fork of Cave Creek coursed within view, and a sheer bluff rose above us. Even today, Idaho holds the most classified wilderness in the United States outside of Alaska. It's as if someone snatched up the middle of a tablecloth the size of Texas with one hand and let it fall in a crumpled pile. That's central Idaho—a convoluted fabric of rock and earth folded by chance into a geological maze of towering ridges and deep canyons. Time alters little in places like this. The bluff, the creek, the mountain lion—they were all part of something to which I, Wilbur, the dogs, and the rest of civilization would never belong. Yet here we were. If we could learn about and understand the mysterious cougars in their hostile domain, I thought, then perhaps we'd all be better off—especially the mountain lions.

Time to get back to work. First, we measured and weighed the cat, easing her up in a net hung from a spring scale anchored to a stout tree limb. "One hundred three pounds," I said while recording the weight in my notes. We took blood and hair samples, tattooed her ears, and affixed both with cattle tags and streamers. We loosely snugged a color-coded nylon rope collar around her neck. Finally, we removed her from the net and placed her, resting, on some dry slabs of bark. We watched as mountain lion No. 1 became more alert, and then we left her alone. When we returned the next day, she was gone, never to be recaptured or seen again.

We captured No. 2 a couple days later—on that Christmas morning several hours before the avalanche hit. After going up a ridge between Cow and Cabin creeks, we hiked through a saddle into the Calf Creek drainage and then over a ridge into the Spring Creek area.

At the bottom of the drainage, we surprised two cougars on an elk kill. The cats fled as we approached and before we actually saw them. The hounds followed their scent and treed one a short distance away about fifteen feet up a small fir tree. It was a young tom, and this time, the darting and processing came off without a hitch. The cat was a powerfully built male, and I gave it a gentle stroke behind the ears before leaving it to recover from the drug and slink away.

Enter a comedy of errors.

After we dealt with cougar No. 2, Wilbur put the dogs on the track of what we hoped would be No. 3, and the hounds spent more than an hour leading us around Horse Mountain. We struggled to follow as the dogs' distant barking gave us a read on their ever-changing location. Suddenly, Duke and Chub were barking treed: filling the canyons with excited yips and prolonged howling. It was their way of announcing that the chase was over, with the cat seeking refuge in a tall tree. Wilbur and I plowed on for another thirty minutes through deepening snow, every step a painful attempt to gain altitude, only to discover that Duke had left the tree and took the pup with him. Not surprisingly, the cougar had scrambled down and run off.

"Damn," Wilbur scoffed angrily as his breath billowed like smoke in the cold air. Although nearly out of breath, I shared Wilbur's disappointment. Then, farther up the mountain, another painstaking climb away, the dogs barked treed again. Channeling our frustration into another surge of energy, we worked our way over and around some of the roughest terrain on Horse Mountain to finally find Duke and Chub, without the cougar, wagging their tails at our arrival.

"Damn dogs," Wilbur grumbled before urging Chub back on the track and coaxing Duke to follow. We combed the whole mountainside again before the dogs cut loose for a third time. That's when we heard the first tumbling stones signaling the start of the landslide.

"Now it's really time to quit," Wilbur declared as both hounds came to heel after the landslide spared us. Dogs leashed again, we slowly made our way down a trail toward Cabin Creek as it grew dark. I flicked on my flashlight and hobbled along, entertaining thoughts of warm food, maybe a touch of mind-altering drink, and a cot in a warm cabin to cradle my weariness. As we continued, my fatigue built and eventually verged on debilitation. Every bone, muscle, and nerve in me began to scream. At about the halfway mark, I stopped.

"I've had it," I confessed. Wilbur slowly wheeled around and beamed his flashlight on me. I was thirty-four years old and spent. Fifteen years my senior, Wilbur still had a full head of steam.

"Go ahead without me. I'll make it back on my own," I said. After spending three months inside classrooms at sea level, I lacked physical conditioning. I was unprepared for the demands of the high-altitude mountains, a heavy pack, and traveling on snowshoes.

"You sure about staying here alone?" Wilbur grilled me. "We can wait."

"I'm sure," I fibbed.

In retrospect, it would have been wise asking Wilbur to wait. But he didn't argue. Like I said, Wilbur wasn't the loquacious sort.

"Rest. Then, easy does it. Stay on the trail," he instructed, disappearing with his hounds into the darkness. I can still hear their muffled footsteps and Wilbur, no longer upset with the dogs he tough-loved so much, encouraging Duke and Chub, "Come on boys, let's go home."

Nighttime was now my only companion. I sat with the flashlight, my butt plopped on my discarded pack, wondering if I could gather some gumption. The day's exertion had taxed me beyond my abilities. I switched the flashlight off, leaned back in the dark against the base of a tree, and thought about family: my wife Shirley and our three girls back home on Christmas Day without their dad. It wasn't their first and surely not the last sacrifice they'd make. I thought about the two mountain lions we'd caught and the one we hadn't and about the enormous responsibility associated with this study and that my career hinged on completing it. So early in the research, we seemed pitted against insurmountable odds. Then I thought about how mysterious and majestic those first two cougars appeared looking down after we'd chased them up trees. I tilted my head back to see stars in the ink-black sky piercing down at me through ragged limbs. I closed my eyes, as if looking inside my beleaguered body for solace.

Gradually, I felt as if the wilderness, after challenging me, had finally accepted my presence, offering more comfort than defiance. I began to feel better—not great but good enough to get up and straighten my stiff knees. I took some deep breaths, eased the pack onto my back, and tightened the waist belt. I cinched the shoulder straps tight, took a few more breaths, reached for energy I wasn't sure I had, and then walked. I walked alone and slowly but determinedly until almost midnight when I arrived at Cabin

Creek, where Wilbur offered a warm glass of water laced with sugar and honey to bring back some energy and jump-start my resolve.

"Sorry," I apologized.

"I knew ya'd make it," Wilbur said, looking me straight in the eye. "You're toughening up."

I'd like to say that I turned in that night with a feeling of satisfaction and renewed anticipation, that it would be easy to unzip the sleeping bag come morning because we'd finally collared two cougars, that the study was truly under way, and that I slept like a content child cuddling a stuffed animal. But my racing mind overpowered my ability to doze off. I kept thinking about the mountain lions and how much work it was to collar only two. The idea was to capture many and as many times as possible. How else could we understand cougar population dynamics and their impact on prey animals? I couldn't shake the word that professional biologists, even my mentors, had uttered—*impossible*.

Then I heard Wilbur ease into a steady snore from across the darkened room. Firelight slipped out of a crack in the woodburning stove and flickered on the cabin ceiling. In the outside world, Lyndon B. Johnson was president, the Beatles' song "I Feel Fine" was topping the music charts, and G.I. Joe was the most popular Christmas toy for American boys. I thought again about my young daughters unwrapping their Christmas gifts. I missed them. My body still aching, my mind finally going numb, I sighed and surrendered to sleep.

Some eight miles away on Horse Mountain, perhaps protected by a rocky outcrop or under cover of a wind-buffering tree, a large male mountain lion also rested. Although he had deftly eluded his would-be captors earlier that day, it would be a short-lived reprieve. Soon he would become cougar No. 3 and, for good reason, be named Rex, as in Tyrannosaurus Rex—but not before the big tom, his entire primal being laser focused on me from two feet away, snarled in my face and glared into my eyes as if declaring, "Go ahead. Collar me, if you can."

CHAPTER TWO

# "The More Ya Learn"

ONE THING FOR CERTAIN: IF COUGARS ROARED LIKE AFRICAN LIONS, Wilbur Wiles and I would have had a much easier time. Instead of trekking up and down steep mountains in hip-deep snow searching for cougar tracks, we might have hiked a few miles up a creek drainage, sat down, paused for Wilbur to kindle his pipe, and cocked our ears to the hills. When we heard a roar, we'd simply gather up our packs and close in with the hounds.

Interestingly enough, apex cats are differentiated into two categories: those that roar and those that purr. African lions, tigers, leopards, and jaguars roar but can't purr. Cougars, bobcats, lynxes, house cats, and all other felines purr but can't roar. It's got everything to do with anatomy. Roaring cats have a stretchy ligament attached to a flexible hyoid bone in the larynx, allowing for a deep roar. Purring cats have ossified hyoids and two-way vocal folds that generate purrs. While roarers (subfamily Pantherinae) might vocally expose themselves, cougars and other wild members of the subfamily Felinae shy away with their purring and are rarely seen by anyone. Like all cats, mountain lions will caterwaul, a wailing vocalization usually associated with breeding behavior.

When Wilbur, his hounds, and I took to the woods in 1964, spurious tales about cougars roaring, screaming, and wantonly killing wildlife, livestock, and humans were common. Remember, this was only three years after novelist Woodrow Wilson Rawls wrote his classic coming-of-age children's novel *Where the Red Fern Grows*, in which a baleful mountain lion dubbed the "devil cat of the Ozarks" attacks young Billy Coleman and his two redbone coonhounds. Such villainous depictions of mountain lions had long been perpetuated by numerous luminaries, including an admired president of the United States. Teddy Roosevelt, a self-described conservationist who led the charge to establish our National Park System, was once obsessed with killing mountain lions. He labeled cougars the "big horse-killing cat, the destroyer of the deer, the lord of stealthy murder." His disdain was underscored in a January 1901 letter to one of his children where he described the bloody dispatch of a mountain lion by his own hands while hunting in Colorado:

> *I ran in and stabbed him behind the shoulder, thrusting the knife you loaned me right into his heart. I have always wished to kill a cougar as I did this one, with dogs and the knife.*

Roosevelt, who eventually championed the role of all wildlife predators, wasn't alone in his earlier misinformed notions and actions. From before the turn of the twentieth century through the 1950s, many people longed to kill cougars for the thrill, the trophy, or the money. Most states offered bounties for dead mountain lions. Idaho had stopped paying bounties by the time Wilbur and I began scouring the Big Creek drainage to study cats. But Wilbur had garnered his share of premiums for dead cougars, and apologizing never crossed his mind. I never held it against him either.

After all, cougars were ubiquitous throughout the country until European settlers marched from east to west establishing their own omnipresence. Pioneers ventured into the unexplored world, and North America's big three predators—grizzlies, wolves, and mountain lions—were indiscriminately persecuted and slaughtered, the big bears and pack canines almost to extinction. Cougars were also licentiously killed. But because of their independent, secretive ways, survivors managed to slink away into areas that most humans found uninhabitable and often inaccessible.

The Big Creek drainage was such a place—a darned good hideout for a stealthy cat, not to mention a lone wolf like Wilbur. He learned how to hunt Big Creek cougars after enduring the Great Depression and driving west in a Model T Ford "to see the mountains." He ended up in the Idaho Primitive Area, staked out a mining claim, and moved into an abandoned cabin on lower Monumental Creek. There he embraced a solely independent lifestyle. In addition to prospecting for gold and mining opal to make ends meet, he hunted wild game for food and used his cougar hounds to help him collect bounties.

"Never ate one," he quipped about killing mountain lions. "Tasted but didn't have the stomach for more."

I saw my first mountain lion in the late 1950s after coming west for college. It was dead and hanging unceremoniously head down from a rope attached to an eave outside the Montana Fish and Game Department office in Missoula. A small, admiring crowd had gathered. Montana's bounty had done a pretty good job of eradicating mountain lions. So when hunters brought the sleek female in to collect their money, the by-then-rare trophy made news, and the carcass appeared in a photograph on the front page of what was then called the *Daily Missoulian*. For the uninitiated like me, the lifeless lioness was evidence that the old saw was still alive: the only good cougar was a dead cougar. I began to wonder if such marauding monsters really roamed the wilds with impunity.

Eight years after I saw that lynched cougar, Wilbur and I woke at Cabin Creek ready to pursue our third mountain lion and resume the scientific quest for answers. Mike Stephen had come back from Taylor Ranch to join us.

"Hungry?" Wilbur asked as I pried myself from the sleeping bag, my still-sore body barking with every move.

"Famished," I responded, easing my legs down into a sitting position on the cot, then standing to see Wilbur, hovering over the wood cookstove, pouring Bisquick into a smoky frying pan.

A slender, muscular man with long, chiseled facial features and close-cropped hair, Wilbur stood about my height, around five feet nine inches, and tipped the scale, like me, at about 160 pounds. He made breakfast the way he lived life: efficiently and with little conversation. I suppose most people who live alone in remote places would be

Mornings started with the crackle of firewood in the sheepherder stove and Wilbur or the author making Bisquick pancakes.

practiced as such. Accepting his silence as routine, I stayed mostly mum, got dressed in my woolens, gathered assorted gear, and then pulled up a wooden chair at a wooden table to a spread of elk steak, pancakes, and hot coffee that Wilbur had placed on the table.

"Good sleep. Plenty to eat," Wilbur said, stepping away from the stove to join Mike and me. "That's the key to survival back here." His chair's legs grumbled on the wooden floor as he sat down.

The Cabin Creek cabin and another cabin eight miles downstream at Taylor Ranch initially served as dual headquarters. Access to each was by foot along the thirty-five-mile river-grade trail or via air into backcountry landing strips at each site. The pilots who shuffled us in and out of this dangerous country known for swirling winds and dicey landing strip approaches were, in my estimation, an elite bunch of skilled artists who earned every dollar they made with each successful landing.

Early on, in addition to the two headquarters cabins, we had five wall tent camps located strategically throughout the study area. We fully stocked all these camps with food, extra clothing, sleeping bags, cots, and other gear in October before snowfall. Collectively, we called all seven locations "home." They provided much needed shelter and warmth during the brutal winter.

"I think we should go up the creek, maybe cut tracks of that cat we missed," Wilbur said.

"Mmm," I agreed, still working on breakfast.

Wilbur paused before eating. "That cougar eatin' a coyote, that still intrigues me. You'd think they'd avoid each other, you know, like cats and dogs."

"Probably the cougar just taking advantage of opportunity," I suggested.

"I suppose," Wilbur said, poking at his breakfast before digging in. "The more ya learn, the more ya learn ya don't know."

"Einstein quote?" I asked.

"Not exactly . . . more of a paraphrase."

"Then . . . a Wilburism!"

Wilbur grinned. "I suppose."

I'd already learned to listen when Wilbur spoke. And at this point in what would become a ten-year project, this latest "Wilburism" absolutely punctuated our circumstances. We humans knew very little about mountain lions. Wilbur knew how to track them, how to tree them, how to kill them quickly and efficiently. I knew how to drug, mark, and begin to collect information about them. But neither of us—nor anyone else in the world for that matter—knew a thing about cougar population dynamics and ecology, nothing about their interactions with prey animals other than killing and eating, nothing about how many cougars lived in the mountains and canyons surrounding us, not a thing about how many elk, deer, and God knows what else they were killing. If stubborn rumors were to be believed, deer and elk populations were being decimated by ever-growing numbers of cougars.

In addition, we didn't have a clue about the human firestorm we'd ignite as word of our work filtered its way into the outside world. We knew nothing about the public uproar and political tumult ahead. Wilbur and I had teamed up not to stir controversy but to unravel mysteries. And there was something Zen about our unlikely union. Coincidentally, he grew up about 100 miles from where I was raised. We were both Iowa farm kids. He, like me, had roamed the Iowa hills and valleys hunting and trapping. We'd played baseball in high school. He spent four years in the military. So did I—he in World War II, me in the Korean War.

The big difference was that Wilbur came to Big Creek with a high school education to make a living off the land. I came with an intense curiosity about mountain lions and the objective of earning a doctorate degree.

And so far, Wilbur was schooling me.

"No elk back here when I first arrived," he said. "Saw the first in 1951."

"Probably worked their way down from northern Idaho," I said. "I read about where they were introduced, up around Bovill."

"Yeah, I hear they brought 'em by train from Wyoming, loaded in boxcars."

"Yup," I confirmed. "There are photos of herds in a corral, waiting to be released."

"Hmm," Wilbur cogitated.

Cougars, on the other hand, had probably inhabited the Big Creek drainage for centuries, living off an ancient mule deer population, bighorn sheep, mountain goats, rodents, and other mammals. The difference in the mid-1960s was that Big Creek cougars had become remnant representatives of the vast populations that once covered the Americas from east to west, north to south.

Wilbur lived alone in his cabin among these surviving mountain lions. I was a visitor with family on the outside. My wife, Shirley, and I lived with our three young daughters in a modern three-bedroom house—a temporary college rental home—in Vancouver, British Columbia.

"I've missed Christmas with my family by design," I said as we finished breakfast. "Shirley and I agreed that I'd have to concentrate on this study. Still, it's tough to be away."

Wilbur got up from the table, addressing my lament with a small nod. "I'll get the dogs. You get the packs, okay?"

With the always excited hounds tethered to Wilbur, often in front, sometimes behind, we carried backpacks weighed down by research gear and emergency equipment, including space blankets for temporary camping, extra pairs of mitts and gloves, and each an extra wool shirt and pairs of wool socks. We were fans of wool. Gore-Tex was still five years away from being invented. Wool soaked up moisture but never lost its insulating qualities.

"Get wet, still stay warm," Wilbur said.

We tied climbing spurs (the kind utility company linemen and lumberjacks used) and ropes to our packs for extracting drugged lions from trees. I had cloth kits custom-sewn to carry the drugs. One of us carried a spring scale that could be suspended from a tree limb to weigh the drowsy cats resting in lightweight hammock-like netting. We had measuring tapes and a Cap-Chur gun for darting the cats. We had binoculars, and I always carried at least one camera. Fully loaded, our packs weighed between thirty-five and fifty pounds.

"What kind ya got there?" Wilbur asked when he first saw my new aluminum-exterior-frame backpack.

"Kelty. Top of the line," I said.

"Hmm," pondered Wilbur, eyeing my purchase like it was dime-store cowboy stuff. He chose to wrap his gear in canvas and lash everything to an old olive-green military pack board.

"You can use it, when I leave," I offered. "It's pretty handy."

"Oh, thanks. But I probably won't need it."

As we set out that morning after Christmas, Wilbur heaved his old military pack to his shoulders, and I hoisted my state-of-the-art version. About a month later, after I'd returned to my family and graduate school classes in Vancouver, Wilbur sent me a letter. Inside was a $40 check and a brief, handwritten note: "Would you order me one of those packs?" I did, and he used it for the duration of the study.

The study area was approximately 200 square miles, mostly within the Big Creek drainage that lies within the 2,000-square-mile Idaho Primitive Area. If you look at a relief map, the mountainous location is pretty much smack dab in the middle of Idaho and includes portions of the Payette, Salmon, Boise, and Challis national forests. It's all public land with a few private inholdings, mostly old mining claims. To this day, there are no roads, and all of it is designated by the U.S. Congress as "untrammeled" wilderness, "where man is a visitor who does not remain."

Its main water course, the Salmon River, is known as the "River of No Return." It and its Middle Fork and South Fork tributaries cut deeply into the Idaho Batholith, a composite mass of granite rock that extends more than 200 miles from north to south and is seventy-five miles wide.

Big Creek, one of the Middle Fork's major tributaries, flows from west to east. The final twenty-eight miles of Big Creek drop sixty feet with each mile, eventually descending to 3,400 feet above sea level at its mouth. Mountain peaks within the Big Creek drainage rise to nearly 9,500 feet. Up, down, around, and over this massive complex, we would trek by foot the next decade for more than 10,000 miles. On December 26, 1964, it's fair to say that as we leashed Wilbur's two hounds and made last-minute checks of equipment, we were at the beginning of the beginning of our quest.

"Let's hunt up toward Brown's Basin," Wilbur suggested, and I had no reason to disagree. "Maybe take another look at where we got that second cat and maybe bump into the third one that got away."

The day wore on, and by the time we made it around Rough Canyon, tracks in the snow told yesterday's story—or at least hinted at the plot. The female with two or three kittens we'd encountered earlier had apparently brought her family back down and crossed Big Creek, then returned up Canyon Creek, over the ridge, and back to yesterday's kill site. I'd already taken a jawbone from the young cow elk after the cougar had covered the carcass with snow, needles, and other debris. Throughout the study, we collected the mandibles off kills to estimate age of the prey. We also inspected bone marrow to gauge overall health.

Cat No. 2, judging from the tracks, had recovered from the drug, walked uphill about fifty yards to rest under a big fir tree, then nosed around the area where we had weighed, measured, and tagged him. Then he returned to the site of his earlier kill.

"Two possibilities," I said. "Either there's a female running with three big kittens, one being the tom we caught . . . or it's the tom alone and the female with two kittens."

Through sifting snow, I looked at Wilbur for affirmation. He nodded and looked up to survey the unsettled weather. Increasing flurries and wind began bearing down on us. "This is good sheep country up here," he said. "The cats could be up there, too, hunting. But we best go back. Too late to turn the dogs loose anyway."

The next morning, while Wilbur tended to his hounds and Mike washed clothes at Cabin Creek, I hiked down the trail to Taylor Ranch, collected more supplies, and returned in time for dinner as the sky cleared.

"No tracks between here and Taylor," I announced.

"So, you're planning to fly out tomorrow, right Maurice?" Wilbur asked.

"As soon as the weather breaks and they can fly in," I said. "Radio-phoned McCall from the ranch, and they said it was fogged in." When we woke the next morning, with still only two cats collared and released, snow was pummeling down. No airplanes would be landing anytime soon. I was beginning to learn that everything in this remote place progressed just as it was formed—at an evolutionary pace. Sometimes you only needed to wait for things to settle out. Reaction was just as important as being proactive. Plan ahead but always have a plan B.

"Let's go up Cow Creek today," Wilbur said. "Weather might break in that direction." Wilbur's plan B turned out to be a good one.

## Chapter Three

# Rex

Wilbur, Mike, and I cut lion tracks in no time. The prints, embedded in crusty snow, revealed that two or three cats had crossed over from Calf Creek. But it was unclear if the cougars might be a lioness

Cougar tracks in the snow not only led to captures but also offered evidence about mountain lion behavior, including depredation on elk and mule deer herds.

with one or two mature kittens or adults traveling alone in the same area.

"One or two days old," Wilbur said as Duke and Chub's eagerness rattled through their chain leashes. The dogs had caught cat scent and knew a chase was imminent. With the hounds still leashed and pulling steadfastly ahead, we followed the tracks up to the crest of Cow Creek, then down, over, and up to the Cabin Creek ridge. The tracks dropped again into the creek bottom and up a draw on the other side. Now the hounds were thrusting even harder, their leashes taut, their initial excited whimpers becoming frantic barks as we rounded a bluff. "I'm turning 'em loose!" Wilbur shouted to Mike and me as we fought to keep pace.

The dogs sped away and within minutes were baying treed. The commotion built as we tried to close in before Duke, Chub, and this third cougar had an altercation. Hopefully, all three were locked in a stalemate—mountain lion looking down from the tree at the two barking, jumping hounds below.

"The lion, it's in that tree!" Wilbur shouted while trying to secure the hounds.

I huffed my way past him to the base of a huge yellow pine and looked up. The cat, much bigger than the other two we'd captured and tagged, glared down from about twenty-five feet above—motionless except for a miffed whip of its long, heavy tail. Based on its large size, we felt certain the cat was a male.

"I'll climb," I said, easing the pack off my shoulders, detaching my spurs, lashing the wide upper straps around my calves, then gathering rope for lowering the cougar to the ground. Wilbur had managed to tie the dogs aside by the time I loaded the Cap-Chur gun with a Sernylyn-dosed dart. The drug would relax but not anesthetize the cat.

"Nice and easy," I whispered to myself while pumping the pneumatic gun several times. "Take your time. He's not going anywhere." I inhaled, aimed, exhaled, and squeezed the trigger. The dart hit his shoulder, causing the tom to barely flinch. I lowered the gun, and we waited ten minutes, then a bit longer to make sure enough calming drug was pumping through his system.

"He should be settled down by now," I said.

"Let's go then," said Wilbur. "Get him while he's numb."

I scrambled quickly up the tree, then slowed down as a thicket of limbs got in the way. Little by little, I weaved up through the branches and drew closer to our third mountain lion, driving each spur deep into the tree trunk with each upward step. Eventually, I was close enough to hear a low rumble emanating from the mountain lion's throat. His tail twitched once, then twice. I assumed the drug was holding him in check and hoped to reach up, gently grasp his tail, loop a rope around a hind-foot, ease him off the limb, and lower him to the ground. But just as I reached for the tail, the tom lunged, and his head came ripping around the tree trunk, causing shards of bark to explode. We were face to face, me looking slightly up, him glowering down, his nose within two feet of mine.

"Heeees," the cat snarled while flashing his teeth. My heart pounded like an arrhythmic bass drum as we stared each other down. "Easy, now," I coaxed the cat. At the sound of my voice, the mountain lion, much to my surprise, started a headfirst descent, ratcheting his way down one side of the tree as I instinctively shinnied up the other side to avoid being bumped into falling.

"There he goes!" I yelled as the cougar scratched halfway down the tree trunk before gracefully propelling himself through the air. He landed on all fours in the snow and ran.

"Let's go! Get him!" Wilbur shouted as the leashed hounds pulled him through the snow. By the time I scrambled down, Wilbur, Mike, and the dogs were a football field ahead of me and closing in on the cat. With the drug finally taking hold, the mountain lion was no match for his pursuers, and he eventually slumped into the soft snow. I caught up in time to help hobble the big cat's legs so that he could no longer crawl.

"Should have waited a little longer for the drug to work," I said between gasping breaths as the cougar continued to settle down. Clearly, this was not a flawless process. To err as a scientist is a humbling path to discovery. From this encounter and others, we eventually learned to identify males and females from distances high in trees as well as to estimate their weight. We adjusted tranquilizer doses accordingly.

Cat No. 3 was a fine specimen. He weighed 142 pounds. Judging from his perfect teeth, he was young but a fully mature mountain lion. The front limbs on big toms are huge and thick like the barrels of baseball bats. You can see and feel the power they must generate when running, leaping, or harnessing prey animals many times their size.

Both males and females are incredibly evolved, top-of-the-chart predatory mammals. Like all cats, they have fewer teeth than other big predators. But each tooth has evolved into perfect puncturing, biting, sheering, and chewing implements, more refined than any of the other big carnivores. Their iron-strong claws retract into protective sheaths when they walk to preserve their pinpoint sharpness. Their eyesight, both peripheral and night vision, is incredible. Their hearing is spot-on. And they have a strong sense of smell.

"Good cat . . . trophy size," Wilbur said, admiring the tom from a hunter's perspective. Little did he or I know that the word "trophy" would become key to securing the future of mountain lions, but more on that later. On this day, with snow fluttering down on the big lion's tawny pelt, I simply admired him. I ran my hand the length of his body, satisfied that his breathing was deep, his heart pumping steadily. The overall sleekness and athleticism of these creatures is demonstrated not so much while they lie drugged for study but when they're free to travel the bluffs and ridges, the valleys and canyons, where they've learned to hunt. Many of us are fascinated by our house cats; their grace, agility, keen senses, and ability to leap and contort in midair. Multiply that 100 times, and you've got a mountain lion.

Naturalist Ernest Thompson Seton lionized cougars this way: "Lithe and splendid beasthood, his daily routine a march of stirring athletic events that not another creature—in America at least—can hope to equal."

"Rex," I said. "Let's name him Rex."

Wilbur, the renowned cougar hunter, leaned over to take a closer look. All these years later, I suspect that he'd begun at that moment to alter his thinking about the animal he'd long regarded as vermin. After a lengthy silence, he responded, "But why not just No. 3?"

"Like Tyrannosaurus Rex," I said. "A big one." Wilbur broke a small smile, as if sharing my exuberance.

While Rex catnapped, we marked his ears with tattoos, cattle tags, and color-coded streamers to help with identification from a distance and on recapture. As with the first two captures, we placed a color-coded nylon rope collar around his heavy neck. Then, with the hounds finally calming down, Wilbur, Mike, and I hefted Rex onto a bed of pine boughs to fully recover.

"Good job," I said. "We're making progress." Wilbur and Mike shook hands, the way successful hunters congratulate one another—victoriously. After we gathered our equipment and packs, the big cat remained still, prone on the mattress of pine boughs atop insulating snow. We watched until convinced that he'd soon be up and about. Then we slipped away. In retrospect, I think the capture of No. 3 marked the beginning of a strong pact between the scientist in me and the mountain lion hunter in Wilbur. We both wanted to better understand an animal so elusive and so mysterious that it had earned the nickname "ghost cat." We were embracing the adventure unfolding before us. Although nothing was said, we'd joined ranks in pursuit of answers. Was the cougar a predator that warranted continued control amid ever-expanding human populations or an integral part of pristine ecosystems worth saving? We hoped to garner the first clues toward understanding.

By New Year's Eve, three days after capturing Rex but no more cougars, seventy-three inches of snow had fallen near the headwaters of Big Creek—a preamble to what would become a detestable winter of bitter cold, record snowfall in the high country, rampaging creeks and rivers—taxing challenges for both mountain lions and the researchers pursuing them. Yet inside our warm cabin, we celebrated the dawn of 1965 by sipping iced tea laced with whiskey and eating Mike's homemade Hershey-bar graham crackers. "To a real ripping time," I offered as a toast. First we sipped from our mugs. Then we gulped. Nobody waited to ring in the new year. Long before midnight, we were all asleep, including the hounds.

The skies cleared the next morning, and Wilbur and Mike moved to the Garden Creek camp to work a different part of the study area. I hiked to Taylor Ranch and flew out with pilot Gene Crosby of Johnson Flying Service to spend the rest of the day and night in McCall. While there, I called a breeder in Cascade and bought a new hound, then made arrangements to have the pup brought to Big Creek for Wilbur to pick up. I also bought supplies, mostly grocery staples and canned goods, and left them with the flying service to be shuttled back to Taylor Ranch when weather permitted. Then I did some belated Christmas shopping for Shirley and the girls before getting in my oxidize-orange 1956 Chevy pickup the next morning to drive more than 600 miles home to Vancouver to resume graduate classes.

"Roads are treacherous," I told Shirley from a telephone booth after driving all day in stormy weather over patchy ice and snow-swept portions of highway before stopping in Othello, Washington, for the night.

"Come safely tomorrow," she said. "We all miss you."

On the final leg toward home, I thought more about Wilbur. Before leaving Big Creek, I told him that he'd done a good job and that my early study doubts had been assuaged a bit by the successful capture of three cougars.

"Not bad for a couple Iowa farm boys," I said.

Wilbur shrugged indifference. But once again, he failed to mask a tiny smile.

# CHAPTER FOUR

# Barn Cat Lessons

HAD I KNOWN AS A YOUNG BOY THAT I'D ONE DAY STUDY THE WORLD'S great cats, I might have paid more attention to the barn cats we had on my family's Iowa farm. As it was, they made for great targets.

"Got one!" I'd yell with glee inside the barn.

"Here comes another one," my older brother Wayne would announce.

We were each stationed on stools under cow udders. I'd expertly twist a teat, give a yank, and nail the adult cats, then the kittens, whitewashing their faces with milk. Wayne would do the same. All the cats, feral and hungry for something other than mice, loved it.

Dad, a stern German who had his rules of the road, didn't.

"Knock it off, you two. We've got work to do."

And work we did—always we worked. The cats knew this, and twice daily they'd line up to consume what they craved. We hand-milked eight to ten head of mostly Jerseys 365 days a year. The small herd filed like clockwork into the barn every morning and evening, each cow assuming an assigned stanchion. Wayne and I moved from one animal to the next. Like everything on the farm, utility defined a cow's value. Same for the cats. They kept the mouse population in check. For that, they were valued. And I'm sure, like mountain lions, barn cats had a social order. They were subject to population dynamics and outside threats, like distemper, which spread unchecked.

Looking back at my upbringing on the farm and the career I chose, the nature and nurturing of those formative years were critical. As with young mountain lions that spend most of their first two years with their mother learning to hunt and survive, I spent the first twenty years with my family cultivating not only farm fields but also innate interests and mind-expanding experiences. In many ways, what I'd become by the time I left Iowa to join the Navy figured immeasurably in how studying predators would eventually consume my professional life.

The Great Depression and I arrived in southern Iowa farm country about the same time. I was born in the family farmhouse on December 5, 1930, a year after the stock market crashed and just before the Dust Bowl loomed on the horizon. We Hornockers—my dad Everett, mom LaRena, older brother Wayne, and younger sister Jeanette and I—lived on eighty acres of former prairie that had been tilled and wrangled over the decades into a self-sufficient farm. We were penny poor, but dirt rich.

Wayne and I wore OshKosh B'gosh coveralls and overalls, just like Dad, and we were expected to do chores and grow into men who farmed, just like our dad. Girls like Jeanette married men who were also expected to be farmers. My brother and I slept in the same full-sized bed clear into our teenage years. My sister had her own little bedroom. Mom prepared meals on a Monarch wood cookstove. We had a wood-burning stove and cut firewood on our property with a circular buzz saw powered by a "one-lung wonder" gasoline engine. It was a hard life. It was a good life. It was a practice in practicality every day of the year.

We lived in Wayne County, nuzzled near the Missouri border, four miles south of Allerton, an agricultural town of about 750 people back then, with a population of under 500 today. We planted soybeans, corn, and alfalfa hay. We had the cows for milk and cream, pigs for meat, chickens for eggs, and a horn-of-plenty garden to provide vegetables and fruit.

Folks say the Depression swept across Iowa's farmland, causing instant hardship. Looking back, I think it mostly augured its way into an already devastated economy. Farmers like my dad had felt the pinch long before the stock market crash of 1929. After Black Tuesday, the farm market took a final plummet, and many farmers surrendered. But not the Hornockers. Dad and Mom would have none of that. We'd make do.

Of course, many rural areas had no electricity back then. No indoor plumbing. We hand-pumped water and shared an outhouse. We used

Great Depression-era Iowa farm kids, circa 1935. The author (right) with his older brother Wayne and younger sister Jeanette. *Hornocker family photo*

kerosene lanterns. Mother had an Aladdin oil lamp that she'd light when entertaining company. We did chores at night with lanterns.

By 1932, when I was a barefoot toddler, cash crops and livestock prices were at all-time lows. Corn brought less than ten cents a bushel, pork a nickel a pound, beef a bit higher, eggs a dime a dozen. Few people had money. And yet my family prospered compared to neighbors who lost their acreage to the banks and other creditors. Dad chalked up our survival to dogged determination and the value of hard work. With the Dust Bowl ravaging vast regions of the country, the U.S. Department of Agriculture, through the Soil Conservation Service, was advancing contour farming as a means to prevent erosion. Experts at Iowa State University preached its virtues. But Dad dismissed it as "crooked row farming" that made tilling more difficult for horses and machinery alike.

"Craziest thing I ever heard of," he groused. "You need straight rows of corn. If those scientists had to farm, they'd starve to death." Maybe he was right, at least during those tight times.

Dad wouldn't tolerate dallying. When one job was finished, we'd set out to do another. As kids, Wayne and I went barefoot as soon as the snow melted in the spring until the first frost of autumn. Not that we couldn't afford shoes; it was just that we couldn't afford to wear them out. Need trumped want. That was our family's approach. When you didn't need to wear shoes, you didn't, even if you wanted to. By the time I turned ten or eleven and got behind a team of horses in the field, my parents agreed that I needed to wear shoes.

My first paying job was as a "water boy" atop a saddle horse. I made fifty cents a day ferrying drinking water around the farm fields to quench the thirst of men on threshing crews. Before combines, farmhands worked through the heat of summer cutting and tying grain into bundles. After the sheaves dried, huge threshing machines moved into the fields to separate the grain from the straw.

While Mom and my sister worked mostly indoors, they also pitched in with outside chores. Mom never drove a car. But she learned to pilot and run all the farm equipment, including our first tractor, which arrived around the time World War II broke out. My mother, a hardworking, confident, and compassionate woman, was the nucleus of our orbit. Not only did she grow and can a lot of the food we ate, she also cooked, sewed, quilted, patched all of our clothes, and darned our socks. She even mended Dad's corn-shucking mittens.

Although electricity didn't arrive to much of rural Iowa until after World War II, Dad had wired a wind charger to a lightbulb in our kitchen. A few years later, he upgraded to a thirty-six-volt charger that provided enough energy to light bulbs in four rooms. Eventually, he bought a gasoline-fueled power plant with battery storage, enough electricity to run all the lights, the kitchen toaster, a coffeepot, and a radio that my parents kept in the living room. There, we'd gather around to listen at night. I remember hearing about the attack on Pearl Harbor in 1941 and the death of President Roosevelt in 1945. By that time, thanks to Roosevelt, rural electric cooperatives were springing up in farming communities across the country as part of the Depression-born New Deal. But that came to our region pretty much after I left home.

Looking back, we practiced a make-ends-meet lifestyle. And it prepared me well for the challenges of the Idaho Primitive Area, as did my early schooling.

Education was a big deal in our family. In fact, it's how my parents met, in circumstances that some would describe as scandalous.

Mom was a young teacher in the local high school where Dad was a student. They courted on the sly and got married when she was twenty-one and he was nineteen. She had no farming experience. She'd led what Dad called "kind of a sheltered life." But she learned fast. I suspect that teaching—and learning—were etched in her DNA. I latched onto the learning part early. During long, cold winter nights on the farm, she'd read by kerosene lamplight to my brother, sister, and me. I have vivid memories of her reading my favorite book, *Bring 'Em Back Alive*, by Frank Buck, a professional wild-animal capturer from Texas who chronicled his experiences of apprehending animals and delivering them to zoos.

Every Wayne County township had its own one-room schoolhouse. Ours was called White School, only a half-mile away from our farm. So we walked. And some of the best teachers I had in my life worked there. They were young women, like my mom, who had just graduated from high school and took what was called "normal training" to prepare them for teaching. I remember all of them. Not only were they inspiring teachers, they kept that tiny school heated, they washed the windows, they often taught as many as six grades and sometimes all eight grades.

We Hornocker kids attended each of the eight grades at White School. The most students it served was twenty, sometimes dropping to twelve or fourteen. Reading, writing, arithmetic. Music, too. We started each day with the Pledge of Allegiance, and there was a Bible verse every Monday morning. Mother was religious, but Dad wasn't. I hated Sunday school. But White School was always good. Learning was fun. The book-mobile came by once a month, and I'd clean the shelves of books about birds and other nature volumes.

My brother, sister, and I graduated from Allerton High School. I was valedictorian of the eighteen-member class of 1949. Perhaps more than anything, team sports taught me the hardest and best lessons. I was and still am shy by nature. But playing shortstop in baseball and guard in basketball tempered my tentativeness. There's nowhere to hide when a line drive comes your way at shortstop or the full-court press must be attacked by the team's only ball-handling guard.

At first, Dad wouldn't let me play basketball because he needed me home after school to do chores. So my freshman and sophomore years were a bust. Now and then, however, I'd scrimmage at school with some of the team members. The coach spotted my ball-handling ability and talked to Dad.

"You can practice three times a week," he finally relented.

My junior and senior years, I was named a member of what today is called an "all-conference" team.

"I'm proud of you," Dad told me one evening after a game.

"Thanks," I responded, beaming ear to ear.

There are a lot of positive and positively corny things that can be said about the way I was educated up to that point. Farm kids of that era were steeped in responsibility, work ethic, basic academics, and a challenge to make the world a better place. This served me well into adulthood, from my four years in the military to the sometimes byzantine world of higher education and ultimately during my years as a scientist.

While leafing through my old records, I found one document from 1942 that hinted of my future. White School teachers filed annual summary reports for each student. Of me, teacher Lenora Kint wrote, "He is a very good student in every subject, and he especially likes science."

Perhaps the thing that prepared me most (or at least complemented my eventual passion for studying predators) was an early intrigue with the natural world and my decision to become a predator myself. As a teenager, I collected the first ten-dollar bounty in Wayne County for shooting a coyote. I killed it for the money and because predator control was encouraged. I was proud at the time but never shot another coyote after that.

And then there were ring-necked pheasants.

"Boy, if I could have a repeating shotgun," I told my dad one day, "I could kill a lot of those fryers." He called pheasants fryers. And he'd often try to bag the birds for dinner by hitting them with the family Ford when they shuttled from the dense thickets to the gravel roads. "What kind of repeating shotgun?" he asked from behind the wheel after taking another unsuccessful strike at a flock.

"One of those pumps." I'd had my eye on a Winchester Model 12.

"Well," he said a few days later, "we can take a look, and I might go half on one with you." I already had the gun scoped out. For about $48, you could order a Model 12 in 12-gauge with a thirty-inch full-choke barrel from the Montgomery Ward catalog. So we ordered one, splitting the cost fifty-fifty. One day, after returning with birds in the bag, I told Dad, "Boy oh boy, I can really slay the fryers now!"

Southern Iowa, contrary to the image of endless flat cornfield and soybean fields, is hilly country with lots of woodlands and little creeks—more like neighboring Missouri. It was and still is wonderful wildlife country. I was interested in wildlife for as long as I can remember. As a little kid, I'd catch tadpoles and keep them in a bucket or any other container I could find around the farm. I caught bumblebees during the day and marveled at them inside a jar. I did the same at night with lightning bugs.

Birds were my biggest interest back then. And not only to shoot them. I knew the names of all the songbirds in our region and could identify each of their calls. I wanted to be a falconer, intrigued that the bird would be the hunter and I'd be the handler. But Dad wouldn't let me keep a "chicken hawk."

Like coyotes, hawks were considered vermin because they occasionally snatched up chickens. Indeed, red-tailed hawks patrolled the fence lines and fields year-round and nested in trees come spring. One day, I spotted a nest and climbed an old cottonwood to take a scientific look at two young red-tailed fledglings. When I got to the nest, they spread their wings and looked at me. Fascinated, I peered back. Then I scooped both up, managed to get them out of the tree, ran home, and confronted the inevitable reception. "Chicken hawks," Dad grumbled. "Get rid of 'em."

I was devastated. It wasn't only that I couldn't keep the birds. It was that in Dad's vernacular, "get rid of 'em" was akin to a Mafia hit order. There was no room in the world for a damn chicken hawk. So I lied. I took the birds away, came back, and told Dad, "They're gone." Actually, I had put them back in the nest. It was a bittersweet act of defiance. I didn't like lying to my father. But I felt good about being a preservationist. The only thing that might have been better is if Dad had let me keep the red-tails long enough to watch them take wing and fly away or perhaps become hunters with me, the boy falconer.

Almost every Iowa farm boy was a natural resource consumer. Most hunted and trapped. I trapped muskrats, minks, even skunks. I got sent home more than once by a nose-pinching teacher after I'd checked my traplines in the early morning and walked into the school building reeking of skunk. For me, nature had already become the ultimate classroom. I learned the country inside and out while hunting and running my trapline. I began to see how everything was interconnected, how the plants grew, how the mice lived off the plants, how the hawks ate the mice. It was ecology, but I didn't even know that term yet. I loved being part of it. Still do.

Curiously, back then, there were no deer, no wild turkeys, no beavers, no raccoons. When I returned many years later as a grown man supposedly steeped in professorial knowledge, I walked my old traplines.

The country was overrun with deer and wild turkeys. The creeks were backed up by beaver dams. Canada geese were on every pond. Raccoons had become pests. Bobcats were common. And, believe it or not, a cougar was killed only a few miles from my family farm. There had been, whether planned or an act of serendipity, less human encroachment and a resulting proliferation of wildlife. Between our home and the town of Allerton when I grew up—a distance of four miles—there were ten active farms and family homes. Now there is one. Small farms have disappeared, and current big-machinery farmers work only the best cropland, leaving fringe areas that develop native vegetation. Such "idled lands" are far more wildlife friendly.

The Big Creek study area in Idaho, its sheer ruggedness having kept civilization at bay, was hospitable to wildlife, especially cougars seeking refuge from outside persecution. A lot of my thinking today is a product of both the wilderness and Iowa. I'd grown up with a self-nurtured mind-set about loving and hunting animals. This outlook put me in good stead for studying an animal such as the cougar—a carnivore in the crosshairs of controversy.

Destiny aside, my adolescent life on the farm was geared toward adulthood in farming. Again, it was expected of me. And the year 1937 underscored this expectation. I was only seven, but my parents, having already toughed their way out of the Great Depression, seemed buoyed by a turnaround in economic prospects. There were bumper crops throughout the region, and suddenly it seemed that everyone we knew was making money albeit not getting rich. By age thirteen, after advancing from water boy to seed sacker on threshing crews, I was entrenched in farming.

High school graduation didn't change the trajectory. My brother graduated, joined the Navy late in World War II, and came back to the family farm. The template set, I worked on the farm with Dad and Wayne. Then, in 1950, the Korean War started. I joined the Navy. If I saw combat and survived, I'd surely return to the family farm.

Little did I know that dumb luck, coincidence, or whatever you might call it was already at work. By the time I left Iowa for the Navy, Wilbur Wiles, who'd grown up on a small Iowa farm just like me, had already been living since the late 1930s in his cabin on Monumental Creek in the Big Creek drainage.

When World War II began, Wilbur hiked out on snowshoes from his cabin over Profile Summit to Yellow Pine, caught a mail car to the tiny town of Cascade, and enlisted in the Army. He was part of the Normandy Invasion, landing on Omaha Beach to fight across France into Germany, earning the rank of sergeant and a Bronze Star for bravery. He survived the great Battle of the Bulge in Belgium and helped liberate starving prisoners from two Nazi concentration camps. After the war, Wilbur retreated back to Monumental Creek.

Nearly two decades after he returned, I hiked into the Idaho Primitive Area, walked up the steps to Wilbur's log cabin, knocked on the hand-hewn wooden door, and accepted his invitation to "come on in, the coffee's almost ready."

We talked late into the night about my proposed cougar study, and I hired him, right then and there.

## CHAPTER FIVE

# Blue Ink

I SIT HERE NOW HOLDING WILBUR WILES'S 1964–1965 FIELD NOTES from the first winter of the cougar study. He wrote them using a

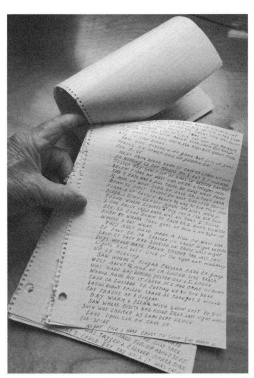

blue ink pen on eight- by eleven-inch white lined paper, later ripped from a spiral-bound notebook. The notes are meticulous. The letters are printed and capitalized. The sentences are both fragmented and complete. Spelling errors are inconsequentially sprinkled throughout.

I close my eyes and envision Wilbur penning words like "Headed up Coxey Creek," "Cold today," or "Got home late, soaked wet." I see him hunkered over the notebook, writing by Coleman lantern light inside one of our wall tents or at the wooden table in his cabin. His words

One page from hundreds of Wilbur Wiles's field notes.

complement my own written record of that first winter when I had to leave periodically to complete my doctoral class work at UBC, in Canada. Wilbur's notes also document his dedication and the depth of his work.

Missing from the notes are hints of how complicated things were getting. People who hated cougars were suspicious of our study, calling it a "sham" and labeling me a "cat lover." (As a side note, I am quite fond of cats in general.) And yet we had no clue of the battle that lay ahead—not me; not Mike Stephen, who hunted with Wilbur for a month after I left for school; and especially not Wilbur, who hunted for three months after Mike departed. To replace Mike, I hired Wilbur's longtime friend Ray Thrall to work with him when I was gone. Ray was a native of the Big Creek community and was at home in the backcountry. He and Wilbur teamed up hand in glove.

After arriving in Big Creek in the late spring of 1965 on the last of several back-and-forth flights made while finishing classes at UBC, I pored over Wilbur and Mike's field notes. The entries gave me a good idea of what they had accomplished in my absence. Mike's notes, written in cursive, documented most of January while I was gone. Wilbur's notes, coupled with my own taken during several visits, told the rest of the story through April. Reviewing these fifty-eight-year-old documents now, I've managed to flesh out and reconstruct the study's infancy.

Finding no mountain lions during the first month, we managed to capture three shortly before and after Christmas Day. Seven more were collared over the next two months for a total of ten different mountain lions. Documentation of captures aside, the notes leave a vivid picture of just how puzzling the Big Creek cats were, how daunting the weather was, how confusing the landscape could be, and how tenuous the project's future became.

Journaling as we did about climbing up a drainage, over a divide, along a ridge, and back around a basin describes where we went but not how challenging the terrain was to travel. Scores of frigid side creeks tumbled down from steep crevices carved by nature over time, each a hurdle to be crossed or circumvented. Distances were logged in straight-line air miles. In reality, getting from one place to another was never a straight line. Nor was it on the level. Gradients, up or down, steep or gradual, always confronted us. Our pursuits were more like forced marches along jagged inclines, through thick brush, over boulders, across streams, around fallen trees and rockslides. Sometimes, while negotiating the impediments set up by nature, I lamented whether the study was worth our time and effort.

Then again, especially after capturing and marking a mountain lion, I'd stop to look and listen. The sounds emanating from the mountainous terrain always had a low undertone, a rhythmic continuity. When the temperature rose, snow melted. Tendrils of water trickled beneath the drifts and sounded like muffled sleigh bells ringing. Tiny tributaries formed and wriggled down slopes to join side creeks. The water continued flowing to merge with Big Creek and on to the Middle Fork of the Salmon River, then into the Main Stem of the River of No Return, joining up with the Snake River churning north from southern Idaho, through the mighty Columbia River Gorge between Washington and Oregon, and finally into the maw of the Pacific Ocean. A timeless progression geared to the pull of gravity. I was mesmerized by it all: by the wilderness where these waters originated and by the creatures that inhabited it. The entire ecosystem seemed to be fighting against the encroachment of civilization to remain pristine. Sometimes I wondered if it might be best to leave the mountains and their lions alone. On the other hand, without scientific probing, the mysterious life history of these magnificent animals might never be revealed, let alone understood.

Then again, I mused, the grueling task of capturing these cougars in the name of science perhaps underscored why no one else had been crazy enough to do it before me.

On January 5, 1965, three days after I left to resume graduate school classes in Vancouver, British Columbia, Wilbur and Mike hiked up Cliff Creek and discovered the fresh trail of a cougar. The lion had apparently tried to kill a bighorn sheep but failed. A maze of tracks, left by fleeing sheep and the pursuing cat, told the story.

Wilbur, after inspecting the evidence, turned his hounds loose, and Duke was soon barking treed. The cougar had climbed a fir tree, about fifteen feet up. Wilbur gave the pneumatic Cap-Chur gun thirteen pumps and shot. The dart missed low. The cat jumped from the tree and raced downhill more than half a mile before treeing again, this time in a fir about forty feet up. She sat for a while, then jumped from a limb of that tree to the entangled limbs of another tree.

*Mike's notes: "This took place over at least a one-half hour period, and at no time did the cat show any effects of the drug."*

Then Mike took aim, hitting the lion in the chest. Both his and Wilbur's shots, with the same 20-mg dose of drug, occurred after they warmed the gun over a campfire. Cold weather had been causing it to malfunction.

*Mike's notes: "She then showed signs and was draped over a limb when she was approached. I let her down with a rope."*

Wilbur and Mike weighed, marked, and tagged the lioness, then administered 3cc of penicillin to protect against infection. The cat soon pulled herself through the snow as Mike and Wilbur lifted her hind-quarters to help her gain traction. Then they waited. Mountain lion No. 4 slowly regained her wits and eventually scrambled into the bluffs above Cave Creek where she'd first been treed. We would recapture her many more times and name her Hazel.

Ten more days passed with Wilbur and Mike hunting unsuccessfully. They took one day off to repair a horse fence at Taylor Ranch. Then rain set in and, coupled with melting temperatures, made tracking difficult. Finally, snow returned. On January 8, they headed downstream along Big Creek toward the mouth of Dunce Creek and found some Native American cave paintings but no cougars. Farther up Dunce Creek, they cut across some bluffs to a high ridge above Big Creek.

*Mike's notes: "Saw 1 old, and 2 young cat tracks but fairly old. Wilbur says game is harder to find than before. Fewer deer and probably the sheep are being forced into the rougher country downstream. The cougar, due to absence of deer, have had to depend more on sheep."*

One thing for sure: We weren't capturing the number of cats I'd hoped to find. Every day, Wilbur and Mike cut tracks, mostly old, and they'd follow until losing them for lack of snow or simply because the cougars had a knack for disappearing. Yet the two men remained optimistic.

*Mike's notes: "We know of at least 6 cats downstream from Cliff Cr., with very little game in Cougar, Goat, and Dunce Creek areas. Female we tracked today was probably one we already found in the area. One foot of crusted snow on south facing bluff area below Snake Cr."*

Throughout the study, we counted browsing and grazing elk, deer, and sheep, documenting them in daily notes and tallies. We assumed the mountain lions would prey on these animals and attack when an opportunity came along. We also continued to collect jawbones and leg bones at kill sites for later examination to help determine the age and health of the prey population.

*Mike's notes: "Jan. 14. Wilbur and I went up Cow Creek and came upon a fawn deer killed by a cougar just after entering the canyon. The kill was at the bottom of a semi-brushy shallow draw. The cougar had jumped the deer and rode him for several yards, then after downing him, drug the deer 75 yards to the bottom which was dotted with a few large Douglas fir trees. There was still some meat on the carcass, but the cougar had evidently abandoned it."*

On January 15, Wilbur and Mike turned the hounds loose on what would become cat No. 5.

*Mike's notes: "The cat had been jumped in the bluffs and ran down hill, and brought to bay in the creek bottom, where he fought the dogs in the creek."*

The cougar held its own and managed to leap from the creek into a large pile of brush weighed down by heavy snow. Wilbur decided, after playing peekaboo with the agitated cat for half an hour, that it wasn't going to come out any time soon. So he and Mike waited.

*Mike's notes: "He finally came out my end of the pile, but it was too brushy to shoot with the air gun. The cat continued up the bottom of Cave Cr. Wilbur got a running shot at him but missed and the cat continued up the bottom of Cave Cr."*

Wilbur and Mike hustled after the cat, eventually releasing the dogs again. After a mile, the hounds had the cougar treed about fifty yards downhill from where Wilbur and I had captured and marked mountain lion No. 1 a little more than three weeks earlier.

*Mike's notes: "The cat after shot with the dart did not jump, but climbed and remained. He could hang on too well as bushy as the tree was. Snow water was dripping down and my hands got numb so had to warm them occasionally, it took 25 minutes to get cat down."*

Mike and Wilbur, after injecting a reduced dose to ensure against overdosing, pulled the tom up from the creek bottom to a more open spot. All the while, the cougar snapped his powerful jaws each time they moved their hands close to his head. So Mike gave him .15mg more sedating drug, and lion No. 5 settled down to be processed. Afterward, Wilbur and Mike searched the area and found evidence of a deer kill.

*Mike's notes: "The kill had been picked clean and by no means was fresh. It didn't have anything to do with No. 5 that we could see, he was just passing through."*

None of us knew at the time that Mike's observation of the cougar "just passing through" hinted of a future revelation pivotal to the understanding of mountain lion ecology.

Cougar No. 6 was darted the next day, January 16, under circumstances other than normal. Wilbur and Mike were hiking to Taylor Ranch along the Big Creek trail, intending to resume their pursuit of mountain lions the following day. Just around the bend near the mouth of Rough Creek, they happened on what looked like a fresh cat track. The cougar had gone up a ridge and then down into a canyon. Wilbur and Mike took advantage of the unexpected opportunity and sent the hounds.

*Mike's notes: "It was an older track than first looked, so the dogs following this track jumped a female with 3 kittens on a 2-point buck deer about ½ mile up the canyon bottom. The deer had just been cleaned up. Bones from an elk and mountain sheep were also nearby in the bottom, but had been killed or died in past years."*

After chasing the female to a bluff west of the kill, around to the north across the drainage, then on to the east side of the canyon, the hounds brought two of the three kittens to bay in a bluff just above the original kill. Wilbur followed and found one kitten in a small cave on the face of the bluff. The other kittens escaped. It should be noted that while we called them kittens, these were full-grown mountain lions under the age of two.

*Mike's notes: "We could get on a similar bluff across a small draw about 70 feet away from the kitten, at the same height. After 2 shots with the dart gun, a third try was to be the last."*

Once again, Wilbur and Mike had to heat the gun over a fire before each shot. On the third shot, Mike aimed about seven feet high (compensating for the dart dropping over the considerable distance) directly over the kitten, which now appeared to be sleeping. When the dart hit, she scurried off the ledge and scrambled up more bluffs and then down a draw. By the time Wilbur and Mike reached the now subdued cat, she'd run about 100 yards.

*Mike's notes: "This marked kitten (No. 6) was one of three traveling with a female."*

Over the next ten days, Wilbur and Mike traversed ninety-six more miles, cutting several tracks but finding no more cougars. Snow piled up, and temperatures dropped. Mike was scheduled to leave the wilderness soon, so he and Wilbur huddled at Taylor Ranch to wait for a plane. They inventoried gear and reviewed marking and dosing procedures. Another storm was brewing as Wilbur set out on his own to hunt his way back home on Monumental Creek. The weather cleared on January 31, and Mike flew out to McCall, drove home to Missoula, and stopped in Grangeville to call me with a report that is reflected in his field notes.

*Mike's notes: "Total mileage from Dec. 5 to January 27 for Wilbur and I in hunting efforts—439 miles. That is 71.6 miles per cat for 6 cats. Old Proverb: It's hard to stay away from the mountains when you've grown up among them. Gary Cooper and Mike Stephen."*

CHAPTER SIX

# Remote Learning

FRUSTRATED BY OUR SLOW PROGRESS TRACKING COUGARS AND STUCK IN classrooms to complete my doctoral degree at UBC in Vancouver, my worries grew. Was I, like an inexperienced young hound, barking up a wrong tree? Were cougars truly the impossibly reclusive animals I'd been warned about? Were they already proving to be too secretive to find in numbers enough to conduct a probe worthy of peer review and

Data collected in the field were recorded each night in notebooks. Here, the author enters a narrative about the day's hunt and discoveries. *Wilbur Wiles photo*

acceptance by the scientific community? For the first time, I mulled the possibility of failure.

Now, as I review all these handwritten field notes from nearly six decades ago, recall events, and reconstruct the study's sluggish progress, an old familiar feeling of frustration wells up inside me. The second-guessing remains palpable but was excruciating back then. Put it this way: Some people work with their hands, others with their head. In the field, I found myself using both, and I loved it. But as winter tightened its grip in Big Creek, my brain, save for the few brief trips I was able to take into the study area, felt distracted in distant classrooms. My hands were dormant, and my heart longed to get back to the physical job of catching cats and the cerebral challenge of trying to understand them.

So once again, I study Wilbur's old notes, appreciating their detail. Despite the challenges of that winter, he kept the study on track, one enigmatic cat at a time, until I could return.

On January 28, 1965, Wilbur, accompanied by Ray Thrall, the other part-time assistant I'd hired who was familiar with the study area, left our Cougar Creek camp with the hounds and trekked downstream eastward along the Big Creek trail. It had rained all night and was still raining when they set out at 9:30 a.m. At the mouth of Dunce Creek, Wilbur found the fresh track of a large tom, probably made earlier in the morning as it headed up the creek bottom.

*Wilbur's notes: "Let dogs go and they went up canyon about ¾ way to top then over ridge in rough bluffs on Big Creek side, between Dunce Creek and Goat Creek. They jumped cat in bluffs, and he ran about 200 yards and treed in a big fir."*

The tree was in the bottom of a narrow canyon dense with brush and snow. En route to the scene, Wilbur noticed that the cat had scraped up a little pyramid of needles and forest debris under a Ponderosa pine tree. These "scrapes," we later determined, were a means of marking their territories.

After an hour of slogging up the canyon, Wilbur reached his baying dogs and tied them aside.

*Wilbur's notes: "Slow traveling, 30 in. of snow in places, and soaked from head to foot from wet snow and rain."*

Dart loaded, gun pumped and ready, Wilbur took aim at the mountain lion perched about twenty-five feet up the tree. The dart hit, and judging from Wilbur's brief description, the processing of cougar No. 7 came off without a hitch.

*Wilbur's notes: "Got dart in his chest, and out, and tagged cat No. 7."*

For the next ten days, Wilbur, Ray, and the hounds hunted with no success. Rain set in for three days straight, stalled, and resumed. Creeks rose, and frigid water collected in the trails. Snow melted in the lower elevations and accumulated in the upper reaches. Wilbur checked known cat crossing areas to no avail. He, Ray, and the dogs continued down Big Creek, staying overnight at various camps. They traveled all the way downstream to the Middle Fork of the Salmon River, then upstream to Fox Creek.

*Wilbur's notes: "Snow all slush. Hills slick and lots of snow slides have run. About 6 in. of snow on Middle Fork. Saw where tom, probably the one I tagged on the 28th had come from Big Horn Bridge up to Dunce Creek traveling in the trail, several times. No new cat tracks."*

Most people might call it quits at this point. But knowing Wilbur, quitting never crossed his mind. Resting was necessary, but bailing wasn't in his DNA. After all, he was working in his own backyard. He knew what winter in Big Creek was like, what the conditions demanded of both animals and humans. Survival was a product of thinking ahead, planning, preparing, being cautious, and overcoming challenges—one step after another, up and down, always forward in cadence with the rhythms of nature. To this day, I can think of no better person to have assisted me than Wilbur. I mean, the guy had been living in the same neighborhood with these reclusive cats for more than two decades. He knew both the country and his carnivorous neighbors.

On February 10, Wilbur's perseverance paid off. Or maybe it didn't. It was a matter of perspective.

*Wilbur's notes: "Went from Doe Creek camp up through bluffs to Toe Head Basin and Cave Creek ridge. Then down Big Canyon from Toe head . . . then up Garden Creek about 1 mile and cut 3 cougar tracks. . . . Let dogs follow them on chain . . . as I came down hill I see a cougar behind a mahogany bush about 300 yards below, watching downhill. Cougar saw me and took off east. Snap on dog chain was frozen and took a little time to get dogs loose."*

Duke and Chub chased the cougar for about half a mile and treed it forty feet up a fir tree encumbered with heavy limbs. Wilbur caught up to the dogs around 4:30 p.m. and fired a dart shortly after 5:00 p.m. as dusk began to shroud the scene. He heard the dart hit and saw the cat jump from the tree. Imagine his surprise when he spotted an identification tag in the tom's ear.

It was No. 2, the mountain lion that he and I had captured just before the avalanche struck on Christmas Day nearly two months earlier. While this surely disappointed Wilbur since he wanted to capture new cats, it thrilled me. It suggested that mountain lions could be recaptured and that our intervention didn't cause them to flee the area or change their behaviors. If we simply stuck to it, kept chipping away long enough, perhaps we could disentangle the secrets of these rarely seen creatures.

Three days later, Wilbur honed in on tracks he assumed were made by No. 2 but never spotted the cat. After another two days of hunting, he discovered a site where a cougar had dug old deer bones out of the snow. Its fresh tracks were nearby. After unleashing Duke and Chub to follow the scent, Wilbur came upon an elk kill so fresh that the carcass was still warm atop the snow.

*Wilbur's notes: "The lion caught the elk in a bluff. He came up from below and the elk had no place to go. He broke her neck and drug her to a ledge. Ate in on the back and opened the elk up in front of the hips and ate most of the hindquarter. Must have ate at least 25 pounds."*

As Wilbur surveyed the kill site, he heard the dogs baying in the distance. For nearly two hours, he waded through hip-deep snow before finding the cat up a tree. Again, the darting, sedating, tagging, and data collection went smoothly. Cat No. 8, a big tom, became another subject in our gradually growing study.

*Wilbur's notes: "Cat was larger than he looked in tree. Didn't look like too old a cat. Teeth in good shape."*

Over the next ten days, Wilbur, Duke, and Chub, accompanied intermittently by Ray and Little Red the pup, scoured mostly downstream portions of our Big Creek study area. Deep snow in the high country had driven elk and deer down in search of food. It stood to reason that the cougars would follow the prey animals.

Sure enough, Wilbur found several elk and deer carcasses from cougar kills. He gathered as much information as possible, including deer and elk jawbones and occasional mountain lion scat samples. He brought his findings back to the camps every night for later analysis and set out the next morning to collect more. By this time, an unusually cold, snowy winter of the kind not seen in the Big Creek drainage in recent years had descended and, in retrospect, probably altered the long-established routines of both predator and prey.

What would become mountain lion No. 9 came down a trail on February 25 and looked Wilbur in the eye from about seventy-five yards away. Wilbur released the snaps on the hounds' chains, and the dogs streaked toward the cougar. The cat stood its ground for a few seconds before speeding away into bluffs where the dogs couldn't follow. Delirious with the chase, the hounds circled above the lion and bayed down at it. Wilbur climbed to where he could see the cat hiding, then clambered back around to secure the dogs before returning to shoot a dart into the lion's flank.

*Wilbur's notes: "Cat took off through bluffs and I got on a point and watched him. In about 10 minutes, he climbed out on the east side of Dunce Creek and was having trouble and went in the brush and stopped. Took about 1 hour to get back to dogs and then to the cat after I got dart in him. He was coming to so gave him more dope and tagged him cat No. 9."*

Mountain lion No. 4, Hazel, was re-treed two days later. With her identification tags intact and no need to dart her, Wilbur caught the dogs, backed away, and let the lioness escape down Big Creek, crossing to the south side before disappearing—more evidence that our capture–recapture methods worked. Catching the same mountain lions over and over was imperative. With each capture, we would note the location, mark it on a map, and eventually delineate territories for each cougar.

A few hours after treeing No. 4, Wilbur found another track and followed it to where a big tom had spent the night in a cave and left early in the morning. The dogs gave chase, and while following them, Wilbur came on another fresh elk kill in the snow. The dogs, after yet another up-and-down pursuit in the bluffs and creek bottoms, finally treed the snarling cat about sixty feet from where they'd treed Hazel earlier that day.

*Wilbur's notes: "Cat done a lot of growling and showing its teeth."*

It was Rex, No. 3, the big tom that had glared into my eyes high in a tree two days after Christmas. He'd been tagged on Cabin Creek more than two months earlier and still wore his collar. Capture–recapture tactics, while excruciatingly slow, were working, and information, though scant early in the study, was mounting. This initial recapture of robust Rex also hinted of the superior place he held in the hierarchy of Big Creek's mountain lion population. Anyway, Wilbur wasn't about to argue the point with the big tom. No need to dart him.

*Wilbur's notes: "Caught dogs and went home."*

The last mountain lion we caught during the study's first winter was No. 10, another big tom. The cat treed near Water Fall Creek along the Middle Fork of the Salmon River in the far eastern reaches of our study area. Judging from Wilbur's cursory description, all went well.

*Wilbur's notes: "Come home after I tagged him, got in after dark."*

It was March 2, 1965. We didn't capture any more cougars that season.

So I collect my thoughts now, fifty-eight years later, and carefully slide Wilbur's notes back into a manila envelope marked "64-65 lion study." Then I put the envelope in a cardboard storage box and retrieve my own notes to review data from that first winter of study and summarize our findings.

We caught and marked the ten different mountain lions—seven males and three females. We found evidence of eight more cougars that weren't captured. There appeared to be an additional mature male, a young male and female, two mature females, and three large kittens within the study area.

*My notes: "Encouraged by number of cats in Big Creek drainage, but must consider extending work to other drainages. Must have enough animals marked to get quantitative data. Possibilities: Main Salmon, in vicinity of Chamberlain Creek; South Fork, from Main Salmon up to East Fork of South Fork Yellow Pine area."*

Something gnawed at me. Of the ten captured mountain lions, all seven males were caught between Taylor Ranch and the Middle Fork, a distance of eight miles. You enter these projects with some preconceived ideas, and I couldn't believe that seven males would coexist within such a small area. It belied the constructs of territoriality. Were the naysayers right? Were mountain lions prone to reproducing with impunity? Could they overrun the country? Did they need to be controlled? Should the bounty be brought back?

I had no answers.

Finally this: Over a period of 111 days, we covered 1,086 miles searching for mountain lions. Simple math: 11.1 days and 108.6 miles per captured mountain lion. Arguably, the return on our investment was not adding up. At this point in the study, the main financial backing came from the Idaho Department of Fish and Game, UBC, and the Idaho Cooperative Wildlife Research Unit at the University of Idaho (UI). We also had support from the Theodore Roosevelt Memorial Fund of the American Museum of Natural History, the Boone and Crockett Club, and the New York Zoological Society.

I was accountable to each of them.

And then there was Dr. Dennis Chitty at UBC. One of five professors on my doctoral thesis committee, Chitty was a critic of the cougar proposal from the get-go. He didn't think the return would be worth two cents.

"These cats won't be easy to catch," he warned. "And you can't just catch and count them, like money. You've got to know the denomination of the coins, not just the total amount, to understand the true value. You must know the makeup of that cougar population to fully understand its function in the environment."

With Wilbur diligently hunting cats in Big Creek and me deep in graduate work, Shirley got word that her father was ill. So she took our youngest daughter, eighteen-month-old Lisa, back to Iowa for a month to help her mother, leaving me with the two older girls, Karen, eight, and Kim, six.

"We'll be fine," I assured Shirley. "You're needed back there. It's important."

I was soon overwhelmed with tending to the kids, tackling the academic gauntlet, and administering the cougar study from afar. So I sought an attaboy from my biggest critic, hoping for a small pat on the shoulder from a straight shooter I respected.

Chitty was a zoology professor at UBC who, four years later, would be elected a fellow of the Royal Society of Canada. Decades after that, he would write a book titled *Do Lemmings Really Commit Suicide? Beautiful Hypothesis and Ugly Facts.* Had I known the latter, I might have solicited solace elsewhere. I was, after all, approaching a cliff of despair.

Chitty was quite famous in England and had moved to Canada to follow the wishes of his Canadian-born wife. He was very British and proper, with a very dry sense of humor. He taught a class titled "The History of Scientific Inquiry," one of the best classes I ever took.

So one day while my daughters were in school, I went hunting for empathy even though Dr. Chitty had already labeled the cougar project "a hopeless study." He had advised me not to pursue anything new because there would be no previous scientific studies to cite. On top of Chitty's skepticism, another one of my professors, Dr. David Suzuki, later known as the Jacques Cousteau of terrestrial science in Canada with his long-running CBC Television program titled *The Nature of Things*, kept snowing me under with his rigorous genetics course.

Before picking the girls up at school, I knocked on Chitty's office door.

"Enter," his voice boomed from inside. I eased the door open and approached his desk. Barely looking at me, he gestured toward a chair. I sat down on the opposite side of the desk and watched him sort through some documents.

"Um, Dr. Chitty," I began, "I'm feeling so inundated with classes and there's been a family emergency involving my wife's father, and other things are going so sour, I think I might just quit."

Silence.

Still looking down and scribbling away on one of the documents, he finally said, "Well, why don't you then?"

I was speechless. I knew he harbored doubts about my thesis. But all I wanted was a word of encouragement, a simple "hang in there" would have helped. Instead, a curt dismissal. Then he slowly looked up, his wise eyes burrowing into mine.

"It's up to you," he said. End of discussion. Calmly, he returned to his paperwork.

I sat dumbfounded for a few seconds, then began to smolder. Slowly, I got up, turned and walked away, closed the door behind me, and began breathing fire.

"By God!" I told myself while returning to my pickup truck, "I'll show him."

I couldn't wait to get back to Big Creek and capture more cougars. Ironically, Dr. Chitty later became one of my strongest supporters and would label my thesis a "landmark" achievement.

## Chapter Seven

# The Compass Swings West

Looking retrospectively at my circumstances that first year—launching a challenging cougar study and fulfilling family obligations and academic demands—I'm reminded that some of life's greatest gifts come disguised as failures, even tragedies. Timing and luck also figure into the formula.

So let's rewind one last time to the farm in Iowa to see how the future can be a product of fluke and how fate opened my eyes to science. The road meanders a bit. But stick with me. We'll get back to Big Creek and those puzzling mountain lions soon enough.

I returned home in 1955 after four years in the U.S. Navy. My father and brother were hard at work, as expected, and I joined them, as expected. I'd spent two years on the USS *Polaris*, a refrigerator supply ship off the coast of wartime Korea, and two more years, mostly in the Atlantic Ocean, sleeping in a fold-down bunk atop a torpedo in the aft of the "killer whale" submarine USS *Grampus* (SS-523).

Because of my farm experience, the Navy decided I would be a good mechanic. I had a choice: either diesel engine school or electrician school. I chose the latter. The electrical grid was on a fast track in Iowa, and my dad always said, "Learn a trade so you have something to do, in case things go sour on the farm." Practical education and training aside, the Navy experience fell short of my expectations. As the lyrics of the 1936 Fred Astaire song go, "We joined the Navy to see the world, but what did we see? We saw the sea." So my return to rural Wayne County, Iowa, to do farm work was not only expected, but also somewhat comforting. Not long after, a feisty farm girl who'd grown up when I was away in the Navy caught my eye.

Shirley Owen, five years my junior, was raised on a farm just north of Allerton. I knew her family when she was a little kid. She knew about me because I'd played baseball and basketball. High school sports were a big deal. Shirley and I found ourselves in similar circumstances—the only choices for dating in the whole town. So we indeed dated, fell in love, got married in March 1956, had our first baby, and seemed destined to do as expected: become a farm family. Like me, Shirley was steeped in thrift, self-reliance, and a work ethic. We made a good team.

A year later, timing and luck turned calamity into good fortune. The region entered a severe drought. Dad, Wayne, and I had to sell most of the cattle and all the other livestock because we had nothing to feed them. We needed to, as Dad put it, "tighten down," which meant I had to find a job outside the farm. So I learned about a roustabout job opening at the El Paso Natural Gas pumping station in Lineville, about ten miles away. I applied, and they hired me. It was a plum job and paid well. All I needed was a physical examination to finalize the deal. In the waiting room of the doctor's office, I picked up a magazine and read a fascinating article about a guy who worked as a forest ranger in Sheridan, Wyoming, on the edge of the Bighorn Mountains. Kind of a day-in-the-life story.

"My God," I said to myself after reading the article and continuing to leaf through the photographs of him at work, "that's what I'd like to do."

Timing and luck. My life's compass suddenly swung west toward the Rocky Mountains.

I longed for a better future for my family and for me. The forest ranger, according to the article, had gone to the University of Montana. So after passing the physical, I gathered ten dollars worth of quarters, went to a phone booth, and called the College of Forestry in Missoula.

"Hello," a voice answered.

"Hello, my name is Maurice Hornocker. I live in Iowa, and I'm interested in studying forestry at your school."

"Well, my name is Ross Williams, and I work here."

Can you imagine that? The dean of the University of Montana forestry school answered the phone himself. More good timing and luck.

I told Dean Williams about the forest ranger article, how I'd been raised on a family farm in Iowa and then spent four years in the Navy. I also shared my hesitancy to even inquire because I was almost twenty-seven years old.

"Well heck, I've got a whole college full of you Korean veterans," said the dean. "How were your grades in high school?"

"I was valedictorian of my class of eighteen students."

"Good enough. Pack your bags and come on out."

I went home, told Shirley about the conversation, and asked, "Do you want to move to Montana?"

"Sure," she said.

It wasn't really that simple. A lot went on between then and leaving Iowa for Montana. And my father almost disowned me on the spot.

"Craziest thing I ever heard of," he chastised. "Someone your age with a family going off to school." I could understand his anger, considering the way he was raised and lived and how he had raised me to live. Bottom line, he wouldn't speak to me for two years.

Shirley and our baby, Karen, moved in with Shirley's parents, and I boarded a train to Missoula with my suitcase and enough money to get along for a while. I quickly established my classes and a routine while staying in a local hotel and looking for an apartment. I found a small one, and Shirley moved out with six-month-old Karen in November 1956, just before Thanksgiving.

With their arrival, more good timing and luck lay ahead.

Montana was on the quarter system, and nonresident tuition was around $150 a quarter—not much by today's standards but a deep reach into our pocketbook back then. Shirley learned through the university registrar that if she worked for six months and established residency, I'd also become a resident and get a break on tuition. So she found a neighbor lady to care for the baby while she worked as a teller at a nearby bank. We became residents, and my tuition fell to about $50 a quarter.

In the classroom, I quickly learned that starting college at twenty-seven years old was a remedial exercise. I was rusty. Most of my classmates were recent high school graduates with minds still in overdrive. While scrambling to get up to speed, I learned about a new degree program called "Wildlife Technology," offered through the university's Department of Zoology. It emphasized biology instead of the saw milling, lumbering, and timber management classes in the College of Forestry that didn't interest me as much.

So I switched and found the wildlife curriculum, taught by a wonderful faculty, to be exhilarating. I thrived.

Meanwhile, Shirley and I bought a little house in a good neighborhood with money she'd earned and profits from selling my livestock and farm machinery. The Veterans Administration provided $132 a month, but we needed more income. So I searched for a summer job.

That's when I first heard the name Dr. John Craighead.

John was leader of the Cooperative Wildlife Research Unit at the University of Montana. He had several projects going, and I was told that he would now and then hire undergraduate assistants. I applied even though there were no openings. Months passed with no word about my application, and eventually I signed up as a choker-setter with a timber outfit out of Thompson Falls, Montana. For the uninitiated, the job entails scrambling around active logging sites and choking heavy cables around the ends of logs so they can be skidded, yanked, and pulled from the forest. It's physically taxing and dangerous work.

"You'll come back with fewer fingers," a forestry buddy warned.

"Or maybe even without a hand!" another teased.

But I needed a job and had my bags packed. Two days before leaving, our home phone rang. It was John Craighead's secretary.

"Dr. Craighead would like to meet with you about a job opportunity we've opened up here at the unit."

I didn't know John Craighead from Adam. His name meant nothing to me even though he was pretty famous by then. I didn't know that he'd garnered global recognition, along with his twin brother Frank, for being falconers and studying birds of prey. And little did I know that he and Frank would one day launch the first comprehensive study of grizzly bears in Yellowstone National Park and bring me along for the ride. All I knew at the time was that I needed a job because choker-setter work was hazardous.

So I hustled over to the wildlife unit, and the secretary ushered me into Craighead's office. A sinewy-muscular, athletic man who'd wrestled in college and taught survival skills in the military, Craighead came out from behind his desk, firmly shook my hand, and wasted little time explaining what he had in mind.

"We're studying pheasants," he began, "trying to measure depredation, you know, plundering of eggs in nests. So we've got these dummy pheasant nests established, and we're focusing on magpies as predators . . . we're monitoring the nests. It would be your job to check those nests daily and report any depredation on them."

The financial compensation wasn't much. But think of it. I would get paid to be outdoors, checking to see if one bird was pecking holes in eggs that were artificially planted by human researchers in another bird's fake nest.

"You bet," I said. "I'll do it." I went home and explained my decision to accept the job to Shirley. She agreed, and I notified the logging company that I wouldn't be coming to work for them after all. The next day, John drove me to the study site and showed me what to do. That was my first experience with John Craighead. It would lead to a ten-year professional relationship, a lifelong friendship, and eventually to me studying mountain lions in the wilds of Idaho.

Once again, good timing and luck.

Like Wilbur Wiles, John Craighead was fifteen years older than me. Also like Wilbur, John was a no-nonsense teacher and mentor. He wanted to get jobs done with efficiency and accountility, and he expected the same from his employees.

"You're a good observer," he told me after a spring and early summer of monitoring pheasant nests. "You seem to see things that other people might not notice." Still an undergraduate, I eagerly became John's gofer. I was taking a full load of classes but jumped at any wage-earning work or learning opportunity that came along. I toiled in the unit's labs and in the field assisting graduate students researching pheasants, geese, elk, bighorn sheep, and other species. It couldn't have been a better-designed learning experience. John even set me up with a small flock of seagulls in my family's backyard to see how many mice they could eat.

"They eat an average of twelve a day," I reported. "But then they fast for a day."

Learning aside, the work helped pay our bills as our family grew. Shirley gave birth to our second daughter, Kim, and we further settled in to Missoula, embracing the western college town atmosphere.

By the time I received my bachelor's degree in 1960, John (eventually joined by his brother Frank) was gearing up his grizzly bear research. John and I had gone to Yellowstone National Park in the summer of 1959 and started the project that entailed trapping and marking grizzlies. Frank joined us a year later. I spent the next four seasons monitoring grizzlies that congregated around dumps both inside and outside the national park. We trapped, tranquilized, marked, and equipped the bears with radio collars for tracking. The study gained worldwide attention and became the subject of magazine articles, documentary films, and Frank Craighead's best-selling book *Track of the Grizzly*. In 1962, I wrote my master's degree thesis in wildlife technology on the population characteristics and reproductive behavior of grizzly bears in Yellowstone. John then hired me as an assistant at the unit, making the grizzly study my primary responsibility.

John and I often went hunting and fishing together. I learned simply from being around him, by osmosis, you might say, the unconscious assimilation of knowledge. Among other things, he schooled me in the realities of wildlife research. It's not only a job, it's a way of life, he told me, a calling that offers one of the purest forms of joy—the reward of discovery in nature.

"If you want to continue the kind of work we've been involved in all these years, you'll have to earn a PhD," he advised me. "That's the only way you're going to be able to establish a reputation, raise money, and do independent research."

So I started, with John's help, to shop around. We eyed a bald eagle project in southeastern Alaska, but funding fell through. There was a potential vulture study in Southern California, but I wasn't interested. John even paid my way to Africa as a candidate to head a lion study. But George Schaller—recognized today as one of the world's preeminent wildlife field biologists—got the job instead.

No problem. Timing and good luck would merge once again.

John and I took a train to attend a North American Wildlife Conference meeting in Detroit. John was slated to give a talk about his grizzly bear research in Yellowstone. It happened that John's counterpart, Paul Dalke, leader of the Cooperative Wildlife Research Unit at the University of Idaho (UI), was on the same train. The three of us had breakfast in the dining car, sitting at a table covered with white linen, silverware placed precisely around white china plates, water jiggling in crystal glasses as the train rattled eastward across North Dakota.

"They've got a new Fish and Game Department director in Idaho," Dalke said. "Woodworth is his name."

"What do you know about him?" John asked.

"A real visionary, forward-looking guy," Dalke continued. "He's really interested in launching a cougar study."

John and I locked eyes, smiled at each other, and began peppering Dalke with questions. He said he didn't know much more than a mountain lion study appearing to be in the works.

Shortly after that trip, John was asked to do another grizzly talk at a sportsman's club gathering in Coeur d'Alene, Idaho. He couldn't go, so he sent me. After the presentation, Frank Cullen, a member of the Idaho Fish and Game Commission, approached me.

"What's your status over there in Montana?" he asked.

"Well, I'm working for John until something I like comes along, and then I plan to do it solo."

"We've got a project coming up that you might want to look into," Cullen said. "You know anything about mountain lions?"

"No," I said. "I've only seen one . . . and it was dead."

Motivated by Cullen's inquiry, I called around to learn all I could about Idaho's proposed cougar study and decided to gain some expertise as fast as possible to give me a leg up. With John's help, I obtained a small start-up grant from the American Museum of Natural History to develop methods for capturing and marking mountain lions. Then I put out the word in Missoula that I'd pay someone $50 if they could tree a cougar and keep it at bay until I arrived to tranquilize it. We ended up getting thirteen mountain lions tagged in about a 100-mile radius around Missoula. It was my first experience working with cougars, and I considered doing a study in Montana. But by spring, nine of the thirteen marked cats had been killed by hunters. Clearly, trying to conduct a study in an area inhabited by so many people would be pointless.

So the wilds of central Idaho became front and center. There, you could escape into pristine backcountry. Few hunters would spend the time, money, and energy to pursue mountain lions in such a remote place. I contacted John R. (Dick) Woodworth, the Idaho director of fish and game, and he literally invited me to conduct the study. Eventually, we drafted a contract between me and the department, with UI as an adjunct to administer funding. Paul Dalke would be retiring in a few years as leader of the UI Cooperative Wildlife Research Unit, and I had my sights on the position. As I would learn from studying mountain lions, when a top cat leaves a territory, there's stiff competition to fill the void.

As part of the contract with the Idaho Fish and Game Commission, we included one year that I'd need to finish the academic requirements to earn a PhD. My doctoral thesis would come as a by-product of the yearly field research. At the time, there were three outstanding wildlife departments: one at the University of California, Berkeley; another at the University of Wisconsin, Madison; and the third at UBC in Canada. I contacted all three, and Ian McTaggart Cowan at UBC got back to me right away.

"Come on up and introduce yourself," he said. So I did. Already an international figure known as the "father of Canadian ecology," I found Ian to be the most inspirational person I'd ever met. A true visionary, he was enthused about my idea to study cougars in the wild.

"It's never been done before, you know that, right?" he said.

"That's exactly why I want to do it," I responded.

I knew that Dr. Cowan's endorsement would lend credibility, if not outright prestige, to the study. To back up his enthusiasm for the cougar study, he offered me a $2,200 scholarship to seal the deal.

Thrilled with his offer, I filled Shirley in and asked, "Do you want to go to Vancouver for a year?"

"Sure." Always game and capable, Shirley, like my mother, shouldered the family household demands and encouraged my career pursuits. She was an invaluable and selfless partner, always helping me attain my accomplishments.

We rented out our home in Missoula and moved, now with three young daughters, to Vancouver for the academic school year. We leased a house and enrolled the two oldest girls in school. The neighbors were wonderful. We lived adjacent to a beautiful park where there was often interesting activity, from kite flying to rugby, from soccer to dog training. We all thrived in the welcoming environment.

At UBC, there was not nearly the emphasis on course work that exists at American universities. In the United States, it seemed they loaded you up with classes for years and then turned you loose as though you were prepared. But it was just the opposite in the British–Canadian system. They look over your academic record, see what you've been exposed to, and then suggest areas that need more attention. Genetics coursework was my shortcoming along with biological theory. So I took the classes, attended seminars, listened to guest speakers, and found it an immensely enjoyable learning experience. They wanted to know your connection to the outside world and how your capabilities might make it a little better—they wanted visionary research. I devoured the philosophy and flourished.

My enthusiasm, however, was not shared at UI, where a snafu brewed and culminated with my barging into a dean's office, pounding my fist on his desk, and demanding he listen to me.

## CHAPTER EIGHT

# Byzantine Bickering

PAUL DALKE, LEADER OF THE UI COOPERATIVE WILDLIFE RESEARCH Unit in Moscow, Idaho, was miffed. You'll recall that John Craighead had introduced him to me on the train trip to a wildlife conference in Detroit and that Dalke had mentioned the proposed cougar study in Idaho.

Months later, after I'd negotiated the proposed three-way contract with the Idaho Fish and Game Commission, UI, and me, I learned that Dalke had pulled out for reasons unknown, potentially killing the study. I called Director Woodworth at fish and game, and he confirmed the news.

"Dalke and the UI forestry dean wanted you to run the study through them instead of the University of British Columbia," he explained.

"But the inclusion of UI as an adjunct is critical since the study will be conducted in Idaho," I explained. "The research being part of my doctorate at UBC was not intended as a slight to anyone."

"Well, we need to clear this up," Woodworth said.

In the proposed agreement, UI was to administer funds, an extremely important role considering the many funding sources I'd need to proceed. And since I alone had to raise those funds, I knew the university's financial oversight would lend credibility to the project.

So Woodworth called Ernest Wohletz, dean of the UI College of Forestry, Wildlife, and Range Sciences, and set up a meeting with the proviso that, if the snafu wasn't cleared up, support by the Idaho Fish and Game Commission for the college in other areas would be reevaluated. Woodworth's not-so-subtle threat worked, and I was promptly invited to the university in Moscow for a hash out. Prior to leaving for the meeting, I wrote a letter to all participants outlining why it was "appropriate" for the university and its UI Cooperative Wildlife Research Unit to be included.

The meeting was scheduled for 10:00 a.m. I drove five hours from Missoula and walked directly to Dalke's office. After massaging our differences and he agreed to rejoin the study, we walked together to the dean's office to set the record straight. Then we sat down and waited.

And waited.

"Dean Wohletz is on an important call," his secretary told us. "He'll see you later in the day."

Dalke and I went back to Dalke's office and waited. And waited some more.

"Let's go back," I said. Dalke balked, I suspect because he knew Wohletz's reputation as a tough administrator bordering on an academic tyrant. But he finally acquiesced and accompanied me back to the dean's office.

"He's still busy," the secretary said. "And it looks like he's going to be pretty tied up the rest of the day."

I flamed out. I'd come a long way. We had an appointment, and here it was three hours later. I stormed past the secretary to the dean's door, threw it open, and marched in. He was on the phone and glanced up at me as I, madder than hell, glared down at him.

"I'll have to call ya back," he stammered and put the phone down.

"I'm Maurice Hornocker," I announced, "and we had an appointment for 10:00. We'll talk now or I'm going home." Then I slammed my fist on his desk.

His eyes widened.

"I believe I can help the University of Idaho," I continued. "I don't need you, and I don't need the university. But I have an agreement to study cougars with the Idaho Department of Fish and Game, and your college was included because I think it's appropriate. But now I hear you've pulled out. I respect this institution. And I'd like to work with your faculty on this. If you're interested, let's talk. If you're not, we're done."

"Oh, well then," Wohletz sputtered, "I'd say we're all interested in this study and what you have to say."

So I sat down across the desk from him, and we talked. Our discussion quickly solidified a professional relationship. He treated me with courtesy and respect after that. I reciprocated, we drafted an agreement, and UI president Ernst Hartung approved it.

Later, after signing a memorandum of agreement in the president's office, we walked back to the forestry college. Dean Wohletz turned to Paul and said, "You know, Dalke, we ought to do a lot more business this way. Less talk, more action."

Dalke said nothing. Neither did I.

On June 9, 1964, the so-called official "Cougar Contract" was signed by John R. Woodworth, director of the Idaho Fish and Game Department; Kenneth A. Dick, financial vice president for the Regents of UI; and me. The legalese stated,

*"WHEREAS, First Party in the performance of functions provided for by law, and for the preservation of the wild life of the State of Idaho, deems it desirable that a study be made of the ecology of the Mountain Lion, and Second Party is willing to cooperate in the supervision and administration of such research, and Third Party is willing to undertake said study . . ."*

The contract then lays out the proposal and its benefits: five pages of detail that describe the study's duration (July 15, 1964, through July 15, 1967), the need for quarterly reports, hiring procedures, the publication of results, the handling of capital equipment, insurance requirements, and, most important, a budget. For the entire three-year study, a total of $24,000 was earmarked by the Idaho Fish and Game Commission.

By today's standards, that converts to roughly $210,000—a pittance even now. Eventually, the Cooperative Wildlife Research Unit at UI, the Theodore Roosevelt Memorial Fund of the American Museum of Natural History, the Boone and Crockett Club, the New York Zoological Society, the National Geographic Society, and UBC underwrote the project with annual financial assistance.

Especially important to me was the contract's final stipulation:

*"It is understood and agreed that Third Party is a candidate for the degree of Doctor of Philosophy at the University of British Columbia, and that the results of the study may be used as a doctoral thesis at the University of Third Party's choice."*

I read the clause and signed.

## Chapter Nine

# Big Creek Personas

With the contract now binding all parties, I left the Craighead grizzly bear project in Yellowstone in the summer of 1964, with encouragement from my longtime mentor. Setting out to visit the proposed Big Creek mountain lion study area for the first time, I drove from Missoula to McCall, Idaho, then eighty miles over up-and-down gravel roads to Big Creek. I was struck by not only the raw beauty of the landscape, but also the smell of decaying fish.

In the eddies along Big Creek, decomposing salmon choked the backwaters. Death's odor was so strong that I had to roll up my truck windows. The riparian areas along the creek were full of scavengers—birds, coyotes, even bears. The Craighead brothers had told me about a good salmon run in Big Creek and suggested I bring a fly rod. The richness of the ecosystem and the tremendous aquatic food source that migrated annually from the Pacific Ocean to this remote region of the state astounded me.

Where the road ended, I hiked and camped my way down the length of the Big Creek drainage, about thirty-five miles to the Middle Fork of the Salmon River, and then retraced the route back up. I wanted to meet the few people who lived in this vast wilderness, including a fellow named Wilbur Wiles, whom, you recall, I'd been told was an experienced mountain lion hunter, perhaps the best in the region.

Glenn and Mary Harper, owners of the Big Creek Store, gave me directions to Wilbur's cabin near the mouth of Monumental Creek.

"But he's not there," Glenn told me.

"He's at one of his mining claims up on Elk Summit," Mary added.

Wilbur was expected back within a week, the couple estimated. In addition to Wilbur, I wanted to meet the people who lived on four Big Creek private properties within the study area. Less than 400 acres combined, the properties represented the only inkling of civilization within a continuum of more than 3 million roadless acres. Eventually, the acreage would be classified as federal wilderness.

While hiking, my head swiveled back and forth, up and down, as I tried to get a read on the land that would become the study area. Radical elevation changes rose up from narrow canyons cut by raucous creeks spilling into the Big Creek valley. Vegetation, including important browse species for elk and deer, grew in four increasingly altitudinous zones: Ponderosa pine at lower elevations, followed by Douglas fir, then spruce-fir, topped by the alpine zone above the tree line. In addition to elevation, these zones were a product of environmental impacts like wildfires, soil composition, exposure to the sun, and insect outbreaks. The lower Ponderosa zone, I surmised, was the principal winter range for elk and deer, providing palatable shrubs and forbs such as mountain mahogany, bitterbrush, rubber rabbitbrush, big sagebrush, and balsamroot. The vegetation would attract wintering ungulates and the cougars that preyed on them.

Harshness aside, clearly the area held a resident mountain lion population though I never saw one that day. To this day, I wonder if one or more cougars watched me as I explored that particular vestige of their range. The Big Creek mountain lions were no different than any other remnant population. They'd retreat to find a food source and avoid being harmed. To most humans, they were like sharks and wolves—the enemy, something to exterminate.

Dewey Moore, the first resident downstream from Wilbur Wiles's place, couldn't have agreed more about a cougar's worthless life.

Dewey Moore, Big Creek resident, claimed, like many critics at the beginning of the study, that cougars were devastating elk and mule deer populations.

"You wouldn't believe how many elk the god-damned cougars killed in the meadow out here last year," he declared after I hiked to his cabin to introduce myself and brief him on the study I'd be conducting.

"Is that right?" I said in a gee-golly sort of tone.

"Damn cats."

Dewey offered the unsolicited testimonial from the porch of his cabin, with his shirt unbuttoned halfway from the bottom, his bare belly sticking out like he'd wintered well.

"You ought to reconsider," he bellowed, "and launch a campaign to wipe 'em out in Big Creek."

When I said I planned to talk to Wilbur about assisting me in the study, Dewey lit into him.

"You're makin' a big mistake if you're bringing Wilbur Wiles on because his dogs ain't no good," Dewey declared, "and he don't know where them damned lions are."

"Is that right?" I repeated, trying to maintain a curious but friendly demeanor.

"I could take ya to every cougar on this creek. But Wilbur doesn't know! He just lucks into one now and then."

About that time, Dewey's daughter, who was visiting, joined us and invited me to dinner.

"And ya ought to spend the night," Dewey said. "There's an extra cot in the cabin."

I accepted their dinner invitation and slept on the porch.

The next morning, Dewey turned into a singsong tour guide.

"I'll tell ya how to take a real shortcut that will take ya to good elk country with a lot of cougars out there, too," he explained. "It's Coyote Meadows. You just take this trail back here, and you'll save a lot of time."

Little did Dewey know that I'd studied plenty of maps, and I knew the son-of-a-gun was trying to send me on an eight-mile wild goose chase.

"Okay," I said, while trying to sound grateful. "I really appreciate the tip." I then hiked in the direction he pointed. Once out of sight, I contoured back down to the Big Creek trail.

John Vines, farther downstream at Garden Creek Ranch, was the next resident. He sometimes called his place Garden Creek Hindquarters as opposed to Headquarters. A former U.S. Army Air Force pilot, John said he flew test planes after World War II until he developed a heart condition and was discharged.

"I went to work for Lockheed in Southern California as a consultant," he told me. Then he got a job as a stevedore

John Vines, another Big Creek resident, not only endorsed the cougar study, but also always offered visitors a "Big Creek lowball." The concoction, which filled a large glass, consisted of Old Grand Dad bourbon whiskey, no ice, and a scintilla of water, if requested.

on the shipping docks in San Francisco, joined ranks with a "girlfriend," and founded a couple of high-end bars and restaurants, one in the Bay Area, the other in Sacramento.

"Long story short, they failed," he said of the enterprises, "as did the relationship . . . so, anyway, I came here, found this 160-acre ranch for sale and bought it for back taxes."

Our conversation took place inside his cabin, where peanut shells covered the floor. "I like peanuts," he explained as he popped a couple in his mouth. "I have 'em flown into the ranch in fifty-gallon drums."

John said he didn't like his neighbor Dewey Moore and vice versa, stemming from some sort of feud years earlier over horses. Unlike Dewey, John embraced the study from the start. After we got established, Wilbur and I always stopped at John's to have one of his "Big Creek lowballs," a glass filled with Old Grand Dad bourbon whiskey and a scintilla of water. I still have photographs of John in the old cabin holding a lowball while seated in his chair in the middle of that peanut shell–covered floor. He later sold the ranch while the study was still under way; moved to a little house in Emmett, Idaho; and died a year later.

Farther down the creek, Rex Lanham, a big-time Boise area contractor and backcountry outfitter with lots of irons in the fire, had established his private retreat. He wasn't home, so I talked to the ranch manager instead.

"I'd like to rent one of Mr. Lanham's cabins," I told him.

"I'll radiophone him tonight, and when you come back up the creek, I'll have an answer for you," he responded.

Lanham offered a small cabin, including split firewood, for $50 a month, which was high. Since I didn't have much choice, I accepted. After I hired Wilbur, we flew supplies in and stocked the cabin for the coming winter. Then, about halfway into the season, Lanham jacked up the rent to $150.

"What's the deal?" I asked when I ran into him in McCall.

"You were using a lot of firewood," he answered.

"The hell we were. We were only there a couple nights a week."

"It took a lot of money to get that firewood in," he insisted.

The study budget was already tight. We couldn't afford the hike. So we moved out. Wilbur had to pack all our supplies down to Cave Creek, and it really put a crimp in everything.

Over the next few years, Lanham would continue to stew, eventually bad-mouth the study, and ultimately threaten to bring in hunters to kill our marked cougars.

Meanwhile, the reception at Taylor Ranch, the farthest-downstream inholding on Big Creek, was the antithesis of the Cabin Creek experience. Jess and Dorothy Taylor couldn't have been more welcoming. A

Jess Taylor, owner of Taylor Ranch, plays a spring-run Big Creek steelhead.

successful Boise businessman and a player in the stock market, Jess had turned the ranch into a viable outfitting business.

"I'd like to rent one of your cabins," I said.

"Well," he pondered. "I think that would be fine. How long?"

"During the winter months, maybe more."

"You could make it your headquarters if you'd like," Jess suggested.

"Thank you. I'll consider your offer once we nail down the study logistics."

Eventually we did just that— rented the cabin for the duration of the project and made the ranch our main headquarters.

Finally, I was about to meet Wilbur Wiles. Remembering my encounter with Dean Wohletz at the University of Idaho, I knew the tables had turned. Wilbur didn't need me. He'd established a fulfilled life in the backcountry. But I needed him. I had much to learn about the land Wilbur traveled and the mountain lions he hunted.

He lived in a one-room log cabin built from scratch with logs he felled upstream and floated during spring high water down to his homesite adjacent to Monumental Creek.

"You come highly recommended," I told him after I knocked on his door, introduced myself, and accepted a cup of coffee.

"Black. Honey?"

"Both," I said.

John Woodworth, the Idaho Fish and Game director, had reviewed state cougar hunting success records and told me that Wilbur was among the top three hunters, if not the very top. We sat on wooden chairs at a wooden table that Wilbur built.

"I've contracted with Fish and Game to do a cougar study back here," I said.

"Why?" Wilbur asked. So I gave my best pitch, then waited for him to light his pipe and answer my request to work with me. As smoke rose and tobacco crackled, I took a quick look around Wilbur's cabin to get a better idea of the man. A wood cookstove was stationed just inside the door, two more chairs were off to the side, two single bunks lined the back wall near a single closet. A countertop and shelves held dishes. Pots and pans hung from hooks. A stout home, I thought, that served Wilbur's needs, which weren't many.

"One thing I will need," Wilbur said after taking a drag on his pipe, "is the summers off. That's when I work my mining claims."

"No problem," I replied. "We can't start hunting until the snow flies anyways."

"That's true."

"So you'll take the job?"

"Yes, I will."

We shook hands. No need for a written contract.

"And I'll need you to erect and stock the camps before we start," I said.

"I can do that."

Wilbur agreed that the camps were crucial to not only the study's success, but also our survival should winter take a bad turn.

"How many horses will you need to build and stock the camps?"

"I've got three," Wilbur said. "Could use another."

"Then I'll buy one. Now, what about compensation? How much do I need to pay you?"

Wilbur paused, then smiled and trained his piercing blue eyes on me through lingering pipe smoke. "Sounds like getting paid for something that I do anyway, live back here and hunt cougars."

"I suppose you could look at it that way. But your expertise is invaluable."

I was receiving an annual salary of $2,000 through a contract with the Fish and Game Department, plus the fellowship from UBC, a total of a little more than $4,000 a year.

"How's $3,000 sound for the winter months, with extra for establishing the camps?"

Wilbur took a drag on the pipe and paused to exhale. "Sounds good to me."

We had a deal. I hiked back out of Big Creek, drove to McCall, and immediately started shopping for a stout packhorse and a winter's worth of provisions.

# Part II

# The Second Season

## CHAPTER TEN

# Defining Boundaries

TERRITORIALITY AND HOME RANGE HAVE BEEN BASIC CONCEPTS OF wildlife biology and management since the beginning of the profession in the mid-nineteenth century. For thousands of years, in fact, all animal populations, including *Homo sapiens*, have traveled a home range and, when necessary, defended their territory. Think of home range as a community and your house and yard as the territory you will defend.

In Big Creek after the first year of our project, we knew there was a population of mountain lions living within the 200-square-mile "home range" study area. We'd captured and marked ten individual cougars and recaptured four of them. But all captures were isolated in the lower end of the Big Creek drainage. And seven of those first ten cats were males. None of this fit the long-accepted concepts of home range or territoriality. If

After tying Red and the other hounds aside, Wilbur climbs to ease a darted lioness down through limbs to the ground.

anything, the cougars seemed to be living on top of each other within a relatively small geographic area. For what reason? I had some theories but no proof. I needed more information to solve the puzzle.

Meanwhile, my family needed a new territory within a new home range.

"I think we should move to McCall," I told Shirley one night after we'd returned from Vancouver to Missoula on completion of my first year of graduate classes at UBC.

"You think what?"

"I think McCall would be a good move, professionally speaking," I explained. "I need to establish myself in Idaho to keep the study going."

"But Missoula is just as close. You fly in and out of Big Creek, so what's the difference?"

Our family, especially Shirley, was established in Missoula. We'd lived there for nearly a decade. We had close friends. The two oldest daughters were in school. We loved the college-town atmosphere.

"Missoula is our home," Shirley said defensively. Looking back, I see the magnitude of what I was springing on her.

"You know," I tried to explain, "I've had my eye on the unit job at the University of Idaho. Paul Dalke is nearing retirement, and that job could come open near the end of the cougar study."

"I understand. But McCall? It's just a timber town in the middle of nowhere. The kids love it here in Missoula. They have friends. We have friends," Shirley persisted.

"Please," I said, "just think about it."

"I will . . . of course. It's just such a surprise."

I really wanted a shot at landing the Idaho cooperative unit job—the same position John Craighead held at the University of Montana. A unit leadership offered the best opportunity for pursuing a career of creative, relatively independent research. John agreed, suggesting that I relocate to Idaho and establish residency. He also described McCall as being bordered by picturesque Payette Lake and a great place to raise a family. During World War II, he and twin brother Frank were naval officers charged with teaching aviators survival skills if shot down. The

Craigheads established headquarters in McCall and moved their families there. The vast adjacent wilderness surrounding the small mountain town of about 1,400 residents back then was their training ground—the same wilderness where I would soon study mountain lions.

But for the most part, Shirley was right. McCall was a tiny lumber town known mostly for its significant U.S. Forest Service presence—nothing like today's glitzy tourist hub with its clothing boutiques, breweries, recreational boating in summer, and nearby winter ski resorts.

Even our family cat, Muffin, seemed miffed at me. After all, he'd recently returned to his territory after being ousted. And what a cat-come-home story it is.

Before venturing off for my required graduate courses at UBC in Vancouver, we decided to rent our Missoula house to two young women, students at the University of Montana. As part of the deal, they agreed to watch over Muffin and tend to his needs.

"No problem!" they told us.

However, when we returned eight months later, we discovered the two students gone (they'd subleased the place) and Muffin missing. Neighbors told us the students had kicked Muffin out as soon as we left. Our daughters were mortified.

"What happened to him?"

"I don't know," I said.

"Will he come home?"

"Not sure, but probably not."

I had no more answers for Muffin's fate than I had for the cougars in Big Creek.

A week passed. We lived in an older part of town with lots of hedges, vegetation, and other landscaping, not to mention numerous feral cats that patrolled the alleys. Was it possible that they ran Muffin out of his territory and that he was now displaced amid his neighborhood home range? We all sulked.

And then, "Muffin is home! Muffin is back," the girls were shouting.

He had just shown up at the door. It was quite a reunion. Our daughters were jubilant. Muffin purred and purred as we passed him around.

He rubbed and circled between our legs. He seemed in perfect shape, and I thought he'd never stop seeking affection.

"Where do you think he went?"

"Where did he live?"

"What did he eat?"

"Did he get in fights with other tomcats?"

My daughters' questions echoed the same queries I'd been pondering over mountain lions. Perhaps another human family had taken Muffin in. More likely, he'd lived on his own, scouring crawl spaces for rodents, plucking small birds from backyard hedges, perhaps snatching kibble from food bowls left on porches for other "outside cats." And then, maybe during a routine neighborhood patrol, he happened by and sensed we'd returned. I like to think that Muffin, relying on innate feline prowess, had reverted to evolutionary skills like stealth, stalk, and the wielding of tooth and claw. One thing for sure: Muffin, the family pet, had restored happiness to our family and given me a renewed appreciation of cats—their adaptability, versatility, and ability to survive.

As we celebrated Muffin's return and Shirley pondered the move to McCall, I returned my attention to cougars. Before long, a mountain lion would appear to materialize out of nowhere, sending chills up my spine and renewing my confidence that the study might succeed after all.

## Chapter Eleven

# Unexpected Ghost

On the morning of July 18, 1965, I flew into Taylor Ranch for a two-day stay with owners Jess and Dorothy Taylor before hopping another flight to Cold Meadows airstrip so I could start exploring the Chamberlain Basin. Hoping to capture more mountain lions during the upcoming winter, I'd decided to expand the study area north of the Big Creek drainage and hire a second crew.

The Taylors were at their magnanimous best, making me feel welcome during my two-night stay. They asked thoughtful questions about the study, and Dorothy prepared terrific dinners. Jess, like most people, didn't like cougars, but he liked the rent money the study was paying him for use of a cabin, and we became reasonable friends. Dorothy, a gracious woman who took pride in setting a table with finery that belied the ranch's remote location, was a realtor in Boise. She and Jess met when he hired her to show a spec house he'd built.

"I'm looking for some art work, some photographs," Dorothy said at dinner that first night. "I'd like a representative series of animals from this area . . . elk, mountain goats, bighorns, mule deer, black bears, coyotes."

"And cougars," I interjected.

"Well, of course."

"I think I can help you out with that." (Later, I assembled some of my best wildlife photographs, had them enlarged and framed, and presented them to Dorothy.)

I turned to Jess. "About the big cabin for this coming winter . . ."

"You can rent it again. Long term, if you like."

"For how much?" I asked.

"Well," Jess, always the businessman, pondered, "how about continuing to pay the rent amount you're paying now, plus paying the radiophone cost through the winter and keeping an eye on the place?"

"Okay, then," and we struck a deal.

Jess was industrious and hardworking. As Wilbur had done on Monumental Creek, Jess built the couple's log ranch house by cutting timbers upstream and floating them down Big Creek. He also built a "duplex" cabin for hunters and guests and eventually constructed an airstrip by hand-clearing a brush-choked part of the property, allowing for pretty much year-round small-aircraft access to the ranch.

"You've done an incredible amount of work," I told him.

"Worth it," he said.

Before dinner, I fished Big Creek for cutthroat trout and jotted "fabulous" in my notes. The next morning, I hiked north up Cliff Creek across from the ranch and found a tree that had been scratched by a cougar. Then, farther up through a basin overlooking the ranch below, I saw two peregrine falcons circling in the blue sky.

Jess, for all his business acumen and backcountry skills, was not a conservationist. He was threatening to kill birds of prey, including golden eagles, in the area.

"They prey on mountain sheep lambs," he insisted. Maybe the raptors did. I wasn't sure and didn't argue. Wilbur had already taught me how raptors and avian scavengers swarmed above deer and elk kills. We'd investigate and often find cougar tracks that led to cougar captures.

Predator control had historic roots throughout the region, including at Taylor Ranch. Enter Dave Lewis, aka "Cougar Dave."

The Taylors bought the ranch in 1934 from Lewis. He was a Civil War veteran and former U.S. Army packer. He also served during the 1879 Sheepeater Indian War, which was fought in the Salmon River country. After the shooting stopped, Lewis retreated to Big Creek as a gold prospector and hunting guide. He eventually took up residence at the ranch site in 1918, built a cabin, and patented the homestead in 1927 (thus making the acreage a legal private inholding within the Payette

National Forest). He ran an outfitting business and earned the moniker "Cougar Dave" for purportedly killing more than 1,000 mountain lions during his tenure on Big Creek. Often, folklore and BS are hard to separate. I was more interested in the current number of cougars, not how many "Cougar Dave" had supposedly slain.

Of course, little did I know that our study findings would ignite a dispute far greater than the debate about Cougar Dave's hunting prowess. This new cougar debate would spill far from Big Creek and eventually to the Idaho legislature in Boise. Fortunately, in July 1965, I had no inkling of the firestorm ahead. And since I still lacked sound scientific findings, I needed to set out and uncover them.

On the early morning of July 20, before summer heat built and rising wind currents negated light aircraft from landing at Taylor Ranch, Gene Crosby flew in from McCall and shuttled me to Cold Meadows landing strip at 7,030 feet above sea level. Looking down as we were landing, I saw elk cows and calves grazing across the meadows.

"Cougar food," my subconscious whispered.

From the airstrip, I hiked twelve miles to Root Ranch in the heart of the Chamberlain Basin along Whimstick Creek, then down to Chamberlain Creek. Signs of cougars were everywhere, including tracks in the trail as I traveled from just above McCalla Creek to Chamberlain Creek. I found where cougars had heaped needles, grass, and other debris into pyramid-like mounds, similar to a domestic cat chaffing up a pile in a litter box. I spotted elk and deer carcasses from last winter or spring, most of which appeared to be old cougar kills.

*My notes: "Hellish good cat country."*

An excellent campsite waited at the mouth of McCalla Creek where it flowed into Chamberlain Creek. There, I found the fishing to be surprisingly poor and barely caught enough to supplement the oatmeal and raisins in my pack.

Lack of food aside and still thrilled by prospects, I felt humbled to be deep in the backcountry with no sign of other humans. But I would soon encounter a formidable creature, a bear, and a big one at that.

On the second night, while camped during a rainstorm where Chamberlain Creek empties into the Salmon River, I woke to a loud "woof." It reminded me of the sound I'd heard a few grizzly bears make while I studied them in Yellowstone National Park. If I'd had a gun, as I did in the park, I would have reached for it. Instead, I lay unarmed and as still as a prostrate statue, eyes pinned wide open, sleeping bag wrapped tightly around my body. Then, "Woof, woof!" Slowly I sat up, and there he was, several yards away—not a grizzly but a very curious and very large black bear. He sniffed the air, woofed again, and stood on his hind legs, his girth silhouetted against the star-pocked night. The rain had stopped, and the skies were clearing. "Woof, woof!" the bear snorted again, turning his head to the side and clacking his jaws.

"Hey!" I shouted, in my deepest voice.

"Woof!" he responded.

"Hey!" I yelled louder while slowly squirming out of my sleeping bag and standing. "Get out of here!"

"Woof!" he answered.

"Go, get out of here. Now!"

And with that, the bruin dropped to all fours, turned, and lumbered away as if he'd grown bored. I like to think that if I had a gun, I'd have taken the same approach—stood firm and talked to the bear rather than pull the trigger. Despite that unnerving encounter, the only gun Wilbur and I carried throughout the study was a dart gun to tranquilize the cougars.

Eventually, I managed to fall back asleep and woke primed to further assess the Chamberlain Basin for expansion of the study. I speculated that the country between Chamberlain Creek and Big Creek was prone to heavy snowfall and offered a natural wintertime impediment that split the cougar population into two separate units. Surely, I reasoned, the cats wouldn't travel over the snow-choked high country during the winter months.

With this thought in mind, I continued to hike, set up another campsite, and turned in for the third night, still pondering winter conditions at this higher elevation. Snowfall and arctic-like temperatures could severely hinder our travel, and I woke to confirmation of my worry—coffee from the night before skimmed over with July ice.

Sometimes, while reflecting on my exploration into the Chamberlain Basin so many summers ago, I feel old and cranky. My memories are remnants of what field research was, but may never be again. Simplicity and intuition have been relegated if not lost. Feet on the ground have been replaced by the latest technology. Yes, remote sensing and all the gadgets and gizmos of the digital era have made the study of secretive species less challenging and the collection of quantitative data much easier. But the technology tends to focus solely on the specific target species, not the environmental forces that can and do alter behavior.

The researcher's immersion into the target animal's environment, I maintain, leads to a better understanding of the animal and its world. Gut feelings garnered while trudging through an apex predator's home range, the direct observation of details within the ecosystem, the confirming or debunking of theories by scouring the earth—these can't be replaced by technical inventions. Nor can technology match the thrill of finally locking eyes with the animal you seek to better understand. Such encounters are organic, aboriginal, primal, and even downright life changing.

It was the fourth day of my Chamberlain Basin exploration, and, to borrow from author Wallace Stegner again, I felt the "prickle" of the mountain lion's presence. Surreal. Zen. Ethereal. Dream-like. Spooky. I've used all of these adjectives over the years when describing the encounter.

I'd gone downstream from the confluence of McCalla Creek and Chamberlain Creek as the day wore toward dusky evening. The trail ahead to the Salmon River was brush choked. Hadn't been maintained in years. But there were elk skeletons, which I presumed had been killed by cougars.

The bones were strewn about, some entangled with vegetation that seemed to be pulling the carcasses back into the earth, and others were rib cages and scapula bones glimmering white in fading sunshine. I don't know why, but something enticed me to turn up a little side trail. I saw no blown-down trees blocking the way. I was tired of negotiating those. So I climbed higher and higher into a steep canyon that topped out into a beautiful little aspen tree meadow. Yellow-green leaves quaked in the breeze and shimmered in the day's fading light. Suddenly, like a dark cloud scudding across the sky, an uneasy feeling overcame me. An unexpected co-traveler was near, and we both stopped.

The mountain lion, a big tom, stood only yards away, frozen in place, just like me. Outlined against the evening light, we peered at one another through wispy aspen branches for the better part of a minute. I could see only his angular face and the occasional twitch of an ear. I grew so still that I may have stopped breathing, but I don't remember. The cat was not crouched for attack. He simply fixed his yellow-brown eyes on me as if assessing my presence and perhaps pondering, like me, the next move. Eventually, he seemed satisfied that I presented no imminent danger, and with one graceful leap from the cluster of aspen trees, the tom was out in the open, his entire body now visible. Once again, our eyes locked. By this time, my heart would have resumed beating. Time seemed at a standstill. Then the cat slowly turned his gaze away and, with one fluid saltation, vanished. No sound. No shadow trailing behind. Just the image of a mountain lion appearing, pausing to observe me, and disappearing as if to say "Good luck trying to figure me out" seared in my memory to this day. It was as if this exquisite king of the food chain had authored the Wilderness Act. In his home range and territory, I was little more than "a visitor who does not remain."

Never again, during all my years of study, would I encounter a free-roaming mountain lion in such an intimate and surreal way. I suspect, however, that these secretive cats often saw me, maybe even studied me, as I was trying to study them.

With the ghostly cougar experience freshly etched in my mind, I hiked the next morning up to Grass Mountain Lookout. At an elevation of 6,400 feet, I determined that the abandoned outpost would be a good emergency stopover camp in case, while hunting, daylight vanished or we got caught in a sudden storm. Ultimately, I determined, three main camps were needed in the Chamberlain Basin area. Root Ranch would be our headquarters camp. To the north, we'd erect a camp at the confluence of McCalla and Chamberlain creeks, and the final and lowest camp would rest where Disappointment Creek flows into the Salmon River. From these three camps, all of which Wilbur and I added to what we called a complex of "homes," I planned to dispatch a yet-to-be-hired second team of hunters to capture, mark, and release cougars.

My notes: *"Looks like ideal area for the study."*

At one juncture toward the end of my Chamberlain Basin exploration, I heard two unfamiliar and incessant sounds that dumbfounded me. The first was a repetitive low-pitched hoot coming from within a vast stand of huge ponderosa pine trees. Unlike any owl I'd ever heard, the baritone five-count "whoo, whoo, whoo, whoo-whoo" continued almost uninterrupted. Creeping deeper into the woods as the volume increased, I finally spotted the source. Dozens of ornately plumed male blue grouse strutted about on the ground beneath the pine trees. They were ensconced on territories trying to attract females with what sounded like an avian symphony. It was breeding season, and I was thrilled to discover them. The bird hunter from my youth also whispered, "You've got to come back in the fall with a shotgun."

I did not welcome the second strange sound, a distant mechanical whining. While hiking above the Salmon River and peering down through vegetation to a slice of water below, I stopped to pinpoint the noisy source, which seemed to be moving. And there it was—something I'd never seen or heard before—a jet boat. It was traveling rapidly upstream, the roar of its loud engine muffled amid twisting canyon walls. The sight and decibel level of the boat reminded me of how far humans had already encroached on the wilderness and how far mountain lions had come to escape their advance.

On July 24, my exploration complete, I hiked thirty miles from Chamberlain Basin back to Taylor Ranch on Big Creek. Thrilled with all the evidence of mountain lions I'd found and the accessibility of the area, my legs felt like wings.

*My notes: "No strain."*

Clearly, it was time to contact Wilbur and get our camps ready for season two of the cougar study. I was, for the first time, awash in confidence.

## CHAPTER TWELVE

# Ten Remote Homes

WE SECURED FOUR CABINS: WILBUR'S PLACE ON MONUMENTAL CREEK, another at Taylor Ranch, one near the mouth of Coxey Creek, and a fourth at Root Ranch. All the other "homes" were twelve- by fourteen-foot wall tents equipped with wood-burning sheepherder stoves. The simple sheet-metal stoves were effective and an absolute must in any mountain camp. Etched on a map, our living quarters extended across the entire study area, including the new Chamberlain Basin complex.

A snow-laden wall tent at the west fork of Rush Creek camp.

"A good camp is like a good cave for a cougar," Wilbur reasoned, "a place to get comfortable, and maybe survive."

I bought all the high-quality canvas wall tents, cots, sleeping bags, and other furnishings, then had the gear either trucked into the Big Creek headwaters area or flown into one of the private airstrips. From there, Wilbur packed the gear on his four horses and transported it to the strategically located sites. It took weeks to erect and stock all the camps.

The camps varied from five to ten miles apart, usually at the mouth of tributaries that spilled into Big Creek. In that country, you never knew where you might be at night after pursuing a cat. You couldn't afford to be located two ridges over from your camp or ten miles away when it turns dark. You've got to have a "home" nearby. We didn't want to spend a cold night trying to sleep under a tree if we didn't have to. So we were adamant about being close enough to a camp to have a warm fire, food, and rest. Sometimes the dogs needed reprieve, especially after a long pursuit, more than we did.

Self-schooled, Wilbur had refined his camping methods and skills out of necessity, using human-made implements and raw wilderness resources. He erected pine poles as support frames for our wall tents. Then he secured the bottom edges of the walls to logs on the ground. We built no wooden floors because bare earth was easier to heat and keep dry. We covered our canvas tents with plastic sheeting so that snow would slide off. Every camp contained two folding cots and two thick polyester sleeping bags. We bought bulk dried food supplies (flour, sugar, salt, pepper, and boxed mainstays like Bisquick) in Donnely, Idaho, from the Hamilton Store, which specialized in backcountry goods. At each tent site, we stored the products, including more than a ton of dog food, in surplus rubberized Navy cargo bags that we hung from poles suspended between trees.

We buried canned goods and covered them with brush piles to stymie raiding black bears before they hibernated for the winter. Despite our efforts, one bear at Cave Creek learned how to climb a tree and shimmy out on the support pole to break it or chew the rope and send the food crashing earthward. Our most tenacious marauders turned out to be flying squirrels, their presence reaching pandemic proportions at the Rush Creek

More than a ton of dog food was flown in each autumn, off-loaded, packed by horses, and stowed at camps.

camp. They'd swoop down from trees, land on the rubber bags, and gnaw their way inside. Although the squirrels didn't eat much, melting snow and rain would gather on top of the bags, seep through the chewed holes, and render large quantities of food inedible. Wilbur tried to trap the aerial demons with minimal success.

"Kind of like dipping water from the ocean," he lamented.

Chainsaws were permitted in the primitive area prior to wilderness designation, and we'd heap each camp with a good supply of firewood. As for the camp menus, our mainstay was elk and deer venison. We shot the animals during the legal hunting season (usually in late November), butchered and wrapped the meat in canvas, and hung it with the Navy cargo bags out of bear reach. The meat was subject to deep freezing and gentle thawing as the temperature either plummeted below zero or rose sometimes into the upper forties. This aging process broke the venison down, and tender cutlets could be removed with the slice of a knife and cooked over the woodstove. I never tasted better game meat. Like predators, we high-graded the stashes, taking the tenderloins first, followed by chops, steaks, and, finally, the last renderings.

"Always eat the best," Wilbur reasoned. "That way, when you sit down to dinner the next time, you'll have the next best to eat."

My favorite camp was Cave Creek. It had a gurgling side creek nearby and an overall comfortable, welcoming feeling. Here and at Taylor Ranch, we did "chores," washing clothes and our bodies at least once a week in big galvanized tubs with water heated on the sheepherder stoves. Waterfall camp, down on the Middle Fork, was in a beautiful swale above the river with a great view. But the best view was from the Rush Creek Lookout camp. That said, Rush Creek was a somewhat unfriendly place. In addition to the pesky flying squirrels, we had to trek a couple hundred yards downhill and then back up to retrieve water from a spring. Often, we melted snow for water, especially when arriving late at night after a day of hunting. All the camps had their own character, and we were always glad to pull into one after an exhausting day.

The only real amenities were little battery-powered AM radios purchased for each camp. Too far from civilization to get decent reception on their own, we rigged wire antennas in nearby trees. And there was an outfit in Riggins, Idaho, that manufactured what they called backcountry radio boosters. The contraptions, little more than a coiled wire arrangement, clipped to the back of the radio and functioned as an extra antenna. We bought several of them and they worked well. We'd listen into the night to various programs and actually became big fans of the Brigham Young University men's basketball team. We kept track of their schedule and listened to most of their games as the fire burned down and we eventually dozed off in our sleeping bags. I tried to stay awake until the games ended. After all, the team was (and still is) the BYU Cougars.

## Chapter Thirteen

# "Only One School?"

Shortly before we got the camps set up for the second season, my family (somewhat begrudgingly) and I moved to McCall. Of course, Muffin the cat, our Labrador retriever Thor, and pet raven Adam came with us. Shirley had finally agreed that the move would put me in good stead with people in the various Idaho natural resource agencies and help my chances to vie for the position as leader of the University of Idaho Cooperative Wildlife Research Unit. In my view, it was one of the best wildlife jobs in government.

So we sold our Missoula home; said good-bye to neighbors, friends, and colleagues; loaded our modest belongings into a U-Haul truck for a friend to drive; and squeezed everyone, including the pets, along with the rest of our personal property into my pickup and the family station wagon.

"What? No sidewalks!" one of the girls remarked when we got to McCall.

"And only one school!"

McCall, the closest "city" to the Big Creek drainage, was still a timber town in 1967 with no big-city amenities, but it did have a rich pioneer history. Mountain men like Jim Bridger, Peter Ogden, and Jedediah Smith reportedly passed through the area.

We rented a house east of town on Payette Lake from Warren Brown, owner of the local lumber company. Regarded as a community pillar, he eventually rented me office space near the lumberyard for the cougar study. As a member of the state legislature, Brown became an outspoken supporter.

Our new house was small but in a spectacular setting: located right on the water with a beach and boat dock. People welcomed us to town, some dropping off meat loafs, pot roasts, Jell-O salads, and other offerings. My reputation as "that cougar guy" confused some residents, but Shirley and the girls endeared our family to the community. And before long, I endeared my family to the world of skiing with three exhilarating words: Little Ski Hill.

None of us were downhill skiers. But nearly everyone in this mountain town of McCall was. Shirley and the girls were interested in learning to ski, but I was concerned about the cost. Our total annual income was just under $4,000—$2,000 from my contract with the Idaho Fish and Game Commission and just shy of $2,000 from the UBC fellowship. For perspective, consider that in 1965, gasoline sold for under thirty cents a gallon and that my hiking boots from Sears Roebuck cost $13. We managed to make ends meet but had little discretionary income.

So I asked a few new friends how I could equip the family on the cheap. They suggested the annual ski swap, when the entire town came together to buy and trade used equipment. In addition, each winter, Warren Brown, the city father and our landlord, provided an after-school bus and driver to transport children to the Little Ski Hill just outside of town, where a family season pass cost $15. Perhaps, I thought, the ski hill could become a family hangout while I was in the backcountry chasing cougars. So Shirley and I did the math and decided we'd need a small loan.

"How much?" Blair Armstrong, the local banker, asked when I approached him.

"Well," I said, calculating in my head, "about fifty dollars."

The banker leaned back in his leather chair, grinned, and said, "Well, I think we can manage that." He wrote me a check for the full amount. We took the money to the ski swap and bought everything: skis, poles, boots, and clothing plus a season-long family pass. By the time I came home from the study's second season in the field, Shirley, who was very athletic, had mastered the sport and was about to become a member of the ski patrol. Our oldest daughter was racing in the Mighty Mites.

And my family had otherwise settled into the little "timber town" like replanted trees in a healthy forest.

So the scientist in me felt set because my family was set. With requisite graduate courses out of the way, I could now concentrate full bore on my treatise and the secretive mountain lions. But first, Wilbur wanted another hound.

"We need to rotate the demands of hunting between four instead of three dogs," he explained.

We located a young redbone hound in Cascade, Idaho, from a good breeder at a fair price. I came out for Thanksgiving and picked up the dog to usher him back into Big Creek for Wilbur. While driving my pickup over Profile Summit on U.S. Forest Service Road 340 at an elevation of more than 7,500 feet, I hit a sheet of ice on a hairpin turn. Out of control, my pickup slid head-on into a horse truck coming from the opposite direction.

Incredibly, no one, including the horses and the new hound, was hurt. But the radiators on both vehicles were smashed. The other driver was a horse buyer from Emmett, Idaho. He was traveling with an elk hunting partner who was following in his pickup that towed an empty trailer. So we unloaded their horses from the disabled truck and transferred them to the pickup trailer. I, with the new hound, accompanied the hunters to the Big Creek Lodge. There, I left the dog with the lodge owner, Glenn Harper, hoping he'd somehow get word to Wilbur, twenty-five miles away on Monumental Creek, that the hound was waiting.

A couple days later, after I had the pickup towed and it was being repaired in McCall, the dog was still at the lodge, tied up and snoozing on the porch. That's when Harry Bettis arrived to help. Harry would eventually become a lifelong friend and research benefactor throughout my career. But not before a brush with calamity.

Harry's father, one of the founders of the First National Bank of Idaho, owned Thunder Mountain Mine, located south of our study area, high above Monumental Creek. And Harry, who'd been working at the

Harry Bettis of Boise, one of the early champions of the cougar study and supporter of continuing research.

mine, rode down to the store on horseback, where he saw the hound tethered to a porch pillar. As Glenn Harper later recounted the story to me, Harry started asking questions.

"So, what's up with the hound out there?"

"Oh, he belongs to Hornocker, the lion hunter," Glenn said.

"Why's it here?"

"Maurice is trying to get him up to Wilbur Wiles. He'll be a new dog for the study."

"What study?"

"They're studying cougars."

"Hmph," Harry pondered.

Harry and I hadn't met, but maybe he'd heard about the "college lion hunter" working the drainage. He'd never met Wilbur, either, but knew of his backcountry reputation and told Glenn that he wanted to meet him.

"I can't take the hound," Harry said, "I've got this horse and pack mule . . . enough to handle. But I'll ride up there and tell Wilbur the dog's here." So Harry, riding with the pack mule in tow, traveled the twenty-five miles down Big Creek and then up Monumental Creek to Wilbur's cabin. He stayed the night and, while visiting with Wilbur, learned a great deal about the region and its history. Returning the next day, Harry decided to take a shortcut up and over a ridge. Apparently, Wilbur didn't know of his plan and hadn't mentioned how big country sometimes gets unforgiving. After slowly gaining elevation for an hour or so, rain turned to snow, and Harry got caught in a ferocious mountain blizzard. Trees blew down across the trail, and pretty soon the mule, scared out of its wits, turned tail and ran off. With visibility reduced by blowing snow and sheer cliffs and bluffs surrounding him, Harry managed to get his horse turned around, find the panicked mule, and make it back to the main trail. Years later, he talked of how he never short-changed the backcountry again by taking shortcuts.

As a sidebar to the near calamity, Harry managed to turn a tip from Wilbur into a financial bonanza.

"John Vines's place might be for sale," Wilbur had said of the Garden Creek Ranch. Long story short, Harry contacted John, settled on a price, bought the place, and later sold the private inholding to the U.S. Forest Service for a handsome profit.

"Best deal I ever made," Harry proudly says to this day. I consider the windfall a just reward for a guy who did a favor for a complete stranger and asked for nothing in return. As for the hound, Wilbur named him Little Red, and he turned out to be a good hunter and companion—so good, in fact, that the dog's untimely disappearance and eventual return would wrack Wilbur's stoic demeanor and bring tears to his eyes.

## CHAPTER FOURTEEN

# Barking Up the Right Trees

Little Red, Wilbur's favorite hound, barking treed after a long chase.

HOUNDS ARE, BY NATURE and training, "trailing" dogs, meaning they chase animals. So you train them to chase the right animals, in our case, cougars.

"It's not that difficult," Wilbur said. "You just don't let them chase anything else."

Because mountain lions can be formidable opponents, big hounds with unnerving hearts are used to hunt them. There are several breeds, but redbone, plott, bluetick, black and tan, and walker hounds seem to be the most popular. The dogs stand about the same height as an adult cougar but aren't nearly as heavy. Temperaments vary. Trained hounds are usually amiable until they're fixed on a chase. The good ones become single-minded and steadfastly determined. Although coat colors differ by breeds, all are muscular canine athletes.

Wilbur preferred redbones. To train specialized cougar hounds, he kept his pups leashed during training hunts. An experienced adult dog, leashed as well, would accompany them until a fresh mountain lion track was found or, even better, a cat was jumped off a nearby kill. "Untrained hounds will chase anything," Wilbur explained, "rabbits, deer, coyotes . . . anything that smells and leaves a scent trail." If the hounds, especially a pup, tried to chase undesired animals, a correction was in order.

"No! No!" Wilbur would admonish.

Hopefully, hunter and the trainee hounds eventually hit a "hot cougar track." Wilbur would release the older, experienced dog first, then the pup.

"Get 'em!" he'd encourage.

Ideally, the pursued cougar would scoot up a nearby tree, the older dog would loudly proclaim victory at the base of the trunk, and the baying pup would charge from behind and join the ruckus. "The old dog raises hell," Wilbur explained, "and the young dog gets the idea."

Pretty soon they're a team—Wilbur and usually three or four hounds traveling familiar country in pursuit of familiar game. Sometimes I'd lead one of the dogs, but Wilbur handled the pack. Occasionally, we'd split up, especially if the tracks got confusing, but always reunited as quickly as possible.

While hunting, the dogs had plenty of water from creeks and smaller streams. At night, they slept in makeshift shelters and ate hearty meals. Wilbur fed them once a day, always at night. "Let them digest a big meal while they sleep," he explained. "Come morning, hungry hounds run the fastest."

## CHAPTER FIFTEEN

# Casting a Wider Net

BUOYED BY THE PROMISING EXPANSION OF THE STUDY INTO THE Chamberlain Basin north of Big Creek, confirmation of continued funding, and the growing alliance Wilbur and I were building, I hired two former colleagues to join the project.

Dave Wedum, who'd been an undergraduate student with me at the University of Montana, brought his experience and enthusiasm as a young biologist. Houndsman Floyd Partney, who worked with me on the exploratory cougar study out of Missoula, brought his four proven dogs. Dave and Floyd agreed to parlay the methods Wilbur and I were perfecting. All of us were stoked.

"We need numbers!" I told them.

More captures and recaptures were necessary to paint a complete ecological picture. So far, we were just this side of a blank canvas. As we launched the second season, I hoped to get enough data to at least hint of a clearer portrait.

Well, we got plenty of data. But we also experienced enormous frustration and a near tragedy.

With all ten camps in order, a second team of hunters ready, and the snow about to start piling up, I was further encouraged by the performance of a new tranquilizer gun I'd designed. The implement would be crucial to the study's success.

The old pneumatic Cap-Chur guns we used during the first season had repeatedly malfunctioned in cold weather. (You'll recall that we often had to heat them over a flame before firing.) So I sketched a new design. A gunsmith in Missoula built a prototype off my design, then another, and both fired perfectly. The rifles had screw-on barrels with a spring-loaded zip gun firing pin. The tranquilizer darts were 32-gauge. So we fashioned a black powder shell the same size to power the dart. With practice, I became proficient, as did Wilbur, Dave, and Floyd. The guns didn't need to be super precise. The barrels had a little bead on the end, and you'd simply point. A mountain lion up to sixty feet away in a tree with a hip or shoulder exposed was enough of a target to competently place a dart.

By mid-November, winter was bearing down on the Big Creek drainage, settling on the high ground in Chamberlain Basin. Wilbur started searching for tracks as soon as snow blanketed most of the lower study area. Shortly after Thanksgiving, I contacted Dave and Floyd to confirm the launch of season two.

"Meet here in McCall to fly in. The weather looks good."

On the morning of November 30, the three of us and Floyd's four hounds boarded two Johnson Flying Service planes piloted by Bill Dorris and Gene Crosby. About an hour later, we landed at Root Ranch. Deep snow covered the ground.

No one greeted us. The place was vacant. I'd reserved the main cabin through the winter, so we moved our gear in, and the planes flew out. Darkness descended. The temperature dropped outside, and I lay awake on a cot full of anticipation as Dave and Floyd drifted off. I couldn't wait to get started.

Wilbur left his Monumental Creek cabin six days earlier and had already captured and marked two new cougars—Nos. 11 and 12, both females.

*Wilbur's notes on No. 11: "The cat at elk kill. Was sleeping nearby. Let the dogs go and treed on south side of creek on steep hillside. Cat up a big fir about 30 feet."*

Two days later:

*Wilbur's notes on No. 12: "Got the dogs tied, cat tagged and put in a good dry bed of fir bows. She looked OK, but will go up tomorrow and make sure."*

Wilbur was hunting with four dogs now: Duke, Ranger, Red, and Chub. We also had Floyd's four hounds working the Chamberlain area: Gypsy, Chief, Freckles, and Dolly.

The morning after we landed at Root Ranch, Dave, Floyd, his four eager redbones, and I hunted up a ridge to Roots Knob and then climbed higher to Grass Mountain within sight of our "emergency camp" near the old lookout. No tracks anywhere. So we dropped off into Root Creek and back up McCalla and Whimstick creeks before returning to the ranch.

*My notes: "Saw no lion tracks. Some fresh elk sign, lots of coyote. Got in about 7:30. Traveled approx 15 miles."*

I awoke the next morning stiff and sore, as did Dave and Floyd. The hounds, however, appeared raring to go. We left around mid-morning along the Cub Creek trail and climbed to a ridge west of the ranch. From there, we hiked over to Wapiti Creek ridge and back to the ranch, logging another five miles.

*Floyd's notes: "Some elk sign, lots of rabbit and bobcat sign. Real good looking cat country, but no cougar sign."*

*Dave's notes: "Up in back of Root Ranch. No game. Lots of coyote and bobcat tracks. No cougars."*

While we were hunting, Root Ranch employees flew in to finish closing and winterizing the ranch buildings we weren't using. They flew out the next morning, and we turned our attention to a third unexplored area—up Wapiti Creek to McCoy Cabin on McCalla Creek. Finally, we hit our first cougar tracks in old snow, left by a small cat, probably a female. Then much larger tom tracks. And fresh.

"Let's turn the dogs loose," I said.

Their snoots full of "feline fumes," as Floyd described the scent, the hounds shot up the trail through some bluffs and in no time had treed a cougar in a fir tree near the top of Chamberlain Creek ridge. We trudged up through the snow thinking we had the big tom. Instead, it turned out to be a mature female, which was actually a good sign. With this female treed, we knew another lion, the big tom, was in the area.

While Floyd tied the hounds aside and Dave got the scale and other equipment ready for processing, I loaded the new tranquilizer gun, took aim at the cat's exposed hip, and squeezed the trigger. The dart hit; the lion catapulted out of the tree to the ground and quickly ran out of sight down a draw.

"Get it!" Floyd commanded, releasing the dogs again. The cat re-treed about three-quarters of a mile down the draw, and by the time we got there, she appeared groggy from the drug. It was 3:45 p.m.

"She's ready," I said and began the difficult climb up through thick limbs. I finally got close enough to see that, even though doped, her ears were pinned back, and she was hissing, growling, and otherwise making things difficult. Eventually, she seemed to relent, and I managed to get a rope around her foot so we could lower her. On the ground, I administered another 10 mg of Sernylyn with a hand syringe at 3:56 p.m., approximately forty-five minutes after being darted with the first injection. At 4:02, I injected another 10 mg.

*My notes: "Cat completely manageable at 4:05. Optimum dosage."*

She weighed ninety-nine pounds and was fully mature. We attached tags to both ears and tattooed the left with "1." We measured her feet and teeth. She tallied seventy-five and three-quarters inches long, including a thirty-and-one-quarter-inch tail. Height at the shoulder was twenty-five inches. We also measured the length of her ears and the distance between them, the circumference of her neck and body, and the distance between her eyes. We, of course, did this with all the mountain lions, but I took special care this time because Dave and Floyd were still learning. We also determined that No. 1's mammaries had not been suckled; thus, she didn't have young kittens with her. We placed her on a dry patch of ground to recover. We had traveled a total of thirty-eight miles to capture our first Chamberlain Basin mountain lion. She would be re-treed a month later at the mouth of Hungry Creek—an estimated seven to eight miles from the original capture site—never to be seen again.

For the next eleven days, we hiked up and down, over and around, covering approximately 100 miles and not capturing a single mountain lion. We did, however, have a close encounter.

*My notes: "Dec. 6, 1965. Hit track of tom approx 1 mile above mouth of McCalla. Cat had investigated old bones along trail. Turned dogs loose about ½ mile above camp. They took cat right through camp and on down Chamberlain Cr. No snow."*

And then:

*My notes: "Lost dogs."*

By December 8, the two dogs, Gypsy and Chief, were still missing. The temperature warmed, and the sky turned blue. No snow for us to track them down.

*My notes: "Damn!"*

We decided to curtail hunting until snow came—and, hopefully, the two hounds would return. Meanwhile, Dave and I hiked back to Root Ranch for supplies, a one-way trip of three hours. We saw one big cougar track and scads of snowshoe hare sign, the likely food source for coyote and bobcat populations.

We woke on December 10 to three inches of new snow (finally), then trekked back to the Chamberlain camp loaded with supplies. We arrived to find two inches of fresh snow and Floyd, but not the two dogs.

"Not sure what to think," Floyd lamented. "No idea whether they stayed together or split up. Been what, three days?"

The next morning, we set out again with our two remaining dogs, Freckles and Dolly, in excellent tracking snow. After seeing no cougar tracks or game, we returned to camp at 7:00 that night, long after dark. Still no sign of Gypsy and Chief. Elk and deer, I figured, had not yet ventured down into their winter range, which might explain the dearth of mountain lions. We did, however, see abundant scratch trees and scrape piles left by cougars, which mystified us.

*My notes: "Never saw anything like it. Floyd neither. Must have been 25–30 different scrape piles. Picked up 9 scats. I'll bet there are 6–8 toms, maybe more, in this area . . . should be ideal later on."*

I speculated that the relative scarcity of elk and deer was linked to the big Thanksgiving Day storm that dumped on enormous amount of snow in the higher elevations. Perhaps the game herds had moved down, resulting in the tracks and signs we were seeing. The twelve days of post-Thanksgiving warm weather had probably enticed the deer and elk back up onto the ridges where snow was still minimal and browse plentiful.

In the creek bottoms, we found elk carcasses, including the remains of several mature six-point bulls, and I wondered if a big tom had killed them. So far in this second season, we had marked only one lion. But from tracks in the snow, we knew a female (with at least two kittens) was in the area, along with a big male and one other smaller male.

My notes: *"Suspect there are lots of males here and several more females. Gypsy and Chief still gone."*

On December 13, we set out from Chamberlain camp, found some older cougar tracks, released the two remaining dogs, but soon lost the trail. About four miles into the hunt, we gathered Freckles and Dolly and headed toward camp. Then, from out of the rays of a setting sun, two emaciated animals emerged on the trail ahead of us.

"Gypsy! Chief!" Floyd bellowed excitedly. After a week of being gone, the dogs were thin and weak, their feet badly worn. But they were alive! Beleaguered as they were, the hounds came ambling up to Floyd with tails wagging. He knelt down and embraced each hound as they panted and then nuzzled noses with equally excited Freckles and Dolly. It was a celebration of survival.

We'd all endured this rude introduction to the Chamberlain Basin. But while I shared in the happy reunion, I was also worried. One captured and marked mountain lion in nearly two weeks wasn't what I'd hoped my expansion plan would render. At best, our success was dubious. Then again, I had no idea of just how disappointing the entire Chamberlain effort would eventually become.

Instead of brooding out loud, I spent the last night of my initial visit to the basin mustering enough enthusiasm to go over recording forms and methodology checks with Dave and Floyd, who, as soon as all four dogs were rested and ready, would go out on their own.

"So we're set, okay?" I asked them.

"Set as we can be," Dave replied as Floyd nodded in agreement.

The plane I'd radioed for early in the day buzzed overhead the next morning and landed, its propeller stirring up a squall of snow until the engine shut down. I boarded with my gear, and pilot Gene Crosby flew me to Taylor Ranch, where Wilbur, hunting upstream along Big Creek, had left me a handwritten message.

"Everything is fine."

## CHAPTER SIXTEEN

# Growing Success—and Doom

DURING THE NIGHT, WHILE I SLEPT SOUNDLY AT TAYLOR RANCH, FOUR mountain lions secreted their way down the Cliff Creek drainage from the north and crossed over Big Creek on the ranch bridge to investigate, among other things, an empty chicken house. With tracks everywhere, the story of their visit was written in the snow. A female and three large kittens, I concluded, arrived a couple hours before I woke. By the time I saw the tracks, the cats were long gone.

After making notes about the incident, I gathered my gear to go hunting, not for the cats but for Wilbur. I noticed that no sheep, deer, or elk were on the slopes across from the ranch, which was unusual. In light of the cougar quartet that had been prowling before daybreak, the ungulates had probably cleared out. Keeping an eye on the hills, bluffs, and cliffs, I began hiking up the Big Creek trail to our Cave Creek camp. Wilbur was gone but had left me a note:

"Left here Dec. 10. Hunting upstream."

So I kept trekking to find him. Eight miles later, I arrived at our Coxey Creek camp. Once again, Wilbur was gone, but his tracks headed toward Monumental Creek. I followed and arrived at his cabin in the dark around 6:30 p.m. Two of his hounds welcomed me with wagging tails. More tracks indicated that Wilbur and his two other hounds had headed up Crooked Creek. I figured he'd be back soon. So I stoked the fire, settled in, and was happy to welcome Wilbur home nearly two hours later.

"Been up north, around Bismark Mountain," he said while shedding his woolens.

"Any luck?"

"Got number three again, Ol' Rex,"

"A recapture, that's great!" I said, recalling the day more than a year earlier when Rex, the big tom, had ripped around a tree trunk and snarled into my face as I tried to capture him.

We wanted to capture as many new cats as possible, hopefully the entire population within the study area. But catching the same cougars over and over was also critical to the study's ultimate success. Take Rex, for example. We planned to pinpoint on a map each site where he was captured and draw lines between the points to eventually define his territory. We'd do the same with other cougars and see where their territories butted up against each other or overlapped.

"The dogs are bushed," Wilbur said, stepping out of his boots as I gave him a warm cup of coffee. "We've had quite a couple weeks."

In my absence, Wilbur, Duke, Ranger, Red, and Chub had captured five new cats. His notes were replete with details of each encounter.

"Let's take tomorrow off," I suggested.

"I got the same idea about three hours ago on the way back," Wilbur agreed as he warmed his feet near the woodstove.

That night, we ate a hearty meal, talked for several hours, and slept well as the outside temperature plummeted to minus three degrees.

During our day off, as Wilbur tended to his dogs and cabin chores, I reviewed his notes. An encounter near Coxey Creek with a lioness and three kittens read like a long, drawn-out hit-or-miss skirmish.

*Wilbur's notes: "I got on a ridge and could hear dogs about 200 yards below me. Found Red with a kitten up a tree. The other dogs running all over the basin, which was about 200 yards wide, baying."*

Wilbur scrambled down into the melee and managed to tie Red at the tree, where the kitten peered down from about thirty feet above.

*Wilbur's notes: "Cat scent so strong in basin I could smell it. Tracks everywhere there was snow."*

Red, Ranger, and Wilbur top a frigid ridge after a long climb.

With Red secured at the tree, Wilbur spent the next hour collecting his three other hounds and searching the thick forest canopy for more treed lions. Unable to find any, he returned to the treed kitten.

*Wilbur's notes: "Decided to tag cat and then look for the rest."*

Wilbur loaded 7mg of Sernylan, took aim, and hit his target. The cat was up about forty feet in a limb-laden fir tree. Wilbur waited ten minutes, donned spurs, and started to climb. The cat also climbed higher to get away from him. So Wilbur came down for more drug.

While he prepared another dart, the kitten descended about halfway down the tree, leaped to the ground, and pounced away into heavy brush.

*Wilbur's notes: "Let Chub go. Saw him line out over a ridge 300 yards from me, so let Red go. Left Duke and Ranger tied."*

Wilbur clambered to the ridge after Chub and Red. But Duke and Ranger were making so much noise in the basin that he couldn't hear the other two dogs. So he went back to the two tethered hounds, turned them loose, and followed. About half a mile away and thirty minutes later, he found all four dogs at the base of another fir tree, baying up at the wayward kitten.

*Wilbur's notes: "Gave cat 10 mg. Sernylan, waited 10 min. Climbed tree, but cat growling. Went up about as high as he could go. So come down and loaded dart with 12 mg. Sernylan."*

This time, instead of shooting from the ground, Wilbur climbed the tree with the tranquilizer gun in hand, got to within about fifteen feet of the cougar, and fired a third dart. Within eight minutes, the young male became manageable, and Wilbur lowered him by rope to the ground. He weighed just twenty pounds but was healthy. The entire capture took more than four hours.

*Wilbur's notes: "If I had doped cat right the first time, think I would have got more cats close. Know there are two kittens, think likely three."*

I set the notes aside and smiled. The more I worked with Wilbur and read his sometimes cryptic but always candid renderings, the more I realized he'd become a priceless partner. Money couldn't buy a better houndsman. And Wilbur seemed to be accepting me. Hell, he seemed to be accepting even the mountain lions—not to be killed for sport and money but to be caught and released for the sake of science and maybe their own future.

"You're doing great work, Wilbur."

"It's not really work, to me." His words lingered amid pipe smoke, and he said no more.

The next morning greeted us with a minus-five reading on the thermometer outside Wilbur's cabin. We gathered gear and readied the hounds, then set out for a quick lunch stop at the Coxey Creek camp before traveling farther downstream to the Cave Creek camp. The temperature never rose above zero. Late in the afternoon, inside the wall tent as darkness engulfed the canyons, we fired up the sheepherder stove and set out the cots and sleeping bags. I managed to strip a couple cuts of venison off a frozen hindquarter hanging from a tree, removed brush from our underground storage site, and exhumed some canned vegetables.

"It's going to get even colder tonight," Wilbur said over the hiss of the Coleman lantern as coffee brewed on the woodstove and we made dinner. "Clear and cold."

He was right. The thermometer registered ten degrees below zero when I woke to find Wilbur kindling a new fire before first light. Soon he was pouring Bisquick pancake batter onto a smoking griddle. Elk steaks sizzled. The canvas tent sealed the aroma of brewing coffee. We devoured breakfast, cleaned up, gathered gear, and secured the camp as the first splashes of sunlight hit the highest peaks. Daybreak in the mountains is always a soul-stirring transition from nocturnal to diurnal hours, especially after a cold and clear night. As Wilbur readied his hounds, I took it all in.

Dawn's dim light had already bathed our surroundings. But actual sunrise erupted moments later as if a switch had been flipped. Beams popped from the eastern horizon and smacked the highest pinnacles with dazzling brightness.

"What do you think?" I asked, taking my eyes off the high country to see Wilbur with three of his leashed-up hounds. "Should we go up the creek?"

"Sounds like a plan." I led the fourth hound as we began our trek.

The sun, after its sudden appearance, had already shifted gears into a lazy rise. As we hiked upward, bright light spilled down the slopes and across the valleys and would eventually linger in the creek bottoms until darkness began its return. Wilbur and I, as hunters who always woke early and worked late, knew the daily cycle well—but not nearly as well, we would learn, as the cougars that hunted both day and night.

About two miles up the Cave Creek drainage, we cut the track of a female lion heading over a ridge toward Cabin Creek. The track was about three days old, so we didn't follow. But we happened on the same track again, this time coming down a ridge from Garden Creek. Then we found a tom's track heading out of the Cave Creek drainage back toward Garden Creek country. By the end of the day, we'd hiked ten miles and caught no mountain lions. But after seeing all the tracks and recalling our previous captures, I was starting to piece together some population dynamic theories.

Bottom line: the kittens Wilbur had captured and marked (Nos. 13, 14, and 15) were probably the offspring of No. 4, a female caught nine months earlier in March. At that time, No. 4 (which we eventually named Hazel) had been in the company of one or two mature males. The most likely (if not only) reason for an adult female to travel with males is to ultimately breed.

*My notes: "This would make kittens No. 13, 14, & 15 about six months old."*

The note, of course, was a product of a simple calculation: a three-month pregnancy resulting in kittens that were now six months old. Population patterns were starting to emerge.

We hiked the next day to Taylor Ranch, and Wilbur inspected the lion tracks I had found fresh four days earlier. "Looks like at least a male and female runnin' together," he said. "Maybe a female and two or three big kittens."

We hunted south the next day up Pioneer Creek behind Taylor Ranch and came upon one set of cougar tracks, probably one of the same cats making tracks earlier at the ranch. Otherwise, the drainage appeared cat-less. So we hiked back down to the ranch, where Wilbur tended to the hounds. I crossed the bridge over Big Creek alone and hiked up Cliff Creek hoping to see birds feeding on a kill but saw none. I photographed some bighorn sheep, peered out across the country, and took a satisfying deep breath. Unlike a year ago, I felt hopeful. Dave and Floyd were working the Chamberlain Basin as Wilbur and I combed Big Creek and its tributaries. The lion's share of winter, with fresh snowfall to aid tracking, was soon to come. In four days, I'd be home celebrating Christmas with my family, a far cry from the previous year when I was fending off physical and emotional exhaustion in the wilderness.

*My notes: "Gene Crosby flew in with mail late P.M. I flew out with him for Xmas."*

As the plane left the ground and rose from the Big Creek drainage, and the distant Chamberlain Basin country came into view, one thing gnawed at me. We hadn't heard a word from Dave Wedum and Floyd Partney since the day I flew out of Root Ranch. No one could raise them on the radiophone there, and they hadn't called out themselves.

CHAPTER SEVENTEEN

# Coalescing Cats

UNLIKE CHRISTMAS DAY A YEAR EARLIER, WHEN WILBUR AND I BARELY avoided being carried off by the landslide-avalanche, I spent the 1965 holiday with my wife and our three daughters in McCall. That same day, Wilbur, as if gifting each of us, caught cougar No. 16.

The tale started Christmas Eve after Wilbur trekked into our Rush Point camp, one of my favorites, you'll remember, because of its spectacular view. The next morning, after spotting some old tracks, Wilbur happened upon fresh ones. With three inches of fresh snow on the ground, he had trailed the cat for two hours when his leashed hounds began barking frantically.

*Wilbur's notes: "Let dogs go. They trailed cat over ridge to next fork east where there were a lot of ravens. Then brought her back around lower down. Treed her about fifty yards below me."*

Wilbur collected the dogs, tied them off to the side, aimed the gun at the cat, and fired the dart, which hit on target. But she rocketed from the tree and hit the ground running. Wilbur released the hounds, and after a half-mile chase, they managed to tree the lioness in another fir. Wilbur caught and tied his dogs a second time. The cat, by this time feeling the strong effects of the drug, lost its grip on a limb, fell about ten feet, and caught and clung to another limb that finally broke. After landing on the steep, snow-laden ground with a soft thud, the cat slid downhill about 100 feet.

*Wilbur's notes: "Got right on her feet. Come back up the hill in a direct line to the dogs. I grabbed her by tail. Headed her back down hill. She went into some brush and stopped."*

Wilbur followed, stalking the dazed cat to where she'd sought refuge in a brush pile. Reaching into the brush, he looped a rope around an exposed hindfoot.

*Wilbur's notes: "She took off. I had to snub her to a tree to hold her. I gave her another 15 mg Sern. And tagged her."*

Enjoying the holidays with my family, I knew nothing about Wilbur's Christmas Day adventure. As he hiked back to camp, a storm front bore down on central Idaho's backcountry.

Forty inches of snow fell in McCall, and then it started to rain. No planes had flown out since my return, and the forecast called for no change in local conditions even though the weather had cleared in Big Creek. So I made some contacts, said good-bye to Shirley and the girls on January 7, and drove to Emmett, where skies had also cleared. There, I hopped a ride with Rex Lanham, owner of Cabin Creek Ranch, in his Super Cub. We touched down late afternoon at his airstrip. Wilbur had radioed out and left a message that he'd meet me at the Cave Creek camp.

Meanwhile, no one had yet heard from Dave and Floyd. They'd been hunting, presumably, for more than a month in Chamberlain Basin. Their silence, I hoped, was nothing more than being consumed by successful hunting. With plenty of supplies at two camps, they'd have no reason to return to Root Ranch, where the radiophone was located. Still, my concern mounted with each passing day.

Wilbur and I hunted five days before recapturing cougar No. 6, a kitten we first tagged a year earlier in the same area, Rough Canyon. At seventy-three pounds, she was in good condition, and we left her with new ear tags and a new collar. The next day, we found her bedded down on a rock ledge against a bluff about fifty yards above where we had examined her. Worried that she had suffered an injury or a bad reaction to the drug, I edged closer, tossed a rock, and managed to hit her. She sprang from the ledge and raced away.

"She's good to go," Wilbur confirmed while keeping his hounds from giving chase.

We hunted two more days before recapturing No. 6 again. I speculated that she was waiting in the area for her mother and littermates to return.

*My notes: "Believe female still has other kittens. Too many kitten tracks in area . . . hard to explain why female didn't return for No. 6 tho'."*

On January 17, we began hunting out of the Rush Point camp, and at 9:00 in the morning, we put the dogs on a tom track we'd found at a cave the previous day. Twelve hours later, we arrived at Taylor Ranch exhausted and dog-less.

"They might have something treed," Wilbur said.

"Think they'll stay the night?"

"They might, especially if they're all together at one tree."

Come morning, no dogs had returned. So we set out to find them, going up Cougar Creek, then taking a trail over into Goat Creek. We cut the old track of a female lion and then a fresh tom track. Following the tom, we saw where two hounds had picked up the same track. For some reason they abandoned it in favor of the cold female track amid myriad footprints in the snow. As we attempted to sort through the maze and kept following what we hoped were the freshest tracks, suddenly there they were—Duke and Chub, trapped on a ledge overlooking a steep bluff.

"We better get up there before one or both of them slip," Wilbur said.

After a short but steep climb, we were close enough to ease around an outcropping, coax the dogs closer, reach out, and get a rope on each. They came to heel almost apologetically, tongues hanging, jowls flapping, tails wagging. After securing the hounds with leashes, we set out to find Red and Ranger and found their tracks by following fresh tom tracks. Wilbur decided to release Duke and Chub, hoping they'd zero in on the two missing dogs. Instead, they treed No. 4, Hazel, along with another kitten.

*My notes: "Found cat tracks all over the area—most I've ever seen. Am positive was at least one, maybe two other kittens also in area & probably treed, but could not find."*

We darted, processed, and released both Hazel (with new markers) and the kitten, which became cougar No. 17. Nearby, I found caves where the kittens had probably been raised. Bones littered the floor inside the caves. I took photographs and checked our records.

Hazel had not been recorded as having kittens when we caught her during the first season. But Wilbur and I now speculated that she was the mother of No. 17, which we'd just captured in the area, and also No. 6, which we'd captured twice a few days earlier. All the tracks and data indicated we were working what we began to call the Rough Canyon Family.

*My notes: "No way to prove it unless we recapture the whole family together."*

We returned to Taylor Ranch at 9:30 p.m. in total darkness with Duke and Chub in tow. There, waiting for us, was Ranger, his eyes squinting with fatigue, his paws crusted with blood, but otherwise excited to see us. Unfortunately, Red was not there.

Wilbur adored Red, the pup Harry Bettis had found at the Big Creek store. The dog quickly became Wilbur's favorite hound and perhaps our best hunter. The loss would be devastating to both Wilbur and the study. Although hounds remaining at a tree overnight is not unusual, we knew the perils this sprawling and mountainous country could deal humans and canines alike.

With each passing hour and then days, Wilbur's hope faded.

*My notes: "Wilbur looked to see if he could find Red's body—he is sure No. 4 killed Red. This is a severe blow—Wilbur depends a lot on Red."*

You have to love dogs to know how Wilbur felt. For him, it was like losing a family member. Having a deep affinity for bird dogs, I understand the anguish Wilbur endured while searching for Red.

"Let's go down the creek a half-mile or so," he suggested on the third morning. "We'll call for him and see what happens."

Wilbur had an old lean-to camp at the mouth of Cougar Creek, where he'd bivouacked a few times over the years. We'd built some makeshift dog shelters at the camp but didn't use the place much. A stiff up-canyon wind blew into our faces as we walked down Big Creek until the campsite appeared about 100 yards ahead. Suddenly, we heard what sounded like barking. Or was it the wind? We edged closer, and Red, who had spotted us, came barking as if defending his territory.

"Red. Red, come here, boy!" an ecstatic Wilbur beckoned. But Red kept barking. The howling winds were sweeping Wilbur's voice away.

Red could see two people but couldn't hear Wilbur's identifying voice. So he kept barking.

Suddenly making the connection, the hound charged toward us. Wilbur knelt down on the ground, and Red ran into his outstretched arms. Wilbur bear-hugged the dog and wept.

"Damn wind," he said, turning away from me. "Makin' my eyes water."

Standing there as the wind swayed the treetops and rays of morning sun broke through the clouds, my eyes also welled up.

"Good dog. Welcome home," I said as Red finally turned his attention to me. He was thin and shivering but apparently uninjured. We figured he'd trailed a cat into some perilous cliffs where the lion holed up or went places a dog can't go. Cougars can do miraculous things in those vertical cliffs. They're like mountain goats. Dogs aren't.

We led Red back to Taylor Ranch, fed him, and reunited him with the other three hounds, and all six of us took the next day off work.

One critter who seemed to never take a day off was No. 3, aka Rex. If you remember, we first caught Rex on December 28, 1964, as he glared into my eyes from two feet away. Barely a year later, we treed him for the fourth time. In three of the four encounters, we jumped Rex off an elk kill before sending the dogs. The first kill was a calf, the second a young spike bull, and the third a mature five-point bull.

We recaptured and retagged Rex for the first time on December 15, 1965, after the hounds pursued him, on and off, for two days. Tracks in the snow showed that he'd hunted through four drainages, both high and low, and eventually stalked a large herd of elk on a ridge between Crooked Creek and Little Ramey Creek. The elk, according to tracks they left behind, had scattered like a burst of fireworks when Rex launched a failed attack.

On January 28, 1966, a little over a month after being retagged, Rex offered more insights into how an experienced mountain lion goes about its business.

*My notes: "This cat, No. 3, is elk hunter."*

I made that entry after investigating the latest of Rex's elk hunting forays. Wilbur, the hounds, and I were following the tracks of a big tom (which turned out to be Rex) in Cabin Creek and over the ridge into Cave Creek. We'd already seen where he had surprised elk on the Cabin Creek side, forcing one animal to blast out from a bluff and trigger a rockslide.

*My notes: "Game all over. Looked like a stock yard."*

Rex then followed several elk right past our Cave Creek camp. We saw where he'd crossed the creek twice in heavy brush while following two or three bulls.

*My notes: "Finally, one put itself in favorable position and No. 3 made final stalk and kill of 5-point bull right at mouth of Cave Cr."*

Stealth, cunning, determination, tenacity—all shaped by evolution into perhaps nature's most efficient killing machine. The more I learned about them, the more I marveled at the mountain lion's hunting prowess. Killer qualities aside, Rex was giving us early indications of cougar territorial behavior.

*My notes: "Cats' territories overlap but they appear to honor anothers' presence."*

I noted the observation after we had tracked Rex up Calf Creek, where he bumped into No. 4, Hazel, and her kittens (the Rough Cayon Family).

*My notes: "No. 3 apparently had gone up Calf Cr. Saw that others were there, immediately made a swing right back and over into Cave Creek."*

Slowly, clues were falling into place. For example, while following the cougar tracks, often we noted scrapes—little pyramids of forest debris sometimes mixed with lion scat and urine. It appeared that these piles served as traffic lights, stop signs, or outright "No Trespassing" signs. From our analysis of the tracks, it seemed that both females and males visited these scrape sites. Also, the cats followed the same routes, albeit not at the same time—visiting the same bluffs, cliffs, overhanging trees, and other places while constructing scrapes along the way.

*My notes: "From now on, will record all these scrape sites, number of scrapes and apparent age of scrapes (difference in age). Scrapes may also serve sexual function."*

In addition to Rex, the Rough Canyon Family (Hazel and her three kittens) were giving us early insights about cougar ecology. On January 30, 1966, we left the Cave Creek camp to pick up the family's tracks. We found where the four cats had come over the ridge into Cabin Creek and turned upstream toward a big cave and then cut down the drainage. We surprised the family eating at a deer kill in the first canyon just below the cave and sent the hounds.

*My notes: "Dogs took them back toward forks of Cabin Creek & treed Nos. 4, 17, and unmarked tom kitten. Another kitten, surely No. 6, was not located but was with others at kill & must have been somewhere in area in tree."*

With Hazel and one of her kittens treed and already tagged, we processed the unmarked tom kitten, which became No. 19.

The dead deer was a young doe. Again, by examining evidence in the snow, we were able to reconstruct the attack. Ambushed and killed at the head of the canyon, the deer was dragged by the lioness down the draw more than 200 yards and cached under thick old fir trees. We found deep fang marks at the base of the deer's skull, but the neck was not broken—evidence that snapping the neck, while probably the quickest and most common approach, was not the only way mountain lions killed their prey.

*My notes: "This completes 5-day record on this family."*

After analyzing the evidence, including other kills in the area, I determined that in approximately twenty days, the Rough Canyon Family had killed four animals. This equated to an average of one prey animal every five days to feed four mountain lions. I mulled over these early observations and initial theories about cougar habits, diet, and territoriality with a growing sense of accomplishment and anticipation of discoveries still to come.

Meanwhile, Dave Wedum and Floyd Partney still hadn't radio-phoned us from the Chamberlain Basin. Being out of communication was nothing new in this vast wilderness. But more than a month and a half of silence had passed. It was time to investigate.

## Chapter Eighteen

# Deadly Silence

On February 1, 1966, Gene Crosby flew his plane into Taylor Ranch and picked me up, and we headed for the Chamberlain Basin so I could check on Dave and Floyd. After six weeks of silence, I was worried about what I might find.

Landing at Root Ranch, we found up to two feet of snow on the runway and herds of elk still on the hills to the east and west but no sign of Dave and Floyd.

"I'll be back in about a week," Gene said with a stern expression, "unless I hear otherwise."

Having equipped his plane with skis for winter flying, Gene wallowed the Cessna 185 down the powder-white runway, gained enough speed, and lifted skyward. I watched him bank toward McCall and disappear over the mountains, then assessed my options amid nothing but the quiet and cold of winter. The ranch was abandoned. No sign that Dave and Floyd had returned, not even for supplies. Where could they be?

I began hiking, sometimes on snowshoes, the ten miles to our Chamberlain Creek camp. Now and then, elk, deer, and some old cougar tracks crossed the trail. But no human tracks. As I traveled, anxiety over what I might find continued to build.

Three hours later, I eased into camp, was relieved to see smoke wafting from the sheepherder stove's metal stack, heard alert barks from the hounds, and found both Dave and Floyd huddled inside the wall tent. Relieved that they were alive, I was not happy with the news.

"Three," Dave said.

That's how many captures they'd made since I left in mid-December. One was a recapture of No. 1. The other two captures included a ninety-seven-pound female, tagged and released on January 12, and a huge, 181-pound male, captured two days earlier.

"None," said Floyd, when I asked about the number of kills they'd located.

"Why haven't you phoned out from Root Ranch?" I asked.

"The radiophone hasn't worked since a couple days after you left," Dave explained.

"So we've pretty much hunted out of this camp," Floyd said, "to the point where we're running out of supplies."

This didn't set well with me. I could tell Dave and Floyd were clearly disgruntled as well. But no use lamenting the obvious. So we turned our attention to remedies.

"All we can do is keep hunting," I said. "Let's see what tomorrow brings."

We found no cougars the next day, but ever so slowly, I began to understand what had been happening the past month and a half. Dave, Floyd, the hounds, and I started hunting up the Chamberlain Creek trail. At the mouth of Mule Creek, I decided to solo my way up toward Deer Creek to check game and snow conditions. All this time, I'd been thinking I might have been wrong. Maybe this slice of the wilderness didn't support a significant mountain lion population. Maybe the expansion into the Chamberlain Basin and the hiring of a second crew had been fraught with failure from the beginning.

Then I cut a lion track. I climbed higher into the bluffs and found three more older cat tracks. Lots of game sign, too, both deer and elk.

*My notes: "Cats have been here, too. Floyd and Dave simply have not hunted high enough. Have stuck only to trail—have worn it out up about three miles, turn around and come back to camp. Plenty of game, plenty of lions in this drainage."*

While I solo explored, Dave and Floyd decided to go off the beaten track and trek a short way up the ridge between Queen Creek and Mule Creek. On the way back, they cut a fresh lion track, turned the dogs loose, and treed No. 2, the big tom they'd captured and marked twenty-one days earlier.

The next day, February 3, we hit another fairly fresh track at the mouth of Queen Creek. The dogs trailed and eventually treed three big kittens. No. 4 weighed fifty-four pounds, No. 5 weighed sixty pounds, and No. 6 weighed seventy-four pounds. The lioness eluded us, but I tracked her for a while.

*My notes: "This female's behavior so like that of No. 4 on Big Creek. Am sure she has brought kittens from a kill somewhere high. This undoubtedly is family I saw tracks of last July at mouth of McCalla Creek."*

On the morning of February 4, I returned to the area alone and did a little more detective work. While following their footprints, it appeared the three kittens had accompanied their mother on her swing across the Whimstick Creek drainage and up the west slope before cutting back down and up to another ridge. Next, the lioness took her kittens into lower ground, where she stashed them and went hunting alone. I continued to follow the female's track and discovered where she'd met up with a tom, and it appeared the two had traveled together for a while.

Then I heard the loud "kraa-kraa" of ravens circling above a small canyon. Following their calls, I dropped down and found the family's kill—a cow elk.

*My notes: "Looks as though family had been on kill 6-7 days. Cats been all over area, all trampled down, trees clawed, ninebark chewed, etc. Three scat stations, scat buried under snow in one, one under fir needles, other one under needles and bark. Kittens had played all over area. Had walked logs (had bitten limbs off logs). Had one big bed under fir, beat down dirty trail to kill from bed. Bed and scat area reeked of cat smell. Took photos. Quite interesting kill."*

That night in camp, I rehashed my discoveries over dinner with Dave and Floyd. Both men seemed downtrodden, as if my success underscored their failures. But that wasn't my intention. I hoped to rally the troops.

"We'll just keep pushing," I said. "Nobody said this was going to be easy."

The next morning, we set out to capture the lioness. Instead, we treed kitten No. 6 again and saw where kitten No. 4 had run in the opposite direction. Then we found what we hoped was the female's track and turned the dogs loose. The hounds took the trail right back down to where No. 6 had been and treed him for the second time that day.

"So this female," I told Floyd, trying to make sense of the tracks she left behind, "has stayed within one-half mile of where we marked the kittens two days ago."

"Dedicated mother," Floyd said with a tone of admiration.

"I must have been within 300 yards of the whole family yesterday," I said. "I circled around the whole drainage and saw no tracks leading out. So the family was right in that relatively small area, fully aware that we were present."

By the end of the day, we were all exhausted, and I figured we had disturbed the elusive lioness enough.

"I'll gather up the dogs," Floyd said as if reading my mind.

We spent the next day resting in camp. I took a short hike to look over a potential new campsite farther up the creek but, figuring we could cover the area from our current location, decided against moving. I found some more scrape sites, including one big one under a spruce tree, then returned to camp.

*My notes: "Looked over Dave's notes. Had talk with Floyd yesterday. Dave today. Don't know what to make of situation."*

I worried that the study's demands, the challenging weather, the relentlessly rough terrain, and the scant captures had long been chipping away at Dave and Floyd's physical stamina and confidence.

The next morning, the three of us hiked nine miles back to Root Ranch so Dave and Floyd could get more supplies. There I might catch a plane back to Taylor Ranch to join Wilbur or possibly return home to McCall. Twenty-four hours later, Dave and Floyd left amid snow squalls to snowshoe back to the Chamberlain Creek camp, and I strapped on snowshoes to set out on my own again.

My notes: "Took hike up trail to where it crosses W. Fork of Whimstick. Tough going, about 2–3 feet snow. Huge tom had crossed creek bottom three times, twice east, once west. I think the biggest I've seen."

I followed the cat's track back toward the ranch and concluded that he'd been hunting elk that were wintering on the ridges above Root Ranch. I also found where he'd leapt onto an old rail fence and walked the top rail for about 100 yards, jumping down in three spots to make scrapes in the snow.

My notes: "Left note about it for Floyd and Dave."

On February 9, I woke alone at Root Ranch to windblown snow and decided against venturing out. I hoped Dave and Floyd might have it easier working at lower elevations where the weather was presumably better. That evening, I decided to tinker with the broken radiophone. I loosened two screws, removed a cover on the microphone, found a loose wire, reconnected it, and got the phone to work. Next, I checked in with Billie Oberbillig in Boise, and she relayed a message to McCall for a plane to pick me up as soon as the weather broke. Gene Crosby arrived the next morning, and soon we were airborne.

I wanted to take some aerial photographs, so we circled over the Chamberlain Creek and Disappointment Creek camps, then the Big Creek and Middle Fork portions of the study area. After a quick stop at Taylor Ranch where I left a note for Wilbur, Gene and I flew to McCall and got weathered in for three days. I spent the time with my family and continued to reassess the situation with Dave and Floyd. I knew they were beleaguered and discouraged.

"Work three or four days each week," I'd suggested before I left. "You need to rest in order to put in an honest day's work in this country." They agreed, and we parted, each of us determined to make the best of it. But it would get worse—much worse.

On February 15, Gene Crosby and I loaded his Cessna 185 with supplies to make an airdrop to Dave and Floyd at the Chamberlain Creek camp. We landed at nearby Chamberlain Airstrip to remove the cargo door so we could later drop supplies by parachute. But we got wallowed in deep powder snow. Try as we did, we couldn't gain enough speed to lift off.

Just then, Bob Fogg, another backcountry pilot, happened to fly over in his Piper Super Cub. Gene, waving his arms, signaled him in, and Bob landed.

"Stuck," Gene lamented.

"I'll try to pack it," Bob said. He got back in the Super Cub and taxied back and forth for about half an hour, packing down the airstrip snow. "That should do it," he said after making several runs and shutting the engine down. Gene, by himself, then took off in his Cessna with all the supplies and flew to Cabin Creek, where the airstrip was relatively free of snow. Bob loaded me into the Super Cub, and, with some difficulty, we escaped the powdery Chamberlain runway and also flew to Cabin Creek. There I reboarded Gene's plane and we flew back to our Chamberlain Creek camp, where Dave and Floyd were waiting for the airdrop.

After circling several times with the cargo door off, I shoved five boxes of supplies, mostly food, out the opening and watched below as five small U.S. Forest Service parachutes opened.

*Floyd's notes: "Mostly clear today so we stayed at camp and waited for the plane to come with supplies. In the afternoon, about 2 o'clock, it arrived. Everything was OK. Only the sugar busted."*

After the airdrop, Gene banked the plane toward Taylor Ranch, where I planned to meet Wilbur. I hoped things would go better for Dave and Floyd.

*Dave's notes: "Cleared off this morning pretty good. Should have gone out, but stayed and waited for air drop so we could take care of it and head for Disappointment (creek camp) tomorrow."*

By February 22, 1966, we had marked twenty-two mountain lions in the Big Creek study area. Wilbur and I were making more sense of population dynamics. We'd documented cougar movements throughout the various drainages and were beginning to understand behaviors, including cannibalism. No. 18, a 163-pound tom, had killed three kittens from a litter of four and eaten portions of each kill. We found remains of all the carcasses, and, as usual, I took photographs.

Camped at Cave Creek, we took the next day off to rest and, among other chores, tend to Ranger, who had a badly swollen leg that needed draining. We injected the dog with penicillin and let the other hounds rest as well. Meanwhile, I knew nothing about the dire straits unfolding more than thirty miles away at the Disappointment Creek camp.

*Floyd's notes: "Stayed in camp today as I think Dave had a light heart attack yesterday. That is what it seemed like to me. He had pains around his heart like he did the night at Root Ranch. Looked awful pale and weak. Am sure the man is sick."*

Dave's own notebook hints of trouble. After a routine entry about hunting on February 21, there are no more entries. I hold the small green spiral-bound notebook today, and the last twenty-six pages are blank.

Floyd, however, left details in his notes.

*Floyd's notes: "Feb. 23, Wed. Dave said he felt better this morning and we had decided to go back over to Chamberlain camp and then to Root Ranch tomorrow."*

The two set out with the hounds, and, about one mile into the trek, Dave collapsed.

*Floyd's notes: "He began to cry and said, 'I can't make it.'"*

So they rested there on the trail. Floyd took Dave's pack and helped him to his feet. Then Floyd let his hounds loose so that he could concentrate on helping Dave. The dogs disappeared hunting. Dave, with Floyd offering aid when needed, struggled back to Disappointment Creek camp.

*Floyd's notes: "He wouldn't accept much help. But made it on his own mostly. Then I went up river to Lantz Bar for help."*

Frank Lantz, who some forty years earlier had floated a wooden boat seventy miles from Salmon, Idaho, to the Salmon River Canyon, lived on the other side of the River of No Return at his gold mining claim (where he would die five years later). Lantz Bar, as it's still known, was located just upstream from a U.S. Forest Service guard station. Floyd managed to yell for help from his side of the river.

*Floyd's notes: "Feb. 24, Thursday. A copter came in and took Dave to Salmon to the hospital this morning. I went with two rangers across the river in a boat to thank Mr. Lantz for his help. I came back to camp about 1:30 and went to try to find dogs that I had to turn loose to help Dave back to camp."*

Floyd hunted for his hounds until dark and then into the next day before Gypsy, Chief, Freckles, and Dolly were all rounded up. The pack, according to Floyd's notes, had split into groups and chased cougars, bobcats, and coyotes all over the drainage.

*Floyd's notes: "I found the pups about 2:30 and two more came in just at dark. So all dogs are all accounted for."*

For almost two weeks, I knew none of this. Wilbur and I had been doing fieldwork. On March 6, I left our Cave Creek camp to get film and pick up mail back at Taylor Ranch. That's when I got the news.

"Everybody in the country has been looking for you," Billie Oberbillig said when I phoned in for messages. "Dave Wedum got flown out by helicopter. Looked like a heart attack."

Stunned is the only word to describe my reaction.

"Is he okay?"

"Not sure. Haven't heard anything."

Gathering my thoughts, I told Billie to relay word to Floyd that he should close all the camps and return to Root Ranch, and we'd fly him out. Two days later, a plane flew Floyd and his hounds back to McCall, and he drove home to Missoula. With Floyd's departure and Dave's hospitalization, the Chamberlain Basin portion of the study drew to an abrupt end.

Doctors determined that Dave Wedum suffered from inflammation of the heart lining, not a heart attack, and he fully recovered. On March 13, 1966, Floyd wrote me a lengthy letter of thanks, an explanation, and an unnecessary apology. "I am sorry things turned out as they did. I realize I am slipping and I am honest enough and man enough to admit it." The rest of the letter is a heartfelt rendition of what turned out to be disappointing for everyone involved.

Dave, who went on to have a stellar career as a biologist and game warden, had hinted in a letter before he was flown out of the discomfort that finally wore him down. He described the arduous demands of the study and quipped, "As you can see, things are really dandy. Be damn glad when April comes and I can come home to a place with a furnace and a grocery store a few blocks away."

Wilbur's take was one of empathy. He knew how the country could exact a toll on most people. "If life was easy back here," he reasoned. "The place would be overrun with people. And it isn't."

CHAPTER NINETEEN

# Basketball's Cougars

THE CHAMBERLAIN BASIN EXPERIENCE WASN'T A TOTAL LOSS. THE BIG tom, No. 2-C, held the record for the largest cat throughout the study, weighing 181 pounds. He even made a foray into the Big Creek drainage but soon left. And one of the females delivered a litter of kittens. She took her young family exploring into Big Creek and got trapped by deep winter snow until spring. She then guided her clan back to her Chamberlain Basin territory, giving us further insight into how home ranges can expand and contract.

But the most interesting events were rapidly unfolding throughout the main Big Creek study area. As Wilbur and I continued to capture and recapture cougars, a less severe winter than the previous year enabled us to get a better picture of population dynamics. During this time, we reveled in our successes enough to become rabid Cougar basketball fans.

Like us, the Brigham Young University (BYU) Cougars were on a roll in March 1966. We managed to catch most of their games on the battery-powered AM radios stowed at each of our camps. Because most of BYU's conference games were played in the Mountain and Pacific time zones, we usually made it back to camp in time for tip-off.

"That Nemelka is quite a player," I observed more than once as the season progressed.

"Sure is," Wilbur agreed. Even though Wilbur was foremost a baseball fan, he appreciated the skill and hard work of a dedicated athlete. Dick Nemelka would earn all-American honors that year and later play professionally for the Utah Stars of the American Basketball Association. By March 19, when Wilbur and I set out with the hounds from our Rush Creek camp, the team had a 20–5 win–loss record and was bracketed that night to play New York University (NYU) in the championship game of the National Invitational Tournament (NIT) at Madison Square Garden.

"Hope we don't get a lion late today," I said. "After all, we might miss the game."

"Can't have that," Wilbur agreed.

So we combed the bluffs toward the mouth of the West Fork of Rush Creek, down the trail, and up to contour the slopes back toward camp—a circuitous route of about ten miles.

"Tracks . . . but old," Wilbur said as we came upon footprints of what appeared to belong to a female. We crossed the tracks two more times, but they indeed looked old—not worth sending the hounds, especially with game time approaching. Plenty of daylight remained when we got back to camp. Wilbur fed the dogs and went to work on dinner while I tuned the radio to the pregame hype. Even though BYU was favored, the team was playing in NYU's backyard.

We sat down to dinner surrounded by wilderness and the sounds of the game far away in New York City filling our tent.

"Anything can happen in this packed-house atmosphere!" the announcer proclaimed. The game tipped off and progressed nicely with BYU building an early lead when the signal started to fade and then fade some more. I picked up the radio from the table and twisted it around to acquire a better read. But the play-by-play announcer's voice and shouting from the crowd grew more and more quiet until—*silence!*

I shook the radio. "I think the batteries are dead," I grumbled.

Wilbur sat across from me, arms folded across his chest, shaking his head. "Seems so," he replied.

"Well, I'll be," I fumed. "And Wilbur, I don't think we have any spare batteries."

Wilbur got up and looked in a few containers. "Nope."

For the next three days, we searched for mountain lions without knowing the game's final score. Not until we reached Taylor Ranch and radiophoned out did we learn that our Cougars won comfortably, 97–84, to claim their second NIT championship. We felt like part of the team.

The cougars we hunted in Big Creek never seemed to play games, except for the rambunctious kittens, of course. Adults were constantly probing the country in search of something to kill for their next meal. Eventually, so did the young cougars. Case in point: No. 19, a member of the Rough Canyon Family and a male kitten of Hazel's, lioness No. 4. We found evidence that she had stashed No. 19 and two littermates, and then gone hunting alone.

*My notes: "So apparently she left them on their own, and they are capable of killing. Looked like No. 19, the male, had done the actual killing."*

This kill, the study's fifteenth, was a huge cow elk, found at the bottom of a draw near where the three kittens were left holed up. Wilbur and I, reading the tracks in the snow, agreed on how the story played out. The young tom, No. 19, had left the other two kittens to venture out on his own. He crept around a bluff, where he spotted the cow, waited, and then took two bounds and landed on her. The cow lunged downhill about 100 feet and sustained a broken neck either from the fall or from leverage applied by the young mountain lion, or both. With help from the other kittens, the tom dragged the elk downhill a quarter mile, which is where we found it.

*My notes: "They are young, inexperienced in hunting, but apparently learned well. They are holding very high, almost beyond game, in deep snow. Could be this is to make hunting and killing somewhat easier—deer and elk, in deep snow, will place themselves in more vulnerable positions."*

Of course, the entry in my notebook was speculative. But it seemed reasonable then, as it does now as I read it again. One thing for sure: cougars, even at a young age, earn the moniker of "apex predator."

*My notes: "It is amazing that such a young, inexperienced animal weighing 80 pounds could kill another animal ten times its weight. The strength of these cats is incredible. They also use surprise and stealth to their advantage."*

Here we were, late in the study's second season. After examining more than a dozen kills, counting game animals every day, and reading tracks, we had initial documentation of how and how many elk and deer were being killed by cougars. Our findings belied conventional wisdom that mountain lions conducted savage killing sprees, leaving countless carcasses in their wake. To the contrary, we were finding that they methodically hunted, stalked, and attacked. Sometimes they failed and took chances at their own peril.

*My notes: "Apparently this is the reason they break an elk's neck. It gets the job done quickly."*

After studying our ever-increasing kill evidence, I posited that mountain lions most often kill by launching onto the prey's back and biting the neck with crushing jaws while using a forepaw to yank the animal's head straight up and back. This leveraging method simultaneously exposes and snaps the spinal cord between the atlas and the axis: the two vertebrae bones closest to the skull. That's where all the documented breaks occurred. Sudden, quick, and expeditious—the product of innate and learned behavior and eons of evolution.

We found that Hazel's kittens, though they were still traveling with their mother, were learning how to kill and becoming self-sufficient. With her family about to disperse, Hazel would soon be looking to breed again. A steady influx of kittens, with lionesses becoming pregnant every two years or so, was presumably key to a sustained Big Creek cougar population.

That said, two week-old orphaned kittens, rescued in Idaho far away from our work in the Primitive Area, were about to provide us with unparalleled knowledge about mountain lion maturation. My young daughters would name them Tommy and Flopsy, help raise them, and to this day, as grown women, consider the two cougars part of our family legacy.

Here's the story. On March 11, I radioed out from Taylor Ranch to talk with Shirley in McCall.

"Homer Ford called," she said toward the end of our conversation. Homer was a conservation officer with the Idaho Department of Fish and Game. "He said he had two cougar kittens."

"Oh," I said. "And?"

"He said they're about two or three weeks old . . . orphaned when hunters killed the mother. He's wondering if you want them."

"Of course!"

Next I called Homer.

"I can bring them to McCall," he offered.

"Okay," I agreed. "I won't be there, but Shirley said she and my daughters will take them in."

"I'll drop them off Sunday."

The kids, of course, instantly loved the kittens. The baby cougars were little guys, two males. And Muffin, our domestic cat, welcomed the newcomers into his lair. I was still in the back backcountry but shared my family's excitement, maybe even more so.

*My notes: "These kittens will tell us a great deal about growth rates, tooth eruption and replacement, etc."*

What an understatement. Tommy and Flopsy would teach us so much more, and not only about cougars. They would tap into our human world and evoke emotions ranging from love and devotion to fear and anguish. They would bond to me like baby ducklings yet retain an innate wildness. They would grow to be adults, and I would fill notebooks with entries about their young lives. And they would teach me how tragedy, like becoming orphans, sometimes has happy endings—but not always.

I'm not sure when or where No. 3, Rex, was born or how many siblings he had, when his mother left him to hunt on his own, or how many fights he had to establish dominance in his part of the Big Creek drainage. But by the time Tommy and Flopsy entered the picture, Rex, the cougar that greeted me with that primal glare when I first tried to extract him from a tree, was establishing himself as a principal character in an unfolding plot.

A little over thirteen months into the study, we had recaptured Rex five times. He'd retained his weight at around 144 pounds but needed a new collar because the old one was wearing out. On the fifth recapture, which started late one day, Rex seemed to make a game of it, zigzagging away from us for at least an hour before finally rocketing up a tree. We left him snoozing on a bed of boughs with his new collar. Then Wilbur, the hounds, and I floundered home through darkness.

*My notes: "Got in to camp at 11:10 PM. After processing Rex. Sat down to eat at 12:15 AM. After cleaning gear and writing up, getting into bed at 2:55 AM."*

Rex wasn't done with us.

The next morning, we hunted up the East Fork of Coxey Creek and found the kill we'd scared him off. The bull calf had been brought down while browsing on mountain mahogany in a rough, bluffy area.

*My notes: "Rex killed him in his tracks, nearly tearing his head off—the atlas-axis joint was torn almost completely apart."*

For most people, nature at the raw predatory level can be unsightly, unsettling, and sometimes unfathomable. For a scientist, it must be viewed as something to be understood. Not to be flippant, but it is what it is. And mountain lions are built to kill. They do it more efficiently than any other predator I'm aware of. Their ability to instantly dispatch prey animals sometimes ten times their size can't be denied or sanitized. I've never watched a mountain lion kill its quarry in the wild, but I've investigated the aftermath enough to know the attacks are necessarily brutal and, in the long run, brutally necessary to the ecological scheme of places like Big Creek.

Rex epitomized such behavior. Ironically, however, sometimes his antics bordered on comedic. Case in point:

On February 28, 1966, we set out in hope of finding mountain lion No. 1, the first cat we captured back in December 1964. We suspected that she was the mother of kitten Nos. 14 and 15. Since we hadn't captured the three of them together, we weren't sure. After a couple hours, we cut a track and turned the dogs loose, eventually finding the hounds above a big bluff but not at a tree.

"I think she's either treed out of sight or in the bluffs," Wilbur said. "The dogs don't know where."

Then we spotted the cat below us, lying directly under a small fir tree. I used binoculars to confirm.

"It's marked. I think it's No. 1."

Wilbur took the dogs above the lioness so he could turn one loose in case she ran uphill when I fired the tranquilizer dart. Crouching and sometimes army crawling, I worked downhill through steep cliffs and around a sharp ledge directly above the cat. I readied the tranquilizer gun, took aim, and, after a couple seconds, eased the gun down from my shoulder and raised the binoculars. Suprise! It was Rex. I could see his new collar as he lounged in the sun. After chuckling to myself, I let out a sharp barking sound. Up the tree Rex scurried, probably thinking those darned hounds were nearby. Eventually, he scurried back down, sidled away, and perched himself in a spectacular spot on the edge of a vertical cliff that dropped between 400 and 500 feet straight down. There he struck an unforgettable pose. He casually folded one front paw over the other and faced me, dead on. Although the light was dim, I snapped several photographs. He looked both confident and miffed. The bright yellow cattle tag dangling from his new collar blared that he was the subject of scientific study.

*My notes: "This is the second time in three days that Rex has fouled our attempt to capture the mother of Nos. 14 & 15."*

And still, Rex wasn't done messing with us.

Several days later, we hunted up Cave Creek, hit tracks, and turned the dogs loose. They took the trail across the creek and around and up steep cliffs where patches of rough ground made for tough tracking. Up high, we noticed an area where numerous deer had been feeding. As we came around a point, Wilbur paused under a small fir tree to study the tracks to see which way the hounds went and determine where the heck the mountain lion might be.

Joining Wilbur near the tree, I looked up. "Wilbur!" I shouted. "Above you! In the tree!"

Wilbur lifted his head, stepped backward, and then stutter-stepped back farther. Rex was so close that he could have reached his big paw down and snagged Wilbur's hat.

"Well, I'll be!" Wilbur said, easing away from the tree.

His golden-brown eyes ablaze, Rex whipped his long tail back and forth. The dogs had raced right past him. We backed off, waited for him to come down, and watched as he disappeared over a ridge. A cougar-size impression in slushy snow revealed where Rex had been sleeping near the tree. When the dogs came running, the big tom simply leaped into the tree and watched as the hounds sprinted past without catching his scent. These repeated encounters with Rex, even when he outfoxed the hounds, were adding to our understanding of cougar population dynamics.

*My notes: "We are getting quite a lot of home-range information on this male."*

Overall, our capture–recapture technique, coupled with close observations of evidence around us, was slowly becoming an exercise in pulling threads that might unravel the mysteries—and debunk some of the myths—surrounding cougar behavior and biology.

For example, despite our failure to capture female No. 1—the supposed mother of kitten Nos. 14 and 15—we'd already confirmed No. 4 Hazel's ability to teach her kittens, one at a time, how to hunt. By extrapolating those findings and inspecting tracks in the snow, we determined that errant lioness No. 1 was bringing only one kitten at a time on hunts.

*My notes: "The females may train the young to hunt by taking them singly— hunting success should be greater with just one youngster along."*

In addition, it became apparent that the lionesses were hunting and schooling their kittens within Rex's territory. How interesting is that? After all, here was a stalwart tom, a loner who seemed to roam with impunity, sharing his area with a female and her two kittens. Unlike the cannibal male No. 18, Rex made no attempt to kill the kittens.

A new term began percolating in my head. I called it *mutual avoidance.* Much more on that later.

In early March, Wilbur and I left his cabin on Monumental Creek and hunted all day. After stopping to chat with Dewey Moore at Acorn Creek, we finally pulled into our Coxey Creek camp to sleep for the night. The next morning, we hunted around Mile Hi and down to Garden Creek before going over a low saddle into the East Fork of Coxey Creek and then back to camp. During this arduous hike, we counted at least thirty-six head of elk and deer and surely missed spotting others. Game had moved back into the area.

*My notes: "This has occurred too frequently to be coincidence. The cats are moving the game around on winter range."*

This rousting of game herds would be further documented and eventually play a crucial part in convincing skeptics that mountain lions were crucial to preventing elk and deer from overbrowsing their food supply. A cat in the area kept the herds on alert. A cat's hunting kept the herds moving.

This became even more clear after we noted the striking difference in winter weather during our first and second years of study. In 1964–1965, snow was quite deep, and game herds crowded into lower elevations. With less snow the second year, elk and deer wintered up to 7,000 feet, eating browse at elevations that couldn't be reached during the previous winter. The game animals were simply taking advantage of the most accessible food sources. The cats were following the herds and, at the same time, having a consistent predatory impact—killing mostly elk calves and older individuals. Each night in camp, with the woodstove and Coleman lantern providing warmth and light, Wilbur tending his dogs and winter loosening its grip outside, I reviewed our notes. Steadily, I began to realize that the Big Creek cougars were slowly telling their own stories. We had to keep trekking, keep observing, and keep letting the mountain lions be themselves.

## CHAPTER TWENTY

# Full Circle

NOW AND THEN, I'D PUSH BIOLOGY ASIDE AND SIMPLY ENJOY THE COUN-try. By mid-March 1966, winter snow was receding from all the drainages, and the Middle Fork of the Salmon River had assumed a more serene character before spring runoff began in earnest. Wilbur and I worked our way down the length of Big Creek and were now hunting out of our Waterfall camp at the far eastern end of the study area. There, the Salmon River was just beginning to swell. Although we captured no mountain lions, I remained awestruck by the wilderness where they roamed.

My notes: *"Spectacular. The Middle Fork is the most beautiful river I've ever seen. The hills at Rattlesnake Creek are my idea of a spot."*

Five days later, after we'd resumed hunting back up the Big Creek drainage, winter weather returned with fury. A storm dropped heavy snow and gusty winds, sometimes at blizzard intensity. Trekking along the slopes was extremely hazardous. In addition to snow, layered carpets of ice built up. With each step, gravity threatened to sheer ice and snow loose and send us careening downward. We avoided hunting several canyons for fear of slipping off cliffs and stuck with areas where footing was more secure.

Over a five-day period, we managed to mark only one cat anew—No. 24, a female—but lost the male that was accompanying her. This was the fifth female we recorded running with a male during the second season. These females had been treed in Rush, Waterfall, Dunce, Goat, and Cougar creeks. We added the unmarked tom to the study area's total population, estimated to be approaching thirty. By April Fool's Day, the

The robust Big Creek ecosystem of sixty years ago produced steelhead trout like this one caught by Wilbur Wiles.

south-facing slopes were finally greening up, and snow continued to recede, which made tracking more difficult. Three weeks later, the second season ended—and on a much brighter note than the year before. We had more than doubled the number of marked mountain lions and recaptured many. While the Chamberlain expansion was disappointing, Dave Wedum had regained his health, Floyd Partney was at peace with his efforts, and I remained grateful that I'd hired Wilbur that day two summers ago at his cabin. Without him, the study would have suffered an early death.

So Wilbur Wiles and I, on April 23, took a thirty-four-mile celebratory hike from his Monumental Creek cabin down to our Middle Fork camp. Steelhead trout had returned to spawn after their toilsome journey back from the Pacific Ocean. We broke out the spinning rods.

I mention this fishing dalliance because the scientific success we were finally achieving boded well for not only the future of mountain lions and my aspirations to understand them, but also the wild country around us. Our work reaffirmed my belief that human beings benefit from being exposed to wild country not only to remind us of our roots but also to lend perspective to our existence. In *A Sand County Almanac*, Aldo Leopold speaks to what my heart was beginning to feel.

*"Man always kills the thing he loves. And so we the pioneers have killed our wilderness. Some say we had to. Be that as it may, I am glad I shall never be young without wild country to be young in."*

The returning anadromous fish that we sought to catch were benchmark creatures. They returned to this wild country to perpetuate their species, to contribute to the pristine ecosystem where Wilbur and I had been tracking mountain lions for two years. It's unclear when cougars entered the picture. But I suspect it was long after steelhead trout began journeying back and forth between Big Creek and the Pacific Ocean.

Of course, we had no inkling of how our work was spurring controversy. We weren't aware that among Idaho's anti-cougar factions, men were getting wind of the study and not liking the smell. I'm heartened all these years later as I page through my notebooks that I filled them with not only field observations and data, but also documentation of good times in cat country.

*My notes: "Fished Big Creek. Got 2 steelhead in hole below Dunce Creek, one about 12 lbs., one about 6 lbs."*

Jess Taylor joined Wilbur and me, and he caught a fifteen-pounder. The three of us smoked the fish, ate well, reveled in each other's company, and soaked in the purity of our feral surroundings.

The juxtaposition of then and now often boggles my mind. I've aged to become an old man who sometimes grumbles about the steady dwindling and threatened loss of things like wild steelhead and salmon runs. I'm left in this new age with the long-ago image of Wilbur as we finally parted at the end of the study's second year, his shaking my hand and saying, "See ya in a few months," then angling his way back up the Big Creek trail, closing camps along the way, stopping to fish, and continuing upstream with his hounds to their home on Monumental Creek. Wilbur would spend the summer mining opals and prospecting for gold.

As for me, I stayed at Taylor Ranch to inventory supplies and organize the cabin for our return in six months. I remember heat waves building during the day, creating spirals of visible updrafts too dangerous for a plane to land and take me home. So I radiophoned McCall and left a message that I'd be staying another night. Then I walked up behind the ranch to enjoy dusk, sat down on a rock outcrop, watched the sun give way to shadows, welcomed darkness in the canyons before returning to my bunk, and welcomed sleep.

In the cool early dawn hours of May 8, 1966, a plane landed with no difficulty, and I flew back to McCall. There, Shirley, after a "glorious" winter of skiing amid the never-ending demands of raising three children, awaited my return. I brought stories of chasing mountain lions, only to find my three young daughters playing chase with two baby cougars inside our home. I greeted them all, including the kittens, with hugs.

Like the wild steelhead, I'd come full circle.

The Big Creek drainage study area looking west from about 9,500 feet above sea level. The creek flows west to east for more than thirty-five miles through central Idaho's rugged backcountry, with scores of side creeks twisting down from the north and south through steep canyons like tendrils to the midrib of a leaf. *All photos by Maurice Hornocker, unless otherwise credited*

Rex on the rocks. The only mountain lion to remain on the study area for all ten years after being captured and released twenty-six times, Rex pauses on a precipice in Toehead Basin between Coxey and Cave creeks.

A cougar stalks until opportunity strikes, then bursts from hiding like a missile to seize hapless prey.

Rush Point Camp, one of our ten "homes" strategically located throughout the 200-square-mile study area.

On the hunt in Brown's Basin downstream from Cabin Creek, Wilbur Wiles and hounds Red, Ranger, and Chub power uphill while tracking a mountain lion.

The author inspects a kill site. Cougar tracks in the snow led to where this five-point bull elk sustained a broken neck and was cached in the snow. *Wilbur Wiles photo*

Lantern light offers a welcoming glow from inside a warm Cave Creek "home" after another punishing day of pursuing cougars.

A morning pause with Red and Ranger before resuming the hunt in the West Fork of Rush Creek.

Wilbur, wearing climbing spurs and using a lowering rope, eases a large tom (tracked and treed in Coxey Creek, then darted and tranquilized) to the ground for processing and release.

Cougar food. A large bull elk silhouetted against a dusky western horizon.

More cougar food. Four mule deer—alert, wary, and still.

A mule
deer buck
in velvet.

Now and then, a cougar "treed" in a cave. Here, Wilbur waits until a drugged No. 4, Hazel, can be eased safely from her rocky hiding place.

Bill Dorris, one of several skilled backcountry pilots who worked on the study, lands his Piper Super Cub, equipped with skis and loaded with provisions, at Taylor Ranch.

A radio-collared lioness is treed near the end of the study. The telemetry phase of the Big Creek research confirmed earlier findings that mountain lions, in stable populations, limited their own numbers through territoriality and had a beneficial impact on elk and mule deer populations.

The "five-star" Coxey Creek cabin, refurbished from an abandoned mining claim, offered a reprieve from tent dwelling.

Wilbur, pant legs rolled up above his knees, and Duke cross Big Creek. Mountain lions crossed creeks by fording through rocky shallows or swimming through open currents.

The author, toward the end of the study, checking radio collar and receiver before leaving a large tom to recover and resume a "monitored" life within its territory. *Wilbur Wiles photo*

The main Taylor Ranch cabin, built by Jess Taylor with logs cut upstream and floated down to the private property in the Idaho Primitive Area.

A male mountain lion roams in springtime sunlight.

A tom drinks from Pioneer Creek.

Wilbur and hounds take a break from the hunt.

Snow-laden Cave Creek camp.

Teeth evolved over eons to penetrate, shear, and chew.

When on the hunt, a mountain lion relies on stealth and cunning more than chase and savagery.

The author's older daughters, Karen, ten (left), and Kim, eight, bottle-feed seven-week-old Tommy and Flopsy a formula prescribed by the Portland Zoo.

PART III

# THE THIRD SEASON

# CHAPTER TWENTY-ONE

# A Pride of Hooligans

EACH MORNING IN THE LATE SPRING AND SUMMER OF 1966, AFTER returning from Big Creek, I stepped out the back door of our McCall home on Payette Lake and whistled loudly.

From a backyard pen, two separate whistles returned like echoes. "Hweet! Hweet!"

It was my way of checking on Tommy and Flopsy—the orphaned cougar kittens—and their way of responding, "Yep, we're still here."

Yes, cougars whistle. If you're surprised, so was I. They don't pucker like a person. But the acoustics, generated through their vocal cords, can be loud and shrill, like when you whistle to get a friend's attention or call a dog to heel. Sometimes Tommy and Flopsy emitted high-pitched and long whistles, other times staccato and chirp-like. In the wild, we would later learn, lionesses whistled to not only locate their kittens, but also issue orders, presumably along the lines of "The hounds are coming, get up a tree!" or "The hounds are gone, go to the cave. We'll eat later."

A bit anthropomorphic, but you get the idea.

When I arrived home after the second field season, Shirley and our daughters were tending the cougar kittens in the house like domestic cats. The kids and baby mountain lions had become a rambunctious pride of hooligans, romping around and pursuing each other over chairs, under tables, in and out of bedrooms. Finally, with everyone exhausted, the little cougars, about ten pounds each, would lie on the girls' laps, purr, and take catnaps. Each cat had a different personality. Where Tommy was aloof,

Flopsy was gregarious. Not surprisingly, they started using the curtains and table legs as scratching posts. By day they'd run and tumble, leap and scamper, and we kept them in a big cardboard box at night. Eventually, they learned to jump out and wake us up with nighttime games of kitten tag, one chasing the other and then reversing the pursuit. Although they took readily to a litter box, within two months, they entirely outgrew our home. Tommy and Flopsy had become too big and too disorderly and were wearing down our furniture and floors. And poor Muffin, our domestic cat, was clearly rattled by bossy playmates who'd quickly grown to more than twice his size.

"It's time," I told the girls, explaining that as the cougar kittens grew, they'd play even rougher and were potentially dangerous animals that could swipe or bite in a whisker of time.

"Switch, switch!" the girls would say, pantomiming cat swipes through the air and nodding in agreement.

So Tommy and Flopsy, still adorned in baby spots, were banished from inside our home. Initially, I made temporary housing in the bed of my pickup truck that I covered with a plywood canopy.

The author's youngest daughter, Lisa, age three, connects with seven-week-old Tommy in the straw-covered bed of the family pickup truck.

They tore around in the straw I'd scattered, slept curled together, ate, and banged about in the pickup bed. Knowing that they'd soon outgrow it, I built a backyard pen with chain-link fencing eight feet tall and topped it with electrified wire. As word of Tommy and Flopsy's arrival spread, some of the townspeople asked to see the baby cougars.

"Here, kitty, kitty!" children beckoned as they approached the pen with me standing nearby to observe. The kittens never showed signs of aggression. Instead, they'd nuzzle up to the fence and purr, rub against the wire, and otherwise belie the behavior of the predators they were fast becoming. I fed them roadkill (recovered by fish and game officers) and frozen jackrabbits purchased from a southern Idaho hunter.

No question: The kittens were cute and fascinating to watch and tend. But my intentions were always scientific. I wanted to learn as much as possible about growth rates, innate behavior, and how personality differences might make one cat more adaptable than the other in their environment. I wanted to know what provokes or arouses one while perhaps not the other. If you've owned more than one domestic cat, you know how different they can be. Still, there's a tendency to think that individuals within wild animal species behave and react nearly the same way. But, like people, they don't.

Certainly, there are similarities—hence the term "cat-like"—and Tommy and Flopsy exhibited some universally shared cat behaviors, especially when communicating. For example, after sleeping in separate locations even for a short time, they'd wake, find one another, rise up to rub shoulders and necks, do lip flutters, purr, and bump heads. I liken these behaviors to humans greeting one another—shaking hands, exchanging hugs, and even kissing on the cheek.

Contrary to most domestic cats, Tommy and Flopsy accepted some training. With a little food coaxing, for example, they learned to enter a dog crate whenever I needed to transport them. By the time they were mature adults, they walked with me off leash and came to me when I called their names.

The backyard pen sufficed for a couple months, but I built a better and more isolated enclosure on a rented site just south of McCall. Each day, I drove over and visited the kittens to feed and observe them. We bonded, in my mind at least, as if I was a benevolent older brother. Both kittens were affectionate, especially Flopsy. I could rub them behind the ears, pat them on the head, and stroke the length of their bodies, and not once did they demonstrate even a tad of aggressive behavior toward me.

Periodically, I lightly drugged them to record their weight and measurements. Keeping records on their food intake, I learned that a jackrabbit dinner five times a week for each cat seemed to satisfy them and keep them healthy. I paid close attention to identifying characteristics, like placement of the ears. All cougars seem to have the same size ears when they're kittens, but as they mature, the ears remain the same, and the head grows. Eventually I realized that, when comparing Tommy and Flopsy to captured female lions, adult male ears are set lower on the side of the head. A female's ears are located more toward the top and appear larger because the head is smaller than a male's. This discovery helped immensely when trying to identify the sex of a mountain lion from a distance, such as sixty feet up a tree.

By the end of the summer of 1966, Tommy and Flopsy were beginning to lose their spots. I built an expansive fenced enclosure at Taylor Ranch amid native vegetation with Pioneer Creek running down its middle. As the kittens took to their new winter home, I shot hundreds of photographs of them amid as natural a setting as could be artificially assembled. Tommy and Flopsy grew to be elegant apex predators even though they never hunted or killed anything. They would eventually touch the lives of many human beings, including Wilbur Wiles, the man I hired because he was an expert cougar bounty hunter.

In the field, I could see that Wilbur had already done a 180. He stopped viewing the cats as mere trophies and began talking about them as part of the wilderness he loved. He, perhaps unwittingly, had opened his mind to discovery. The cougars we captured and recaptured fueled the learning process and touched something primal inside both of us. These wild mountain lions became feline tutors, and both of us welcomed the schooling.

"The more ya learn, the more ya . . ." Wilbur didn't have to finish his Wilburism.

Soon to enter the study's third year, I knew there was still much to be learned. Of course, I didn't know that one lesson would hit like a stake to my heart. Despite all attempts to be objective, dispassionate, and dedicated to cold hard facts, I learned in a most unnerving way that wildlife scientists can make mistakes, be forced to take extreme remedial action, and sob in the wake of tragedy.

By late November 1966, Wilbur and I had resumed hunting. I flew to Taylor Ranch the day after Thanksgiving with Bob Fogg. After stowing gear, we flew up the canyon to Dewey Moore's airstrip, and I hiked the remaining five miles to Wilbur's cabin on Monumental Creek.

"How was the trip?" Wilbur asked.

"Good. Except I've got a bad cold," I told him. "I feel weak."

"Well, let's see what I can brew up," Wilbur said. He concocted a hot drink laced with so-called medicinal spirits and advised, "Get some sleep."

I slept well into the next morning and spent the rest of that day recouping. By Sunday, November 27, I was good to go. So we hiked from Wilbur's cabin to our West Fork Rush Creek camp twenty-two miles downstream, each with fifty-pound packs filled with essentials and all of our cougar processing gear.

*My notes: "Straightened up camp, laid in provisions. Two lions had come up trail below camp about 3–4 days earlier, had come up past camp."*

We hunted the next two days without success and ended up following some old cougar tracks over Rush Creek ridge. They failed to pan out, the hounds showed no indication of a cat nearby, and we decided to stay the night at our Rush Point camp.

"So remind me about why you'll be leavin' come morning," Wilbur said as we sat down to dinner.

"There's that meeting in Pocatello."

"Oh yeah. That's right. It should be interesting."

A meeting with several state legislators had been set up by John Woodworth, director of the Fish and Game Department, and Arlie Johnson and R. J. Holmes, both members of the Idaho Fish and Game

Commission. Among other things, they planned to discuss a possible closure of recreational cougar hunting in the Big Creek drainage pending completion of the study. They wanted me there to explain why it was a good idea.

"We need you to talk with the legislators," Woodworth told me, "in case the closure becomes necessary. Just tell them what you've found so far in your study and explain the best you can." The explanation, of course, was simple. Our marked cats had become too valuable to be killed as vermin, as Idaho law still allowed. Anyone, including professional hound hunters, could kill cougars year-round without a license and with no obligation to report the kill to authorities. Both Wilbur and I worried about how this could impact or even destroy the study. The word I got was that some people suspected we would rig the study and call for an end to cougar hunting. Concerned about potential sabotage, I was eager to make a preemptive pitch to protect the Big Creek mountain lions, at least until the study was complete. Unfortunately, I got delayed.

"No go," word came from the flying service in McCall. "Weathered in." After leaving Wilbur and hiking from Rush Point to Taylor Ranch, I was forced to stay the night and miss the meeting. The following day, Bob Fogg landed his Cessna early, and we flew to Pocatello, where I met after the fact with Woodworth, Johnson, and Holmes. They filled me in on the meeting with the legislators.

"We discussed the closure in that area, and we're encouraged," Woodworth said.

"Good, at least the door's open, right?" I asked.

"If necessary, we'll be ready to take the necessary steps," Johnson assured me. I flew with Arlie back to Boise and stayed the night with him and his family before flying to McCall on December 2, only to be weathered in for another week, although fortunately at home with my family. On December 9, Bill Dorris called to say the weather was clear for me and my two special passengers to fly back into Taylor Ranch.

Tommy and Flopsy took to flying the same way they were about to adapt to their new pen at Taylor Ranch: no sweat. They willingly entered their dog crates, and we loaded them aboard Bill's Cessna 182. They purred and slept during the flight. On the ground about an hour later, they followed me from the airstrip up to their new home. I got them settled into their shelters, checked the fence, and watched in amazement as they explored the enclosure, making scratch posts and scrapes and otherwise seeming to accept their circumstances, except for when I was away from them.

*My notes: "Both kittens, particularly Flopsy, extremely affectionate. Flopsy would put his head against me and purr and whistle and was reluctant to let me leave. Both kittens adapting to new environment well, but are lonesome."*

Wilbur arrived later in the afternoon with his hounds after hunting for more than a week. He'd captured and marked one new cat: a kitten. He was enthused to meet Tommy and Flopsy, and they seemed intrigued to meet Wilbur.

"Watch this," I said, then whistled.

Both cats whistled back and sauntered over to greet me and meet Wilbur. "Well I'll be damned!" Wilbur said.

That night, in our Taylor Ranch headquarters cabin before heading out to hunt in the morning, Wilbur talked about the comedy surrounding his capture of the kitten—the first cat of the third season. He kindled his pipe, exhaled, and began his story.

"Cut a tom track about two miles east of Bear Trap Saddle, going over a ridge into Canyon Creek." He stopped to take another drag and exhaled. "Dogs acted like it was fresh, so I let Ranger and Red go." Wilbur, with not many words, always had a way of engaging a listener. He utilized economy not to make a long story short but to get to the salient point. This story, however, was about the fiasco between the beginning and end.

"Sounded like Ranger and Red were headed toward Bear Trap. Went after 'em. But then I hear Ranger down Canyon Creek. So I cut back and found a female track. And then I could hear Red barkin' treed above me and Ranger below."

"Ha," I said, envisioning the building debacle.

"Well, I found Ranger, and he'd run out of snow and was havin' trouble picking up scent, and then he heads out anyway. So I let Chub go, but he didn't bay on the track."

Between my increasing guffaws, Wilbur continued.

"Then I heard Red tear across Canyon Creek and start baying treed again." Wilbur went on to say that he went to find Red but found tracks where Ranger and Chub had joined up and gone over the ridge into Doe Creek.

"Then, as I went up a hill, I saw two kitten tracks and then found the dogs had treed one kitten. But before I could get to it, the kitten jumped, and the dogs treed it again about 100 yards away."

"So, all the dogs are loose, chasing how many cats?" I interrupted.

"Not sure. All I know is I've got one up a tree. It's 1:00 in the afternoon, and I used seven darts before I got it drugged."

"Seven!"

"They kept hittin' flat. Kitten was up about thirty feet in a limby fir. By the time I'm done with the kitten, it's getting dark, so I cut for the West Fork Rush Creek camp."

"And the dogs, where are they?" I asked.

"Got me? Not sure. Anyway, the snow's about knee deep on top before I got to camp. Chub got in about five minutes after I arrived. Ranger and Red come in about 1:30 in the morning."

Story over. Pipe smoke hung in the air.

"Well, Wilbur," I said, "I can't tell you how much I appreciate your effort."

"Well, don't then," Wilbur said. "This is what we do, me and my hounds. We like it. And we get paid to do it."

"Not as much as you're worth."

Wilbur took another pipe drag. "Let's hunt up Goat Creek tomorrow."

Then silence. Wilbur was ready to move on. So I got up, opened the cabin door, stepped out, inhaled, and whistled. Two whistles returned.

*My notes: "Flopsy and Tommy adjusting nicely. Are concerned and seem frightened when hounds bay. Flopsy and Tommy both are still extremely affectionate."*

Two days later, while traveling up Cliff Creek, we came across a cougar track about one day old. We followed with the dogs leashed. The tracks took us to where the mountain lion had zeroed in on four elk. The cat had approached to within seventy-five feet of the prey before launching its attack.

*My notes: "Elk spooked but cat caught yearling cow within thirty feet. Cow went down once, got up and jumped once, and went down again for good."*

When we found the kill, the meat in its hams was still warm. We'd spooked the lion off his meal shortly after he'd attacked and broken the elk's neck. The hounds treed him about two miles away, and we tagged the second cat of the third season. We got back to Taylor Ranch after dark.

*My notes: "George Dovel and his wrangler visited on way out with horses. Kept us up until 2 a.m. Also stayed around this AM after breakfast."*

Within the next two years, George Dovel, a skilled backcountry pilot, outfitter, and small outdoors newspaper publisher with a lot of statewide connections, would play a major role in the cougar study, but not in a good way from my perspective. A few hours after George and his assistant left, Billie Oberbillig, operator of the Oberbillig Mobile Telephone System in Boise, Idaho, called to alert me that John Woodworth, fish and game director, wanted me again, this time to fly out for a meeting in McCall with the Idaho Outfitters and Guides Association.

*My notes: "Damn!"*

Trouble was brewing. Bob Salter, assistant director of the Idaho Fish and Game Department, had addressed members of the Idaho Fish and Game Commission on an urgent matter. The November 11, 1966, meeting minutes read as follows:

*"Mr. Salter advised the Commission of a potential problem in the cougar study being conducted by Maurice Hornocker. Apparently a cougar hunter with three dogs has moved into Big Creek and intends to stay all winter. It was suggested that the Director arrange a meeting among those concerned to see if something could be worked out so that the research study will not be hindered."*

Word of our Big Creek project had indeed leaked out.

CHAPTER TWENTY-TWO

# Cowboys with Clout

IN THE MID-1960S, THE IDAHO OUTFITTERS AND GUIDES ASSOCIATION was a formidable political lobby composed mostly of skilled hunters, horse and mule wranglers, houndsmen, and stereotypical rednecks who'd turned their passion for the outdoors into businesses. As the environmental movement spread from the eastern United States to the western states, people feared their leisure-time passions and professional livelihoods would be destroyed. For the most part, the outfitters and guides were a rough-and-tumble, straight-talking lot. Members wore western garb, including cowboy hats with salty sweat stains around the headbands, riding boots, and snap-button chambray shirts tucked into Wrangler denims or Frisko jeans held up by suspenders. Others wore belts festooned with Buck knives or perhaps even a pistol or revolver.

They wielded a lot of political clout, especially when it came to stoking anger over predators like "those damn mountain lions."

All these years later, I must admit to having harbored some preconceived ideas about these good ol' boys. And I'm sure they had prejudices about the college-student cougar lover they planned to confront.

The standoff was set for December 16, 1966, at the Shore Lodge in McCall, the only place in town with a conference room big enough to accommodate the expected crowd. About 150 people showed up, with the outfitters and guides prepared for a showdown. I arrived alone with my data and a slide projector.

When the dust settled, no blood was spilled. But demarcation lines had been drawn.

*My notes: "Talked to general session on Dec. 16 and showed pictures. Quite a discussion followed pictures."*

One of the slide pictures featured Wilbur and Rex, by then a trophy-sized tom. Dressed in his everyday woolens and stocking cap and sporting climbing spurs, Wilbur was using a rope to lower Rex from a tree to the ground for processing. The picture would eventually be published in *National Geographic* as part of an article I wrote about the Big Creek cougar study. But there in the darkened conference hall of the Shore Lodge with the slide projector's fan humming amid the suddenly silent crowd, Wilbur Wiles stood out on a screen bigger than life. He was doing something few people in the room could imagine: gently lowering a treed mountain lion to the ground to be released, not killed.

"For those of you who may not know, I'd like to familiarize you with Wilbur's hunting prowess," I told the crowd as I let the image sear into their minds before reciting the statistics. I went on to explain that, according to Idaho Fish and Game Department records, a total of thirty-four mountain lions had been reported killed in Big Creek from 1960 to 1964. Wilbur had killed twenty of them for bounties.

"I hired him because he's the best at what he does. And he's out there right now, catching and releasing more mountain lions, while I'm here talking to you. Not because we want you to stop hunting them," I told the crowd, "but because we hope to get enough answers to ensure huntable populations for the future while determining the impacts mountain lions have on elk and deer herds."

The silence was punctuated by a few grumbles and the sound of people rustling in their metal chairs. The irony, of course, was that the outfitters and guides were a lot like mountain lions. They worked territories (assigned through the state Outfitters and Guides Licensing Board) for exclusive use. By edict, they practiced mutual avoidance by agreeing to respect their peers' designated boundaries. This, like in a cougar population, limited the number of outfitters in a specific area.

Regardless of my attempts to open a few minds, some movers and shakers weren't impressed. During another general session I attended the following day, Steve Jordan, an influential outfitter known throughout Idaho, attempted to turn everything I'd said on its head. After challenging my findings and interpretations, he introduced a resolution calling for reinstatement of the bounty system.

*My notes: "Spirited discussion followed."*

Voicing support for my work and opposition to Jordan's maneuver were Bob Salter, the assistant director of the Fish and Game Department; Joe Blackburn, regional supervisor for the Fish and Game Department; and Sam Defler, U.S. Forest Service supervisor of the Payette National Forest. Several outfitters, including Rex Lanham, owner of our initial Cabin Creek Ranch headquarters who had suddenly jacked up our rent, spoke in favor of Jordan's resolution.

Jordan, after consulting with his counterparts, eventually withdrew his call for a return to bounty hunting but only after fish and game officials assured him that the agency planned no change to the cougar's legal classification for at least two years.

Meanwhile, out in the hallway, Rex Lanham and another outfitter cornered me with a different proposition.

"I'll support the study," Lanham said, "if you do me a favor."

"What's that?"

"Let Wilbur take Daryle Lamonica on a mountain lion hunt."

I'd heard of Daryle Lamonica, a backup quarterback for the Buffalo Bills in the American Football League. (He'd eventually earn the nickname "Mad Bomber" and play for the Oakland Raiders, be named American Football League's most valuable player, and compete in Super Bowl II, albeit losing 33–14 to the Green Bay Packers.)

"Who's Daryle Lamonica?" I asked Rex, simply to get a rise.

"Why, you need to pay more attention to the scores," he grumbled.

"Look. I know who he is. But what's he want from me?"

"He likes to hunt," Lanham answered. "And I'll pay Wilbur good money to take. him cougar hunting."

"Wilbur won't do that," I responded.

"Well, why not?" Rex demanded.

"Because he's working for me, and I don't want Daryle Lamonica or anyone else coming into the study area to hunt the marked cats. Even if he doesn't get a cat, the precedent will be set—everyone will want to come in. Wilbur and I just won't do that."

"Well then, I'm gonna bring my own hunters in there. Nothing to stop me. No law against shooting those cougars, marked or not," Lanham rebuffed.

"You're right, Rex," I said. "There's no law. But why would you want to do that?"

"Because you, you and these other cat lovers are part of a sham. Ya know, I don't know how you ever talked Wilbur Wiles into joining it."

Come Christmas 1966, snow kept piling up in McCall, and I enjoyed being with my family, especially at the Little Ski Hill, where, along with Shirley and our daughters, I was learning to ski. But I must admit, a big chunk of me was with Wilbur, who remained in the study area. I'd later read two unsettling entries he made in his notebook during the time I was in McCall.

The first—December 27, 1966:

*Wilbur's notes: "Saw where two men on horses had come to Cave Creek trail, about ½ mile above tents down ridge from east. Come down to our tents. One held horses and other had gone in both tents. On to Lanham Ranch. Must have come over ridge as no tracks going up."*

The second—January 4, 1967:

*Wilbur's notes: "Saw where three men on horses, with dogs, had come from Lanham Ranch, up Cave Creek beyond our camp, one going into tent. Gone back to mouth of Cave Creek, up Big Creek a short time ahead of me."*

At that point, Wilbur knew nothing of my dustup with Rex Lanham and his threat to send in hunters to kill the study's marked cougars.

As these mystery men on horseback prowled the study area and Wilbur dutifully went about his work with the mountain lions, I looked forward to the arrival of Ian McTaggart Cowan, my major professor at UBC. He flew into McCall the day after New Year's Day 1967 and was excited to hop a Cessna into Big Creek to see the area. Unfortunately, bad weather interfered once again.

"Socked in," the flight report repeated three days in a row.

Dr. Cowan was a powerfully built Scotsman standing six feet, six inches tall. But he assumed a down-to-earth demeanor that put people at ease. He laughed and interacted with my daughters, was gracious to my wife, and ably bantered with townspeople, including the local game wardens who considered him a celebrity. I put him up at the Shore Lodge, where two weeks earlier I'd addressed the crowd of outfitters and guides and dueled with Rex Lanham.

"How'd the talk go?" Ian asked.

"They were . . ."

"They were ready for you, right? I can only imagine," Ian empathized.

During the three days we were weathered in, I showed Dr. Cowan the town, took in sites around the lake, drank a lot of tea, and talked in depth about the study.

"I can't wait to get back into Big Creek," I said. "Luckily with Wilbur Wiles on the hunt progress is being made in my absense."

"Tell me about this Mr. Wiles," Ian inquired.

So I filled him in. At the end of my laudatory and somewhat lengthy introduction, Ian expressed disappointment at not being able to visit Big Creek to meet Wilbur.

"We're lucky to have such a man," he said.

I thought it interesting that he used the pronoun "we." Ian seemed invested not only in me as his graduate student but also in the study as something special. "These kinds of projects are never easy," he said. "That's what makes them all the more important to complete."

All these years later, I sometimes use the word "malleable" to describe Dr. Cowan. "Adaptable" might be better. He knew how to go with the flow—as long as things flowed in the right direction. I think that, based on his wealth of experience, he considered the Big Creek study to be on course. After all, he'd spent a lot of his early career in the wilds of British Columbia and Alberta and knew the difficulty of research in harsh environments. He and my mentor, John Craighead, were friends. I doubted that two more approachable humans had ever walked the backcountry. Ian, like John, could talk to anybody and listen with equal attention. So, after Dr. Cowan flew out on January 4 (which, by the way, was the same day Wilbur found the tracks of the three horsemen with their dogs), I was raring to get back into the field. The next day, I tried to fly into Big Creek, but clouds thick with heavy snowfall closed in once again. Finally, on January 9, I said good-bye to Shirley and the girls and landed at Taylor Ranch. Wilbur was out hunting, but caretaker Arlow Lewis was on-site. While tending to ranch chores, Arlow also cared for the captive mountain lions.

*My notes: "Tommy and Flopsy overjoyed to see me!"*

## CHAPTER TWENTY-THREE

# Mystery Tracks and Mutual Avoidance

THE DAY BEFORE I LANDED AT TAYLOR RANCH, WILBUR CAPTURED, tagged, and released mountain lion No. 28. It was a young, 110-pound male treed on a south slope of Big Creek, about one-half mile from the mouth of Coxey Creek. He took me to the site so I could backtrack the tom. Wilbur and the hounds had jumped the cougar off a kill and treed him about 100 feet away. I planned to follow the cat's tracks backward, hoping to gain insight into not only how he killed the small elk calf, but also where he traveled from and how the hunt had played out. Entering our third season, Wilbur and I were getting pretty adept at reconstructing mountain lion hunting scenarios from tracks left in the snow.

"Looks like he came from the east slope of Coxey Creek, hunted the west slope, back and forth," I said.

"And then topped out over onto the Big Creek side," Wilbur added as his hounds, all leashed, nosed around in their canine-detective manner. Judging from the tracks, the tom entered an area of steep bluffs and then a steep canyon area where he encountered a small herd of resting elk. The lion, with the element of surprise on his side, stalked and then charged toward the unaware elk.

"They tried to escape upward," I said, pointing to their tracks in the snow. "Couldn't go down because of the steep cliffs."

Wilbur nodded in agreement.

"Look here," I continued, assessing the evidence. "The cat cornered the calf against the bluff and leaped on it." We looked farther ahead. "The elk went down . . ."

"Twice," Wilbur said, pointing to a large divot in the snow where the cougar and calf tumbled a second time.

"Then the struggle," I added, picturing the final moments in my mind before, again, a broken neck.

In our Coxey Creek cabin later that night, I entered all these observations into my notes along with a description of how No. 28 dragged the dead elk down a steep slope more than 300 yards before caching it. An inspection of the carcass showed that, after two days, the tom had eaten the belly, liver, kidneys, three-quarters of the rib cage, and one hindquarter.

"Gorged on it," I said.

"With such a full belly, no wonder he didn't run far before we treed him," Wilbur added.

After eating our own elk dinner that night, I asked Wilbur if I could review the journal entries he made when I was weathered in at McCall a week earlier. He gave me his spiral-bound notebook. Paging through, I abruptly stopped.

"What's this?" I asked, pointing to a December 27 entry and then, flipping a few pages forward, another on January 4. "Something about men going into our tents?"

Wilbur leaned over the table and looked. "Oh, yeah. Was meaning to tell you about that. Didn't think much of it since nothin' appeared to have been taken from the tents. Figured they were just checking out our campsite."

"Normally, I'd agree," I said, "except for the run-in I had with Rex Lanham at the outfitters meeting."

"What run-in?"

I told Wilbur about Lanham wanting him to guide Daryle Lamonica on a cougar hunt.

"Daryle who?"

"Daryle Lamonica. He's a pro football quarterback, and Rex has some connection with him. Lanham said he'd back our efforts here if you'd take Lamonica hunting. Said he'd pay you a lot."

"What did you tell him?"

"I said hell no. Wilbur's working with me."

"Good."

I smiled at Wilbur and said, "But what really stood out is that Lanham threatened to bring his own hunters in to kill cougars, marked or not."

After sitting silently for a moment, Wilbur nodded and replied, "Well, you're right to be suspicious. Now, after hearing what he told you, I'm concerned." We went on to discuss how, nine days after my encounter with Lanham, Wilbur saw the first set of human tracks and found the second set about a week later.

"Seems they're on the hunt," Wilbur concluded.

"Oh, can't be sure of that," I said. "Let's hope not. But if they are, there's nothing stopping them, no law or regulation against it."

Wilbur shook his head and grumbled, "Ought to be, though."

After a restless, worry-fraught night of sleep, it was clear in my mind that all we could do was keep working. "Let's go back to where No. 28 made his kill," I said. "I'd like to look at those other cat tracks you found."

By the time we cleared the breakfast dishes away, put on our wool jackets and hats, checked gear, leashed the hounds, and set out for another day of hunting, I'd managed to refocus. My brain was occupied with the potential thrill of discovery. We spent the entire day scouring the area around No. 28's kill. Back in camp, over bright light from the hissing Coleman lantern, I rendered our findings and my thoughts to writing.

*My notes: "Yesterday, after marking No. 28, Wilbur noticed a track of another cat in trail below hill. Believed this to be larger cat. Today we picked up track and followed it up trail to Lime Creek."*

John Craighead, through his own child-like excitement, had instilled in me the thrill of being the first to unravel any of nature's many secrets. That's why, as Wilbur and I probed the area around No. 28's recent kill and set out to follow the second set of unknown tracks, I sensed we were closing in on something significant—not the scream of major discovery but the steady assemblage of key puzzle pieces.

"Look here, Wilbur," I recall saying as we followed the new cat's trail. "He hunted these mahogany brush bluffs and approached the top of the ridge up there." We trudged to the top and could see where the big tom had broken into a full run, chasing three deer out of their beds, following them downhill, but failing to catch any. More tracks indicated that the cougar then slowed down, resumed its prowl, and suddenly pursued a second time. After chasing a small herd of about three or four deer for approximately 200 yards across an open area, he gave up again.

But the third time, a charm!

*My notes: "He approached a rocky, bluff area and started to run, then bounded down into rocky mahogany outcrops and nailed calf elk."*

Several elk had been resting, and the cougar surprised them, attacking the small, easier-to-kill calf, then skidding the carcass about 150 yards downhill into a canyon bottom where he cached it under a fir tree.

*My notes: "Striking thing is spacing of cats. When this cat went up trail, after crossing from the south side of Big Creek, he had to pass within 100 yards of cat No. 28, a much younger smaller animal (110 lbs. vs. 151 lbs.)."*

The bigger cat we followed, much to my delight, turned out to be Rex. We captured and released him later that day. Although he'd lost all of his markers and his collar, we knew him well and confirmed the identity by the tattoo on his right ear.

*My notes: "Another striking example of mutual avoidance."*

Rex, now wearing yellow cattle tag No. 6 after being processed, had to have known that the younger, smaller male was in his territory, not to mention nearby with a kill. Yet, rather than attack or run the young tom off, Rex veered from the trail.

*My notes: "Rex went straight on past No. 28 and his kill, although normally I'm sure he would have gone right up the trail into that country to hunt. Instead he went on about one mile to Lime Creek, and then up into the hunting country."*

I contemplated mutual avoidance once again. Look at it from Rex's perspective. Why fight like cats when he and the younger tom had what they wanted—wide-open spaces to hunt and all the food they needed to thrive? In his mind or innate propensity, Rex probably figured, *See ya later, young tom. Enjoy your meal. I'm headed home. Just realize, this is my territory. Don't make a habit of visiting and sticking around.*

While this latest example of mountain lions avoiding one another added to the evidence of mutual avoidance, it also portended an even more crucial dynamic at work—one that involved younger cougars (like the No. 28 tom) out on their own for the first time. What I would call a "blinding glimpse of the obvious" was still months away. But the realization, when it hit like a lightning bolt, would be one of the final key pieces in the Big Creek mountain lion puzzle.

After hunting two more days with no success and snow falling steadily, Wilbur, the hounds, and I left the Coxey Creek cabin and headed toward our Cave Creek camp. Along the way, we stopped to visit John Vines at his Garden Creek Ranch.

"Come on in," John beckoned, "we'll have a lowball!"

Wilbur tied Ranger, Red, Sam, and Chub outside. Then he and I kicked the snow off our boots, let our packs thud to the front porch floor, entered the cabin, and warmed our hands over John's crackling stove while he mixed the drinks.

"How goes the hunting?" he asked, uncorking a bottle of liquor.

"Hunting's good," Wilbur said. "But the catching . . ."

"Remains spotty," I finished Wilbur's sentence.

*My notes: "John in good spirits."*

Somewhere in all my memorabilia of the years spent in Big Creek, I have an almost comedic photograph of John sitting in his rocking chair holding up his lowball in a toast, the floor around him covered in peanut shells. By that time in 1967, he'd eaten his way well into the first half of a fifty-gallon drum full of peanuts. And clearly, he hardly ever swept up the shells.

"At the rate I'm eatin' 'em, should finish the second drum come late spring, early summer," he calculated. "Time enough to get next year's drums flown in."

We toasted to his peanut-eating discipline and nursed our lowballs. A second round of drinks was never necessary (or requested). Whiskey and a mixer constitutes a standard highball. In contrast, a John Vines lowball was made of Old Grand Dad bourbon whiskey in a tall glass. He added a splash of water—but only if you insisted.

"You got a lot of walking ahead of ya, so drink up boys! Here's to better hunting." We toasted and talked another hour. Wilbur and I left John's cabin on a high note courtesy of John's lowballs. We tacked another five miles onto the day's trek before reaching our Cave Creek camp near dusk. We agreed. Even then, a pleasant lowball buzz lingered.

John's toast to better hunting proved prophetic. The following Saturday morning, January 14, 1967, we left camp and within half a mile spotted ravens and magpies circling overhead. The scavengers appeared to have zeroed in on a kill, but we couldn't tell the exact location. So we climbed up a ridge to get a better look.

*My notes: "Heard ravens fighting, as if on kill back down creek on west side. Wilbur spotted where something had run down hill."*

We descended, crossed Cave Creek, and immediately hit a fresh track. Wilbur unleashed and sent the dogs. The kill was right in front of us, a small elk calf. It had been dragged off a slope and cached under a fir in the creek bottom.

"Probably three or four days old," I said as the sound of baying hounds faded up the canyon. We stood, listened, and then—

"I think they've got him," Wilbur said. The distant baying had turned into a clamor of canine barks, yelps, yips, and howls—auditory chaos signaling the end of a short chase and the beginning of another capture. The hounds had followed the lion up the drainage through two canyons and treed it. The dart hit true, but the cat launched from the tree, and the chase resumed. Wilbur, who had gathered the dogs, turned Chub and Sam loose again, and they overtook the drugged cat in the creek bottom.

We arrived, and the stalemate ended with Wilbur pulling his dogs away from the lethargic but hissing lioness.

*My notes: "Adult female, No. 29, a beautiful russet colored cat."*

As we weighed, measured, tagged, and collared our latest catch, more pieces came together. I recalled that a year earlier, in almost this same spot, we encountered a family—a lioness and two kittens. We managed to capture one of the kittens, No. 14 (and later No. 15, twice). Their mother had continued to elude us. Until now.

*My notes: "This cat also has a small track, exactly the same as mother of 14 and 15. Photographed cat and marking techniques."*

We named her Bessie.

The following morning, as the Green Bay Packers and Kansas City Chiefs prepared nearly 1,000 miles away to play inaugural Super Bowl I in the sun-soaked Los Angeles Memorial Coliseum, Wilbur and I set out with Ranger, Red, Sam, and Chub. We traipsed up, down, and around the Cave, Cabin, and Cow creek drainages cluttered with old cougar tracks left by a female with kittens or a lioness in the company of a tom.

*My notes: "Could not tell . . . tracks too old and melted out."*

We continued to contour our way around a canyon when the hounds suddenly got excited. As we approached the bottom of a draw, we spotted a cached kill, its bones gleaming in the shadowy light, jutting up from beneath the snow.

"Get 'em!" Wilbur ordered, releasing the four dogs. The hounds raced away and treed two kittens a couple hundred yards up a hill. "I'll circle down and see if I can find the female," boomed Wilbur's voice from amid the ruckus.

I shot up past the kill and arrived at the tree to tie off the frenzied hounds and start preparing darts for the kittens above. Then from below me, "Found her!" Wilbur yelled. "She's treed and marked." I left the two kittens with three hounds baying at the base of the tree and took Ranger to rendezvous with Wilbur and the marked lioness.

"It's No. 4, Hazel!" I said when we got her on the ground. The last time she was caught and released was February 16, 1966, one month short of a year ago. At that time, she was in the company of male No. 22 in the Cougar Creek drainage. Two weeks before then, we captured her in the Cabin Creek drainage with two kittens, No. 17 and No. 19.

*My notes: "So have good record of breeding interval on this cat. I re-marked No. 4 while Wilbur went on up to take care of kittens. We drugged both and processed."*

The new male kitten, No. 30, weighed thirty-two pounds. The new female, No. 31, weighed twenty-seven pounds. Both had lost their spots except on the underside and inside of their legs. Overall, they retained a kittenish appearance with soft kitten fur. This was our sixth capture of Hazel.

"She's got another family since we last saw her," I marveled.

I noticed that Hazel was no longer suckling her latest offspring, which meant these new kittens would soon be on their own. She would likely breed soon after and have another litter within months. The timely capture on that day added to our growing understanding of reproductive intervals and perhaps the dispersal of young.

"It's been a good day," I said.

Wilbur looked up at building clouds and added, "But looks like it's about to end."

A mix of rain and snow began to fall. The wind picked up, and nighttime closed in. By the time Wilbur, the hounds, and I returned to camp, I'm confident that Hazel and her two kittens had reunited and retreated from the advancing storm, maybe beneath the protective canopy of a tree or into the shelter of a cave.

*My notes: "Got in long after dark, soaking wet. Came in a howling rain and snowstorm. To bed at midnight after notes, drying equipment, etc."*

In the twelve miles we had traveled that day, we marked three mountain lions. John Vines's lowball toast to better hunting had worked. As we eased into our cots for a good night's sleep, Green Bay Packers fans continued celebrating into the early morning hours after their team beat the Chiefs (my favorite team to this day) 35–10 in America's first Super Bowl.

Successful hunting also warranted celebration. So we decided, after waking, to take two days off and hiked from Cave Creek to Taylor Ranch. Along the way, we happened upon old tracks left by two or three mountain lions just above the ranch across from Rush Creek.

"Most likely another female and kittens," Wilbur speculated. The group had left footprints all over the flats and up and down the trail. Instead of pursuing, we continued on to tend to matters at the ranch, including the captive lions.

*My notes: "Tommy and Flopsy overjoyed to see me."*

Feeding two growing mountain lions was challenging. Having been raised mostly on roadkill and jackrabbits, a more natural diet of elk and deer seemed appropriate if not important. So I approached the Fish and Game Department with a proposal that I be granted a special permit to collect "specimens" in connection with the study. As we analyzed the cougars' elk and deer kills, we were documenting a pattern of mostly young and old prey. Hypothesizing that cougars were selecting these ungulates not by age but simply as the most vulnerable and opportune targets, I proposed that I hunt in a similar fashion. Armed with a rifle, I'd harvest the first available specimen I came across. The age and physical health of the animals I took would then be compared to the mountain lion kills. Additionally, the carcasses of the animals I killed would be fed to Tommy and Flopsy.

Officials accepted my proposal and issued the permit.

*My notes: "Chores at Taylor Ranch. Mail day, but plane did not show. Took specimen, cow elk."*

Apex predators don't always get their way. Sometimes, like their prey, carnivores fall victim to nature's unforgiving forces. Death might be accidental and quick, or prolonged and agonizing. Mountain lion No. 18, the one we called "Cannibal Tom" after he ate three kittens a year earlier, became a case study.

On January 18, 1967, we left Taylor Ranch and stayed the night at our Rush Point camp after finding no fresh sign of cougars in the area. The next morning, we set out in off-and-on snow that continued the rest of the day. We contoured through canyons in wet, ankle-deep snow toward our West Fork camp and eventually encountered old cougar signs seemingly everywhere.

"I bet we've seen tracks of at least five lions," I said.

"Or more," Wilbur agreed.

As we picked our way along a ridge above camp, a mountain lion suddenly burst from a small cave. It had apparently been sleeping when we approached. Bolting away, it charged high into the bluffs, appearing to head back toward Rush Creek. Wilbur unleashed the dogs, and they quickly treed the lion, only to have it leap to the ground, run, and tree again, this time in a fir tree laden with limbs. From the ground, I could see markers on the cougar's ears but couldn't make a positive identification. So we darted the lion, waited for the drug to take hold, lowered it to the ground to check markers and tattoos, and were stunned by the cat's emaciated condition.

"No. 18," Wilbur said. "Looks like he's had a tough time of it."

We gently maneuvered Cannibal Tom into netting, then heisted him off the ground to be weighed. The spring scale, attached to a rope looped over a tree limb, slowly oscillated up and down before registering.

"One hundred and thirty-three pounds," I said as Wilbur recorded the weight.

I checked our records. The first time we captured Cannibal Tom was three days short of one year ago and only a half-mile away. A month after that first capture, we caught him again near the mouth of Rush Creek.

"That was on February 18, 1966," I recited from our notes while looking at the scale in a bit of disbelief, "and he weighed 163 pounds."

"So he's lost more than thirty pounds in a year," Wilbur said.

"Thirty-three to be exact." We checked his teeth, examined him externally, and found nothing that might cause or contribute to such a drastic loss of weight. After processing the tom and refreshing his markers and collar, we left him on fir boughs to recover and then backtracked toward his cave.

*My notes: "His droppings, found at the cave's entrance, contained numerous tape worm segments—this might be a factor in his weight loss."*

We had no idea if the mountain lion was slowly wasting away or if he was gradually recovering. We'd unceremoniously yanked Cannibal Tom from the ecosystem, assessed his condition, made notes, and left him lying on fir boughs in the snow. Would he survive in such a compromised condition? Did he have enough fight to stay at the apex?

Our abandonment was justifiably scientific but, at the same time, coldly Darwinian.

# Chapter Twenty-Four

# "Everybody's Got to Eat"

A series of storms engulfed the entire study area starting on January 20. Snow descended at a blinding rate for three days, and we found ourselves struggling on snowshoes simply to get around much less hunt. At one point, Red got loose and took a track over Lookout Ridge. So we let Ranger follow. Eventually, we determined that the track, fast filling with snow, was that of Cannibal Tom. No need to follow, so we caught the hounds. I was glad to see No. 18 was still up and running.

On January 21, the temperature rose, and snow briefly turned to rain. Trees dripped around us like leaky shower faucets. Elk and deer seemed to have pulled out, perhaps sensing another onslaught of foul weather. Then the temperature dropped again.

*My notes: "Snowing all day, really piling it up. Snow has covered old tracks—tough trip. Deep snow. Game has pretty well pulled out and it looks as this storm will move bulk of game on down drainage."*

We holed up at our Rush Point camp on January 22. It snowed all night and into the morning. Just before noon, the skies cleared, but the temperature plummeted further. We hiked our way to Taylor Ranch, arriving just in time to meet the mail plane. Equipped with skis, it landed like a carrier pigeon into a pillow of powdery snow. Inside our cabin, I read a letter from Shirley and the girls first, then some fish and game correspondence—welcome words from the outside world. Wilbur had no mail and didn't seem surprised or disappointed.

"I think I'll photograph Tommy and Flopsy in the morning," I told Wilbur.

"Still clearing up," he said after peeking outside. "Light might be real good."

Wildlife photography back in the early 35-mm film days involved learning about light, mastering the equipment, exercising immense patience, and often stumbling into dumb luck, especially when mountain lions were the target. Just like the lack of cougar science, a dearth of photographs existed. The cats mostly hid from people, which meant photos from the wild were usually of treed mountain lions looking down at baying hounds before being shot by bounty hunters or sportsmen.

Since the beginning of the study, I photographed each lion we captured and managed to get some compelling images. But I had few candid shots of cougars simply being cougars. Tommy and Flopsy changed all that.

The cougar pen at Taylor Ranch was designed and built for the cats to live in a spacious natural habitat. Inside the pen as I entered, both cougars always greeted me with whistles, purrs, and nuzzling. If I waited long enough, they'd return to more cougar-like behavior. I learned to meld into their environment, observe, and become a wildlife voyeur. Eventually, they got so used to me armed with my cameras that I could take them for photo sessions up into the bluffs behind the ranch.

"Come on boys, let's go." No leash, no ropes, and no tethers of any kind. They simply followed me, and I'd bring lots of film. I used Nikon cameras. In the 1960s, all cameras were heavy metal mechanical marvels as opposed to today's lightweight digital, mostly plastic models. No enclosed minicomputers back then. No autofocus. No "easy" mode. But the gear was stout. I swear, after shooting thirty-six precision frames with a Nikon F, a person could use it to pound nails. Although some cameras had light meters, cutting-edge technology pretty much ended there. And I never knew if I got the great shot—not until the roll of film

Flopsy, roaming the bluffs outside his pen at Taylor Ranch, offers the author a classic wild cougar portrait.

was spent, packed back to the ranch, sent by plane to McCall, mailed to a lab for developing, and returned in reverse fashion maybe three weeks to a month later.

While photographing wild cougars in their wilderness environment was fraught with failure, getting Tommy and Flopsy on film in their "artificially natural" environment was like starting a football game with a three-touchdown advantage. All I had to do is walk with them off leash to the bluffs above the ranch. Game over! Great pictures of both cats exploring and simply being cougars.

But not the day Flopsy clamped down on the entire process.

*My notes: "Photographed Tommy and Flopsy in bluffs above cabin. They behaved nicely—esp. Tommy. He explored bluffs and all over, offered excellent shots."*

Flopsy was less cooperative. Earlier that day, I noticed that he limped, like his right hind leg was bothering him, perhaps having wrenched it in some way. Otherwise, he was his same affectionate self. I decided to set him up for a portrait.

*My notes: "I carried Flopsy and put him on ledge in bluff for one shot. He didn't like it and came right down."*

So I carried him back to the ledge a second time. "Come on, Flopsy," I coaxed. "Just stay here long enough for one shot." As I pivoted to walk a few feet away, he jumped down and was back at my side. "Look, Flopsy, just one shot," I said, about to pick him up a third time.

*My notes: "The third time I tried it, old Flopsy growled and took my hand in his teeth real firmly as if to say, 'Now, that's enough!' He didn't bite, but I'm sure he would have if I tried to move him again."*

These photo sessions went on for the better part of a year, and many of the resulting images appeared in scientific publications and magazines and on the covers of several books. When I look at my notes and the pictures more than sixty years later, I can almost hear Tommy and Flopsy whistling and purring as I approached them with a Nikon slung over my shoulder. Their portraits are a legacy of what I took from them in the name of science and what they gave me in the name of trust.

For the next four days, Wilbur and I hunted out of Taylor Ranch. We covered nearly thirty miles, probing upstream from the mouths of Cliff, Cougar, Dunce, Goat, and Rush creeks; contouring the canyons in between these multiple watercourses; and negotiating windswept ridges cleaned of snow on one side while inundated with the roofs, faces, and scarps of dangerous cornices on the leeward side. We counted thirty-one elk, nineteen deer, ten bighorn sheep, one mountain goat, and scads of ravens, magpies, and other avian scavengers.

At one kill site where tracks showed that coyotes had brought down a deer, a cloud of birds took flight as we approached. Among the swarm were three golden eagles, so gorged with carrion that they managed only downhill flight before landing a safe distance away. It appeared that a small number of coyotes had closed in on a fawn and attacked. We collected a femur from the remains and, after later examination, found the bone marrow to be in poor condition. The deer, perhaps taxed by winter and in the early stages of starvation, was vulnerable to the lesser predators.

When compared to mountain lions, coyotes are inferior killers, especially when trying to overcome big game. Canids are more likely to join birds and other scavengers to clean up at cougar kill sites. We often found evidence of coyotes scattering bones and other carcass parts after competing among themselves, then running off with any tidbit of nourishment they could grab.

"Everybody's got to eat," Wilbur summed up the science at such scenes.

We would soon find that at least one adult male cougar had also become a scavenger. Or perhaps "robber" is a better word. But first we needed to unravel some kitten mysteries.

On our fifth day of hunting out of Taylor Ranch, we split up after entering the Rush Creek drainage. Wilbur, with three hounds, hiked high, while I, with one hound, descended. Eventually, I crossed the creek atop rocks and found where a female and a kitten had come together. I followed their tracks, climbed higher, and whistled for Wilbur. We met and followed the two cats around a bluff into a canyon where Cannibal Tom had earlier killed three kittens. Tracks indicated that the lioness made a failed attempt to kill a deer. Then, as we followed, the tracks appeared fresher.

"I'm turning 'em loose," Wilbur said. Within about five minutes, the hounds treed kitten No. 25 on the next ridge. We had marked this cat fifty-five days earlier on the West Fork of Rush Creek. So once again, we darted, processed, and left her lying on fir boughs to recover. Then we circled the area for the female. The dogs eventually treed female No. 12, first captured in late November 1965, more than fourteen months earlier.

"Looks like a one-kitten litter," I said.

"Unless she's lost some," Wilbur added. After all, we were in Cannibal Tom's territory.

"But we can't be sure of that," I said. "Let's go with what's most likely." Later that night, January 28, 1967, I reviewed our records and wrote the following:

*My notes: "Believe we have 3 litters of this year's kittens—No. 12 and her No. 25; No. 4 with Nos. 30 and 31; and the unknown female mother of No. 27."*

Next I speculated about the lionesses:

*My notes: "Believe No. 12 has only 1 kitten, a female; No. 4 only 2 kittens, a male and a female; and the unknown female, two or three kittens, one a male."*

That's an average of two kittens per litter. Again, while speculative, it seemed to be early evidence that mountain lions were not propagating with impunity, overrunning the study area, and wantonly killing prey.

We left Taylor Ranch the next morning and hunted in a cold rain toward our Cave Creek camp, cutting an old track of a female that we decided not to follow. Within a short distance, we came upon a much fresher tom track heading toward Brown's Basin. Wilbur turned the dogs loose, and they made a straight-line pursuit up the canyon, then east into some rough bluffs. After climbing for about twenty minutes, Wilbur and I topped the ridge and saw Red about 200 yards below us, barking at a lone tree across the draw from where we'd jumped Hazel and her two kittens two weeks earlier. Meanwhile, we could hear Ranger barking in the bluffs above. The younger dogs had pulled off and come back to us.

My notes: *"Ranger really raised cain. We worked on down to Red and tied him."*

By this time, fog had set in below the ridge, and rain continued to fall, creating an eerie mist that swirled throughout the bluffs as a gentle breeze seemed to say, "Hush." The hounds eventually fell silent.

Then we spotted the cougar crouched on a rock outcrop about 100 yards away. As we approached, he slipped down, like a fleeting phantom, around and out of sight. The dogs started barking again. We kept searching, peering through the fog that hovered over the bluffs.

My notes: *"I looked up and saw cat's switching tail right on edge of rock outcrop—dropped sheer 150–200 feet from where he was."*

Wilbur headed back up the bluff to catch Ranger, who had resumed a round of frenzied barking. I put the binoculars to my eyes, focused through the murk, and waited for the cougar's long tail to stop switching. It did. Then I saw round ears, followed by yellow eyes, clenched mouth, and finally the entire head and neck. As I honed in some more, the cat looked back with a familiar glare.

"Rex," I muttered. "Of course."

We'd recaptured the big tom eighteen days earlier. I could see that he retained all his markers and collar. So there was no need to tranquilize and process him again.

Wilbur returned with a panting Ranger, and I said, "Guess what? It's Rex."

"Figures."

I raised my camera, held it as still as possible in the fading light, focused on the big tom, and shot more than a dozen frames, hoping the Nikon not only captured Rex wearing his collar and the bright yellow No.

6 cattle tag but also recorded the severity of the world where cougars had retreated.

*My notes: "Poor light."*

I realize now, nearly six decades later, that as I continued to trip the shutter and twist the lens wide open to collect as much light as possible, the portrait of Rex clinging to the cliff (making a portrait for the cover of this book) portended something more ominous. It reflected not only his immediate circumstances but also the precarious future of all mountain lions at the time.

We treed Bessie, No. 29, the next morning about one mile upstream from our Cave Creek camp. She'd been captured and processed sixteen days earlier and still had her identifying tags and collar. No need to immobilize and process her again.

About one-half mile from where we left Bessie treed, we found evidence of a kill—a mostly eaten calf elk. We assumed Bessie, the mother of Nos. 14 and 15, had killed it. The calf had been attacked on a fairly open bitter brush slope, dragged downhill, and cached under mahogany vegetation. The killer slept in needles under a pine about forty yards away.

*My notes: "Believe No. 29 made this kill and had left it few days ago."*

Next evidence of an opportunity taken.

*My notes: "No. 29 went on up west slope of Cave Creek and appeared to be hunting elk in the creek bottom. Believe it killed and ate a rabbit in bottom."*

To survive, wild animals need to act when opportunity strikes, take the path of least resistance, make the most of challenging situations, think on the run, and adapt to unexpected circumstances. This is crucial for apex predators—carnivores that roam at the top of the food chain amid what we researchers call the highest trophic dynamics. In the 200-square-mile Big Creek study area, mountain lions had no predators above them—except Wilbur and me with our tranquilizer darts.

And, of course, the mystery men on horseback with dogs and high-powered rifles.

## Chapter Twenty-Five

# Making Brains Sweat

ON THE LAST DAY OF JANUARY 1967, JIM GRABAN, A FISH AND GAME
Department photographer, flew into Taylor Ranch to spend several
days documenting the study. The agency, by this time, was deeply
invested in our work and needed to take a public relations stance as
political rumblings built throughout the outfitter-guide, livestock, and
wool growers' associations. The department's media people wanted to
be prepared with photographs and press releases to answer questions
and inform the public.

Members of the Fish and Game Commission had already been
alerted about the brewing storm. There was talk that a hunter from
the town of Cascade had been wintering at Dewey Moore's ranch and
killed two of our marked cats. Rex Lanham's threat to bring hunters and
hounds into the study area kept rattling around in the back of my mind.
And there were those worrisome human tracks Wilbur had found visiting our camps and going inside our tents while I was in McCall, along
with horse and dog tracks on the trails. All of it left me fearing the worst.

If someone wanted to sabotage our work, killing lions would be
easy. The rationale was fear—fear that the study was the first step
toward outlawing mountain lion hunting. A paradox had surfaced: the
deeper we got into the study, the more critics spread fear of a hunting
closure. The more they threatened to kill our study cougars, the more I
contemplated pushing for the closure.

For the next five days, with camera-laden Jim Graban accompanying us, Wilbur, the four hounds, and I scoured known cougar haunts upstream between Taylor Ranch and Cabin Creek. I had called Jim earlier by radiophone to say we'd be in the Cave and Coxey creek country. He didn't seem too keen about searching for us on his own and said he'd rather fly in to meet us at Taylor Ranch the following Monday. Just before he landed, we treed Bessie, No. 29, in bluffs above Cave Creek. Unfortunately, Jim missed the action.

Wilbur and I, of course, were well conditioned to the rigors of the hunt, and Jim, after a day or so, did a good job of keeping up. Although daytime temperatures were rising slightly, they dropped well below freezing every night. This caused treacherous walking atop crusted snow, so much so that Wilbur opted to stop tracking in some areas, including steep bluffs.

"Not worth it," he flat out declared.

The day after Jim arrived, heavy morning snow negated our plans to negotiate ridges between Cave and Coxey creeks. So we stopped to have a quick chat with John Vines (too early for lowballs) before retreating for the night to our Coxey Creek cabin. The next day, we made a circuitous hunt among a maze of tracks that I thought might belong to two toms working the same area. But after some exhaustive circling and probing, I concluded that it was probably one cat—and most likely one we knew well by now.

*My notes: "The tom we were after may well have been Rex. The tracks followed the same route Rex did last time. Further, this cat went directly to the kill Rex made 1-11-67 and dug out old hide. If was Rex, he made quite a trip from Brown's Basin country, where we got him 1-29-67."*

On the morning of February 2, 1967, Jim, Wilbur, and I left our Coxey Creek cabin with the hounds to follow tracks left by another cougar that Wilbur discovered the evening before. We intercepted the track on a slope about 100 yards above the cabin. The cat had approached, reversed direction, gone back up a hill, crossed our own tracks from the previous day, negotiated a ridge, and descended toward Big Creek. It crossed the creek, and the dogs treed it.

Peering up at the hissing cat perched on a limb, I could see it was marked. "It's No. 15," I said. Wilbur had recaptured the young female twice two months earlier, once in Garden Creek and again in Buck Creek. She and No. 14 were the kittens of No. 29, Bessie. We first captured the kittens almost a year earlier. It appeared, based on my inspection of more tracks, that the youngsters, while perhaps in the same area as their mother, were now hunting on their own.

*My notes: "Believe this cat is living, in part, on rabbits—had tough time killing fawn deer in Garden Creek."*

I also revisited old evidence left by another cougar—and a big cougar at that.

*My notes: "Inspected kill No. 11 again today. Made by quite large male, believe bigger than Rex, at least larger track."*

The next day, I ended up tracking Wilbur instead of mountain lions. The dogs had been trailing feverishly, noses vacuuming scent from both the ground and the air. Amid the excitement, we thought the dogs had possibly left a treed lion to pursue another lion. So Wilbur set off after his hounds as Jim and I explored. We didn't find a treed lion but eventually found fresh tracks left by Wilbur.

*My notes: "Tracked Wilbur around into deep brushy canyon. Found Wilbur with drugged cat—cat had jumped a tree and entered a cave."*

"Interesting pursuit," Wilbur said, as he tended to No. 32, a seventy-nine-pound female. "I thought the dart hit true but wasn't sure." With the hounds tied, Wilbur tracked the lion, eventually locating it backed into a dark cave. He retrieved a flashlight from his pack and reloaded the tranquilizer gun.

"Then I crawled in with the light and gun. She was growling and upset. But I could tell she was drugged. So I reached into the darkness and grabbed her by a back leg."

Wilbur had just pulled No. 32 from the cave when I arrived. We fitted her with a collar, tagged and tattooed both ears, and left her settled in a dry spot back inside the cave.

"She's resting nicely," said Wilbur, offering the lioness a gentle pat before turning to leave.

We hunted unsuccessfully the next two days, finding some old tracks but nothing fresh. The recent temperature fluctuations had left the ground covered with slick, crusty snow, making it treacherous for us to travel and possibly forcing game animals down into the bluff areas, where there was less snow.

*My notes: "This makes it tough since there is little snow on these south-facing slopes."*

The following day was February 6, 1967. Wilbur and I left our Cave Creek camp and hunted our way back to Taylor Ranch. Jim Graban packed up his exposed film, hiked to Cabin Creek, and flew to McCall, then on to Boise. Wilbur and I, on our arrival at Taylor Ranch, discovered more disturbing tracks in the snow.

*My notes: "Someone had been to Taylor R., had gone directly to cat pen. Probably last Sat!"*

I pondered the worst-case scenario. Our marked mountain lions had already been threatened by Rex Lanham and others. We'd found evidence of hunters working the Big Creek drainage. And now, with this latest sign of intruders leading to Tommy and Flopsy's pen, I worried they would become targets.

For now, both cats came purring. I eagerly reunited with each through the fencing, then inside the pen as they rubbed against me. I observed that Tommy and Flopsy had pretty much eaten all of specimen No. 3, a 168-pound mature doe that had been shot thirteen days earlier.

*My notes: "Growth of captive kittens has slowed considerably during past 2–3 months. Also their overall appearance has changed but little."*

I whistled, and they followed. Their pelage had become much darker on their upper bodies and heads. Tommy and Flopsy, the two orphan kittens who'd rampaged around our home with my three daughters, were now almost a year old. Their maturation was a fascinating sidebar to the even more fascinating story that their wild counterparts were steadily revealing.

The next day, I flew home to McCall. Wilbur hunted for twelve more days but captured no more new cats. No. 32, the young female we left in the cave, would be the last new mountain lion captured and released during the third season. After averaging just over ten new lions each year, most were now recaptures. I suspected we had pretty much identified and marked the entire resident Big Creek mountain lion population. The fieldwork was gradually transitioning to analysis. Explaining the population dynamics of these cougars and their impact on elk and deer herds—that was a looming challenge. The pressure was intensifying. My doctoral thesis hinged on making sense of our findings. The Idaho Department of Fish and Game wanted facts about cougar depredation on deer and elk herds. After three years, I'd overcome the study's physical demands. Now the mental demands—converting raw field data into a coherent dissertation—were bearing down. If brains could sweat, mine was saturated.

# Chapter Twenty-Six

# Clinging to Life

As February waned and melting snow continued to recede up the south-facing slopes and make tracking difficult, Wilbur took some well-deserved time off to straighten up around a couple camps and work on his taxes, of all things.

"Our Uncle Sam knows I'm back here," he explained. "Still demands his share."

On February 19, University of Idaho graduate student Ted McKinney flew into Taylor Ranch with me to begin an elk–bighorn sheep study in the Waterfall area of Big Creek. The next day, Wilbur and I hunted from the ranch up the bottom of the Rush Creek drainage and followed some old tracks high onto a ridge. We then picked up a fresher set going down through some bluffs. The hounds treed No. 11 after a short chase. She was pregnant, and we estimated she'd give birth within two weeks. The lioness, our records confirmed, had been running with a tom in November 1965. She'd lost one ear tag and one marker but still wore her collar.

*My notes: "Processed, marked and left in bough bed under tree."*

Next, we inspected the surrounding area and found that the pregnant cougar had killed an elk calf and dragged it about 150 yards over downed trees and into a canyon before the carcass got snagged in a brushy creek bottom.

"I can't explain this," I said.

"Me neither," Wilbur concurred as we surveyed the remains she left in the inhospitable creek bottom. Why the lion had gone through so much work instead of simply caching her kill in an easier, closer place made no sense to us.

"Whatever the reason, she did a first-rate job of burying her scats," I said. Wilbur poked his walking stick around the wide area where the cat had scraped hardpack snow over her droppings and topped it off with brush and grass.

*My notes: "Displacement activity? Seems as tho' she couldn't bury carcass, so just had to bury something."*

Laboring back up the ridge on snowshoes, we returned to our Rush Point camp and, after dinner, assessed the current circumstances.

"In the past ten days while you were gone, the elk have gone high," Wilbur said.

"And the deer moved low," I added.

"They're probably feeding on green grass sprouting in the lower elevations," Wilbur said.

"Could be, or maybe the severe crusted snow drove them down where they found the grass greening up," I suggested. "The elk could handle the hard snow better . . . and the deer, once down, stayed on the grass."

"Makes sense," Wilbur agreed. I jotted our observations into my notes and wondered what impact, if any, this situation might have on the way mountain lions hunted. Had weather conditions divided the prey and made them more vulnerable for the mountain lions to attack?

The next morning, we found evidence of somewhat baffling mountain lion behavior. At the lower end of Rush Creek, we intercepted the tracks of two kittens together and then an adult female that joined them. We assumed they were a family. The kittens had scurried all over, up and down the draws, walking on logs and churning up the snow and soil. We eventually treed one of the kittens, No. 25, and the mother, No. 12. Half of the lioness's tail had been bitten off, probably in a fight defending her offspring. We were right.

After finding the remains of a fawn nearby, the dogs treed No. 18, the still-thin Cannibal Tom. You recall that he killed and ate three kittens a year earlier. Our conclusion: Perhaps weakened from the severe weight loss and unable to hunt normally, he'd stolen the fawn kill from the wounded mother and her fearful offspring.

*My notes: "The female probably fled with her kittens when this cannibal male appeared. This is the first instance we have had of one cat stealing or driving another from a kill."*

With Cannibal Tom treed, Ranger upped the excitement a notch. The dog managed to climb twenty-five feet up the fir tree to within a few feet of Cannibal Tom. The cat spat at him but didn't attack.

*My notes: "Ranger goes completely insane at tree."*

Wilbur threw off his pack, climbed the tree, and grabbed Ranger by the scruff of the neck within six feet of the snarling tom. "Damn dog," Wilbur grumbled while managing to retreat with one arm around the still-barking hound down through the limbs to the ground. The chaos didn't end there. The other two hounds had No. 25 cornered on a bluff, with the cat recoiled on a thin rocky point eight feet below.

*My notes: "Full of fight, she lashed out at the dogs."*

After Wilbur's nearly two weeks of not finding lions, this day stood out. Albeit chaotic at times, we caught cats. I managed to photograph most of what happened and fell asleep that night with a sense of satisfaction and absolutely no idea of just how harrowing tomorrow would become. My life would literally hang in the balance.

The Rush Creek drainage, where Cannibal Tom roamed, was mostly steep canyon country with sheer cliffs, jagged ridges, and avalanche-prone terrain that became especially dangerous as winter gave way to spring. Heavy snow melted during the warming days and froze solid again at night. Additional snow would fall, followed by more days of melting, nights of freezing, and then more snowfall. This counterpunching weather pattern resulted in layers of snow, ice, snow, and more ice clinging to cliffs until gravity triggered small avalanches. We found ourselves in such an area on February 22.

*My notes: "We crossed over and climbed up—quite treacherous. Snowslides had run, making icy runways to the bottom."*

My boot-clad feet went first, followed by my pack-laden body and my arms grasping for anything to stop the descent.

"Wilbur!" I shouted. And then, as I slid away on my belly, my gloved hand caught a small, leafless mahogany bush (the kind elk browse on) protruding from the snowpack. I grabbed, and the bush halted my descent. Not quite dangling, I nonetheless clung literally to life. If the bush or my grasp gave way, I'd slide to the edge of a cliff and plummet straight over. I doubt anyone could survive such a fall.

"Don't move!" Wilbur shouted from above me. "Hang on and don't move." He tied the hounds to some rocks as I continued to cling with one hand. Taking his hatchet from his pack, Wilbur started chopping footholds into the ice. He then secured a climbing rope to a small tree, held the rope with one hand, chopped more footholds with the other hand, and worked his way down.

"When I get close, I'm going to throw the rope just above you so it slides close enough for you to grab with your free hand," he said in a matter-of-fact way that belied the terror that was consuming me.

"Now this is important," Wilbur instructed. "Don't let go of the bush until I tell you."

"I understand," I grunted.

"Take hold of the rope when it comes, then don't let go of the bush until I say so," he repeated.

"Okay."

With his boots anchored in the icy footholds, Wilbur coiled the rope and flung it high overhead. It hit the slick slope and came sliding over to me just as he had explained it would. I snatched the rope with my free hand.

"Now, let me know when you've got a good grip on the rope."

"Got it!"

"Keep hanging onto both the rope and the bush," Wilbur continued. "And when I say, 'Now!' let go of the bush and grab the rope with both hands. Ready? Now!"

I don't recall letting go of the bush and grabbing the rope, it happened so quickly. But I can still feel the surge of adrenaline as I slid away from the bush with both hands welded to the rope. I do remember sliding on my belly with increasing velocity across the frozen snow, then back to the other way like a pendulum until gravity held me still. I looked down beneath the slope that dropped several hundred feet to jagged rocks. Then I turned my head up toward Wilbur. He literally held, in his woods-strong hands, my only chance of survival. He began pulling. Slowly, ever so slowly, Wilbur inched my weight back from the precipice, one step at a time, making sure his feet were secure in the footholds he had chopped. He gathered up short coils of rope, keeping the length I held taut, ever so gradually pulling us both to safety.

"You saved my life!" I gasped as we stood facing each other on firm ground.

"Nah," Wilbur said while gathering his gear and the hounds. "Well, maybe."

To this day, people often ask me about the perils of pursuing dangerous apex predators in the name of science. And I say it's not the animals but the country that's more likely to eat you.

Five days later, after hunting with no success, we treed the pregnant female, No. 11, again. All her markers were intact, and seeing that she'd probably give birth within the next ten days, we left her alone. Continuing down Rush Creek, we saw lots of game sign in the timbered pockets and open slopes. As we approached No. 11's kill for another inspection, large tracks indicated that someone new had fed on it. More than half the carcass was gone.

*My notes: "Dogs excited, so turned them loose and they took track right up canyon toward Pioneer Creek, then turned back up drainage in rough bluffs and high timber. Treed cat near top in second canyon up from kill."*

It was Cannibal Tom.

*My notes: "So this male had 'stolen' another kill. Looked as though he had spent two days at kill. He had left it, however, and gone hunting—was hunting hard in bluff areas (quite a lot of game high on north slope)."*

We now had two verified instances of this lion stealing other cats' kills. Cannibal Tom had a new title: "Thieving Cannibal Tom." Interestingly enough, the new moniker spoke more to the carnage he'd wreaked on his own species than on the prey he hunted.

On February 28, we traveled twelve miles, hunting from our Cave Creek camp, up Cow Creek, over to Cabin Creek, and up to the forks of Cabin Creek. Though we captured no cats, my reading of tracks in the snow was slowly confirming my theories on cougar territoriality. Not long after leaving camp the next morning, we cut the tracks of a female and two kittens. Wilbur and I were sure it was Hazel, No. 4, and her offspring, Nos. 30 and 31—the Rough Canyon Family. They appeared to be living, perhaps year-round, in the Cabin, Cow, and Spring creek contiguous area.

*My notes: "Territoriality is fascinating—there is absolutely no overlap of territory of females with kittens."*

Hazel had spent part of her time last year in the Cougar and Cliff creek drainages. This year, another female, No. 12, and her two kittens, No. 25 and probably No. 27, took over that area. Hazel stayed with her family in the Cabin Creek drainage.

*My notes: "This is further evidence of advanced evolution of felines. Cats are at top of mammalian evolutionary process—most specialized, fewest number of teeth, very intelligent, capable of killing wide range of prey, including very large animals, adaptable to wide range of ecological situations, etc."*

While reviewing notes more than a half-century old, I pause to recall the long-dormant thrill of discovery.

*My notes: "It is reasonable to accept idea that a more complex system of territoriality should also have evolved. This is mutual avoidance. No aggression in a stable population. Mutual avoidance does away with poor economy of fighting. It also makes for better hunting conditions—respect for presence of another cat makes hunting success much more likely."*

The key words appear in the third sentence of my notes: "stable population." Our Big Creek study area, because of its remoteness, approached a benchmark natural cougar population—a model of stability. Hunters, including Wilbur Wiles, had stirred things up in the past, especially during the bounty years. But three years into our study, we were finding that the cougar population reestablished itself. Territories, or home areas, were occupied and appeared well defined. All the cougar condos, if you will, were full. "No Vacancy" signs in the form of scratch trees and scrapes appeared to be strategically placed and respected. Although males and females (those without kittens) sometimes wandered through common hunting territories, seldom did it occur at the same time. Males, as illustrated by Cannibal Tom, didn't allow females with offspring to hunt in the same territory. Toms would sometimes kill kittens and steal family kills. But resident toms, like Rex and the cannibal, simply steered clear of one another.

*My notes: "It has been more economical, in the evolutionary process, for these individuals to recognize another similar individual's hunting territory and then to NEVER encroach on another's territory. This is one of the most exciting and fascinating aspects yet of this study!"*

# Chapter Twenty-Seven

# "Craziest Son of a Bitch"

On March 6, 1967, following another week of hunting with no new captures or recaptures, I flew home from Taylor Ranch to McCall. Wilbur and the hounds continued to hunt up Cliff Creek, over into Cougar Creek, then Goat Creek—wherever tracks and better prospects might lead them.

In McCall, rumors persisted that at least two, possibly three, of our marked study cougars had been killed by hunters. One of the rumors led me to Cascade, Idaho, for a sit-down with Bill Smith. He was the cougar hunter who wintered in Big Creek at Dewey Moore's ranch. Smith purportedly killed at least two of our collared cougars. He agreed to talk at his home, and I prefaced my questions with acknowledgment that there was nothing illegal about killing cougars in Big Creek, marked or not.

"Got that right," replied Smith.

"I'd just like to know which cats were killed," I explained. "We've been collecting as much information as possible, and it's crucial to know if any cats and which cats have been removed from the population, either naturally or by hunters."

"Both had collars," Smith, a burly man of few words, confirmed.

"Where did you get them?"

"On Acorn Ridge."

I probed some more, and he changed his mind about the collars.

"The female had a collar . . . tom was unmarked."

"What color was the female's collar?"

"Kinda orange. She had no ear tags."

Then Smith changed his mind about the Acorn Ridge kill site, at least for the tom.

"Followed him for three days out of Ramey Creek, up to headquarters, and treed him there." Later in the conversation, Smith said he never treed the tom but that the male fought his dogs in a rocky area before he shot it.

"It was a big old tom. Had made five kills in three days."

"What were the kills?"

"Two elk, one deer."

Things weren't adding up. He had contradicted himself several times.

*My notes: "I am skeptical of whole story—I think it is doubtful he killed any cougar at all. I believe he would have skinned them, or at least scalped them, to make his story better."*

I dismissed his account as unreliable.

Another rumor surfaced that seemed more credible. Gene Nichols, an outfitter from Challis, Idaho, reportedly killed one of our collared cougars up Rattlesnake Creek outside the study area. If true, I hoped to learn which cat and exactly where it had been killed. I worried that, based on my initial encounter with the outfitters and guides, my inquiry might be rebuffed.

But I cinched up my belt, mustered some courage, and drove four hours from McCall to the mile-high cow town in Custer County. Challis was and remains a small community rooted in ranching, farming, mining, and straight talk. I'd retrieved Nichols's home address from the state outfitters and guides directory. So I parked in front of his house, walked to the front door, and knocked.

"He's not home," his wife said pleasantly after I introduced myself. "He's at the tavern. You can wait here until he returns."

"Oh, that's okay," I said, "I'll go downtown."

"Suit yourself."

I drove a few blocks and parked my ratty orange pickup truck across the street from the tavern. I forget the name. But I'd heard stories of good ol' boys fighting their way in and out of such places simply for recreation.

It was dark on the street. Inside, through the windows, I could see a dozen or so silhouettes seated at the bar, all wearing cowboy hats.

"What the hell," I mumbled to myself, "I'm here, so I'm going in."

A bit unnerved, I stepped out of my pickup, seized a quick breath, marched across the street, walked up to the tavern door, peeked inside, and turned tail. Back in the pickup, I decided to wait. Nichols would eventually come out. I had an idea of what he looked like.

Ten minutes later, one of the bar silhouettes walked out the door. Although I didn't know for sure at the moment, Gene Nichols stood on the steps. He peered up the street and down the street, then fixed his eyes across the street at me in my orange pickup before sauntering over. I slowly cranked down the window.

"You Hornocker?" he asked when he got to the truck.

"Ya."

"Well goddamn it, I'm Gene Nichols," he said. "Come on in. The boys wanna meet ya."

"They do?"

"Yeah. Come on over. I'll buy ya a beer."

It turns out Nichols's wife had called the tavern to tell her husband that I was looking for him. Inside the bar, much to my surprise, I was treated like a hero. Most of the patrons wanted to shake my hand, and the beer flowed.

"We don't agree with what you're doing, tryin' to save them cats," one cowboy shouted over the cacophony, "but damn it, you're doin' it. You're doin' the work."

"It's true," Nichols confirmed when things quieted down. "We know what it's like in that country. It's hard work. And you're doing it. And wor-kin' with Wiles. Well, we all know and respect him."

Nursing my beer, I was reminded that hiring Wilbur underscored my brilliance.

"A toast to Wilbur Wiles!" I declared, and the cowboy hats nodded.

Later that night, after Nichols invited me and several others to his house for barbecued steaks and a lot more beer, he handed over the collar and tags from the male lion he'd killed and poked a map with his index finger to show me where the cat had died. Rex or one of the other dominant resident males had probably forced the lion out of our study area.

"You're welcome," Nichols replied after I thanked him for the information. "Still don't like cougars, though."

Sometimes criticism sprang from unexpected places—like remote Campbell's Ferry ranch on the main stem of the Salmon River. Frances Zaunmiller Wisner lived there alone and wrote a popular newspaper column (flown out on the weekly mail plane and published by the Idaho County Free Press in Grangeville, Idaho) about her day-to-day life in the wilderness. Occasionally, Frances helped us relay radiophone messages from our Taylor Ranch headquarters (where transmission and reception could be sketchy) to Boise or McCall. Despite a proclivity for privacy, she attained a public persona through her writings and was dubbed by the media as the "last of the mountain women."

Frances and I, as the study progressed, became radiophone acquaintances.

"Thanks for the help," I'd say.

"Don't mention it," she'd respond. She never had a thing to say about the study. Nothing critical, positive, or otherwise.

Finally, we met. I'd joined three Fish and Game Department officials on a ten-day rafting trip down the River of No Return. Dave Neider, a regional biologist, knew Frances well. So we pulled the raft ashore at her place and walked up to her cabin, and Dave knocked on her door.

"Well, Dave," Frances said in a welcoming tone, "how are you?"

"I'm fine, Frances." Dave introduced the others and then, "I'd like you to meet Maurice Hornocker, the cougar guy."

Frances, graying and bespectacled, wearing an ankle-length skirt, blouse, and light sweater, peered past Dave, looked me up and down, drilled my eyes with hers, and snapped, "You're Hornocker?"

"Yes ma'am," I admitted.

"Well, now, you're the craziest son of a bitch I've ever met . . . standin' here on the steps of my cabin." Frances shuffled around Dave to get a closer look, parked herself in front of me, and said, with hands on hips, "Catchin' them cougars and turnin' 'em loose. I never heard of such a crazy goddamn thing in my life!"

Not the reception I expected. Frances, shaking her head as if in disbelief, then turned and invited us all in for coffee, wasting no time filling our cups to the brim and giving me a tutorial on how cougars were running rampant.

"I used to shoot deer in the garden, right out of my kitchen window here," she lamented while pointing like she was about to mount a Winchester, "until the damn cougars started killin' 'em all."

I listened, nodded politely, and said nothing. What else could I do? Not only was I her guest, but I figured it would benefit me to learn more about the critics' perceptions. Besides, Frances was no dummy, that's for sure. She had opinions, like most people who detested cougars, that were rooted in experiences I'd never had.

The point being, I was beginning to understand where people like Frances Zaunmiller Wisner, Gene Nichols, and Bill Smith were coming from—the heart of mountain lion country where cougars remained listed as vermin. To them, eliminating mountain lions was laudable. So fibbing to a "cat lover" about killing study lions was no big deal. Collecting the collar and ear tags as proof of one fewer marauder was admirable. Scolding the college kid before welcoming him into your home for coffee, well, that probably felt darn satisfying.

The debate, however, was increasingly being waged outside the wilderness as well.

"The Cat: Good Guy or Bad?"

In early June 1967, that headline in the *Lewiston Morning Tribune* appeared below a large black-and-white photograph of a mountain lion about to be shot and killed. The photo caption read, "An Idaho Cougar Pauses on a Ledge of Rock to Snarl at a Hunter and His Dogs."

I read the lengthy feature, written by respected reporter Ladd Hamilton, while back in my McCall office adjacent to the lumberyard. It started with a quote from "government trapper" Billy Reed:

*"I trailed a cougar from daylight to noon, when I turned the dogs on him. He killed three deer without eating any of them. Cougars kill for the joy of it."*

More of Reed's quotes sprang brazenly from the article:

*"A cougar will kill a deer every night if he can get one."*

*"They're a restless animal. Come dark, they start hunting whether they're hungry or not."*

Ferris Weddle, an outdoor writer and avowed conservationist, was interviewed and attempted to counter the cougars-are-monsters viewpoint:

*"When a cougar makes successive kills, it's because the animal is being chased by men and dogs and can't return to eat what he has slain."*

The story summed up the increasingly heated debate with this single analytical sentence:

*"Depending on who's talking, the cougar is gentle or savage, curious or cruel, a scourge or a blessing."*

Hamilton ended the article with this:

*"The Idaho cougar has not been studied closely enough to determine very much about his eating habits, although it is assumed that he lives chiefly on deer."*

I was not contacted for comment, which surprised me. Months before, I'd embarked on what I later dubbed the "Johnny Cougar Seed" phase of the project. As early as March 1967, invitations to speak arrived from surrounding states as well as from within Idaho. I attended informal gatherings and official meetings to give public presentations about the study, sowing the seeds of understanding cougars wherever I could.

For example, I traveled to San Francisco to attend the North American Wildlife Conference and also addressed a Boone and Crockett Club conservation committee meeting. At both events, my talks seemed well received. People asked insightful questions. They applauded. Back in Idaho, I continued to spread the word, like the time I drove to Payette and talked to junior high and grade school students. I enjoyed the younger students because they'd ask, "Why?"

"I don't have an answer for that," I sometimes told them, "but I love your curiosity, and I'll try to find the answer."

I was also interviewed by local radio stations and received a warm reception before a presentation at the Payette Rod and Gun Club. I traveled to the college town of Moscow, Idaho, where I was invited to speak before the Northwest Section of The Wildlife Society. From there,

I drove my pickup almost nine hours to Pocatello to give a talk during the annual meeting of the Idaho Wildlife Federation.

Unlike the rancorous outfitters and guides meeting in McCall more than a year earlier, audiences expressed fascination about mountain lions and the research project. They appeared impressed by the combination of colored slides and facts I presented.

"Cougars are supreme apex predators," I explained. "And we're just beginning to understand them." I did my best to impart that the cats were neither a blessing nor a scourge but rather a critical part of an important ecosystem.

As March gave way to April 1967, the third season of the study was winding down. In a final effort to catch cats that year, Wilbur and I covered 112 miles in eight days. The snow line was nearly gone on the south-facing slopes and steadily receded up the north-facing slopes. Big Creek, long free of ice, continued to rise. We treed no lions during this time. But we scoured several kill sites and confirmed previous findings, including the fact that cougars break the necks of their prey to kill them. Evidence at one kill was particularly graphic.

*My notes: "Kill was calf elk, female, in fairly poor shape. Was killed right in trail, dragged about 50 yards across flat into thorn thicket and buried. Elk's neck broken in two places, mouth full of Oregon grape leaves—killed instantly."*

I ended my own predatory efforts on April 2 by collecting specimens 11, 12, and 13 (all deer). If you recall, fish and game authorities had granted me a special permit to harvest deer and elk not as a selective human trophy hunter but as if I were an opportunist cougar taking the easiest animal available. When comparing the cougar kills to my kills, the results were strikingly similar—mostly older, younger, and infirm deer and elk. Opportunity was the key for both me and the mountain lions. Instead of high-grading healthy animals, we were culling the herds— weeding the garden, if you will.

After conducting a health analysis on the collected animals, the carcasses were fed to Tommy and Flopsy as part of our nutritional study.

"Amazing," I told Wilbur, "how they eat everything."

Meanwhile, as the weather turned spring-like in the Idaho Primitive Area, political whirlwinds intensified. Rumors persisted that hunters had killed some, perhaps many, of our marked cougars. Believing this might be true and that more collared mountain lions could be shot, I considered pushing immediately for a hunting closure to protect our next study season. But I feared such a move would be akin to rolling a grenade into the state's legislative halls that might trigger a premature and unnecessary political war.

I needed time to think. I needed to go fishing and consult with two men already steeped in fighting controversial conservation battles.

John and Frank Craighead, the celebrated and sometimes cussed at Yellowstone National Park grizzly bear researchers, accepted my invitation and flew with their spin casting rods into Taylor Ranch on April 24, 1967. Wilbur and I met them the following day. Big Creek's steelhead trout were more than cooperative.

The author (center) flanked by brothers John (on the left) and Frank Craighead after some successful fishing.

*My notes: "Wilbur caught and released a 31-inch female at Drift Hole. I caught and released 34-inch female at Goat Creek Hole."*

The next two days were even better.

*My notes: "Fished with Craigheads. Wilbur caught 5 big steelhead in lower Big Creek. Kept two. Frank got 33-inch female at Goat Creek Hole. John small female in hole below Dunce Creek. I lost 2 small ones at Bluff Hole and hole below Bluff Hole."*

With the fish eagerly biting, I decided to keep casting before asking for advice. John and Frank were already embroiled in their own controversy. In his award-winning book *Track of the Grizzly*, Frank would later write, "The year 1967, as I have indicated, was a watershed both for the grizzly bear in Yellowstone and for our ongoing field study." The furor was centered on Yellowstone's garbage dumps, where scores of bears foraged for food. As I explained earlier in this book, I worked under John's tutelage during four summers documenting grizzly bear behavior at the dumps and wrote my master's thesis on the findings.

"Events in that year," Frank wrote in his book published in 1979, "were to significantly affect both the bears' future and that of our research—unfortunately, in both cases for the worse." The National Park Service wanted the bears to remain in the backcountry away from tourists (who routinely visited the dumps to view the bears). So authorities decided to close the refuge sites abruptly. Fearing that such a cold-turkey approach would cause the habituated bears to raid nearby populated campgrounds for food, the Craigheads pitched a phased closure of the dump sites. Both sides wanted the same outcome but disagreed on methods.

With all that as a backdrop, I told John during a break in our fishing about threats to the cougar study and my contemplated push for a hunting closure.

"Stick to your principles," he said, his words an echo from when he was my major professor at the University of Montana.

"Like I told you when you were a student, if you stand on principle, you'll make enemies," he said.

"I'm afraid I've already got enemies."

"Then keep standing," he asserted.

Although the Craigheads lost the grizzly debate in Yellowstone, their theory was proven correct several years later. By suddenly closing the garbage dump sites where the bears had fed for decades, instead of returning to the backwoods for food, the bruins searched campgrounds and visitor areas. Run-ins escalated, and hungry grizzlies were shot.

John would eventually win the Aldo Leopold Memorial Award, the highest honor bestowed by The Wildlife Society for distinguished service to wildlife conservation. But on that long-ago spring day, rather than ruminate over our problems, we opted to ply Big Creek's currents. When the Craighead brothers later flew home from Taylor Ranch, in between rain squalls, each had his limit of steelhead. Wilbur and I kept fishing and closing our camps for the next five days. I caught and released more than a dozen steelhead. One in particular continues to leap into my mind today.

*My notes: "Caught beautiful 10 lb. male at drift hole. Held him up to admire him and he jerked free and escaped. This fish put on the most spectacular aerial display of any I've caught. Leaped three times immediately after being hooked, later leaped twice more. Beautiful blood-red male, a magnificent fish."*

That night, Jess Taylor and I smoked and ate two. The next day, I cleaned the headquarters cabin, stowed gear and supplies, and flew home to McCall.

*My notes: "End of field season!"*

# Chapter Twenty-Eight

# The Blinding Glimpse

I write today atop a desk cluttered with manila envelopes stuffed full of field notes and numerous other cougar documents yellowed and frayed after being in storage for more than a half-century. One missive amid the heap is titled "An Analysis of Mountain Lion Predation upon Mule Deer and Elk in the Idaho Primitive Area." It's my UBC PhD dissertation.

I began writing the 115-page thesis in the late spring of 1967 in my rented second-floor McCall office located above a defunct warehouse. Determined to assemble a cogent treatise, I launched what quickly became a stutter-start effort. I was crippled by confusion.

Territoriality was key to the thesis. Our findings showed that all resident Big Creek mountain lions established territories. These territories, I was about to postulate, were in part the product of what I called "mutual avoidance." The term was new, and I assumed it would be challenged. My hypothesis was that after a cat establishes a territory, it avoids other cats that have territories. As long as a sustaining food source was available, these cougars mutually agreed to live alone and engage in little or no fighting. Their solitary behavior, I suggested, creates a stable population and limits overall cougar numbers.

The theory seemed sound, except for one critical first-season finding that circumvented explanation. We'd captured ten lions that year in a relatively small area. Seven of the ten were males. How could that be? Were multiple male lions actually *sharing* the same territory? Could conventional assumptions be true? Were cougars tolerant of one another and prolific enough to warrant population control by humans?

I could almost hear my critics chanting outside the office window, "Bring back the bounty!"

Then one night, while reading the findings of a marten study, of all things, I was struck by a glimpse of the obvious. Like cougars, marten (weasel-like carnivores of the Mustelidae family) are solitary animals that meet only to breed. They establish territories and respect the territories of others. Then a word exploded from the literature: "Transients!" Transient martens routinely frequent the established territories of resident martens, but they don't stick around.

"Holy man!" I yelped. "That's it!" Like transient martens, most of the young male cougars captured that first year were either passing through or about to leave the region in search of their own territories. That's why we never recaptured them. They left the study area. How blinding. How obvious. How exhilarating!

From that point forward, the thesis steadily came together. Having only hunt-and-peck typing skills, I composed longhand day after day, night after night. I worked with a desk lamp and overhead fluorescent lights illuminating the maze of strewn-about documents. Now and then, I crumpled pages into baseball-size wads and shot them like basketballs into wastebaskets. When I finished the first cursive draft, I hired a woman who lived on a farm south of McCall to do the typing. She pounded out the pages, I'd edit, and she'd retype. Back and forth we went into the late summer of 1967 until I finally thumped the final sentence with a period.

It read, *"Lion predation appears incapable of limiting elk and deer populations in the Idaho Primitive Area, but the effect and influence of such predation is of great significance in maintaining, or in seeking to maintain, ecological stability in a wilderness environment."*

In other words, deer and elk were good for mountain lions, and mountain lions were good for deer and elk. I could hear the bring-back-the-bounty boys shouting, "This guy's nuts!"

The numbers, gleaned from the study, spoke for themselves:

- Thirty-nine mountain lions were captured over three years.
- Twenty-six of the thirty-nine were recaptured sixty-two times, adding up to a total of 101 captures.
- The population averaged 30 percent adult males and 70 percent adult females.
- Over three years, the population included an average of three resident territorial males, six resident territorial females, six to eight annual kittens, six to eight subadults, and three or four transients.
- The deer and elk populations increased over the three years.

The findings were the product of our walking and snowshoeing more than 3,720 miles during 430 days of tracking. The thesis represented the rigors of demanding field research, and I was proud of the document.

Then came the pinnacle of academic scrutiny—the oral defense of the treatise, in this case a formal European type of exam at UBC before a five-member faculty committee in a big lengthy hall with a lectern up front and seating for at least fifty fellow graduate students, some of them ready to take aim at me.

Armed with a slide projector, its carousel loaded with pictures taken during the fieldwork, I stood in a sport coat, tie, and pressed pants before the committee and students. The stars of the presentation were Rex, Hazel, Bessie, Cannibal Tom, and all the other study cats. Wilbur, of course, played a strong supporting role. Portraits of him working where mountain lions roam seemed to impress the group.

I spoke from notes and sometimes read directly from the thesis. Committee members had already read the dissertation, grilled me in private, and for the most part left questioning to the students. A mix of zoology, wildlife, ecology, and life sciences graduate students filled the chairs. A few tried to undo my work.

"Why didn't you use more statistics?" one asked.

"I didn't need to."

Actually, I'd used several statistical methods, two of them for computing total population: one called the Peterson Index; the second called the Schnabel Method. The outcomes supported my observational counts. But the questions kept coming.

"Well then, if you don't rely more heavily on statistics, how are you going to define your population?"

"We marked them all."

"How can you be confident about marking the entire population?" the student persisted. I rotated the slide carousel to a photograph taken from the mouth of Big Creek looking west into the drainage's snow-covered crags.

"You should see the country," I said, letting the image sink in. "It's entangled with steep-wall canyons." Cougars don't like deep snow, I explained, so they're confined to the lower elevations, where there's less snow.

"And there's only one low-elevation entry into the fifty-mile-long Big Creek drainage. You're looking at it." Murmurs filled the room as students fixed their eyes on the projector screen. Before them was a dramatic image of Big Creek emptying into the Middle Fork of the Salmon River amid wedged canyons.

"Any new mountain lion," I said, "that travels into that drainage in winter has to come from the Middle Fork country. They can't come over the top. There's too much snow. They can't come from any direction but the east."

More murmurs.

"It's like a house with only one entry. And we patrolled the entry." The walkway leading to the entry, I explained, was covered with fresh snow where tracks would be visible. "We could tell if cats had come in or gone out."

I moved on, sharing more interpretations of the data, including the blinding glimpse of the obvious. "Transients," I said, letting the word hang a bit. "The number of lions classified as transients indicates that many animals were only passing through the area. The fact that these lions did not establish residence, because all the condos were full, supports the view that the Big Creek population remained stable."

I was relieved to see nodding heads.

"Data suggest that twenty-three resident lions were present on the area during the study's first year," I said. "After the second year, I estimated the population at twenty-two lions and then twenty-three the third year. Again, these data suggest a stable population."

More nods of agreement.

"Mortality factors are less clear. The rugged terrain, plus the fact that carcass remains are quickly consumed or carried off by scavengers, makes mortality data difficult." I talked about Cannibal Tom but dismissed cannibalism as a major check on cougar numbers.

"That said, a mountain lion's first six months of life are probably quite critical, particularly when the lioness takes her kittens from the cave where they're born and begins to wean them."

"Why's that?" came a question.

"The female must leave them unattended while she hunts," I explained. "We have evidence the young may be left alone for as long as two days while the mother hunts. Under these circumstances, the kittens are quite susceptible to predation and accidents, not to mention starvation in extreme circumstances."

Key to understanding mountain lion population dynamics, I suggested, is the importance of dominant males that occupy specific territories and practice mutual avoidance. I let the term linger again, then continued. "We captured No. 3, Rex, nine times. We captured Cannibal Tom, No. 18, six times. The boundaries of Rex and Tom's territories may abut," I said. "But I am certain they don't overlap."

By this time, there was more listening and less questioning.

"Take one of these dominant males out of the population, through hunting by humans or some kind of natural cause," I said, "and the dynamic changes. A level of chaos may even develop. But eventually, an adjacent dominant male may expand or move his territory to cover the vacancy. A young male progeny of the local population may take over, or perhaps a transient could move in. Each scenario can lend renewed stability to the population."

Some of the graduate students leaned toward each other whispering, which, I hoped, conveyed growing acceptance.

"We found that cougar predation helps the prey population," I said, explaining how the cats cull unhealthy deer and elk, dampen drastic prey numbers fluctuations, and move herds throughout winter ranges, thereby limiting overutilization of critical browsing vegetation.

"The mere presence of a lion or family of lions in a local area or drainage doesn't appear to alarm deer and elk," I said. "When a kill is made, however, the reaction is striking. Prey immediately leave the area, crossing to the far side of a drainage and sometimes leaving the drainage."

Again, I pointed out, all this interaction stems from a single lion (or perhaps a lioness with mature kittens) hunting—not from great numbers of cougars preying at the same time in the same area on large herds. "We calculated that a total of sixteen lions were actually hunting during the winter in the Big Creek drainage. That computes to one adult lion per 12.5 square miles, or one lion for every 234 prey animals."

All of which brought the thesis defense to what many people, especially hunters in Idaho, wanted to know: How many deer and elk were mountain lions killing?

"I believe that a mature lion in the Big Creek area kills one deer every ten to fourteen days during the winter," I said without equivocation. "This interval is longer when elk are killed, and I'm certain the intervals are considerably longer in summer, when many smaller prey species are available."

My declaration flew in the face of "government trapper" Billy Reed, who had recently claimed in the *Lewiston Morning Tribune* story that a cougar kills a deer every day. In addition, my thesis covered enough kill and consumption detail for me to say, "The computed number of elk required to sustain an adult lion per year is five to seven. For deer, the number is fourteen to twenty." Based on statistical analysis, I continued, the sixteen Big Creek mountain lions annually killed ninety to 112 elk, or 224 to 320 mule deer.

"Bottom line," I said while reading directly from my thesis, "elk and deer populations were limited by winter food supply, not lions. Predation by cougars was inconsequential in determining ultimate numbers of elk and deer. Lion predation, however, is a powerful force acting to dampen and protract severe prey oscillations and to distribute deer and elk on restricted, critical range."

I turned off the slide projector light, let the fan cool the bulb, straightened my tie, and called for the hall lights to be brought back up. I sensed that the committee members, based on their questions and laudatory comments, were on my side. The session was recessed, the students were dismissed, I was asked to leave the room, and the committee deliberated for about fifteen minutes before calling me back in to have Dr. Cowan say, "Congratulations. You passed."

On December 6, 1967, the dissertation was filed in the library at UBC. Within the next two months, I would receive word that hunters with hounds had shot and killed three of our marked mountain lions in Big Creek. Although I never found proof of their deaths—no carcasses, no tags or collars, no bragging admissions from hunters—Hazel and her two kittens were never seen again, nor were their tracks that Wilbur and I learned to recognize so well.

PART IV

# THE FOURTH SEASON AND BEYOND

# CHAPTER TWENTY-NINE

# Survival of the Family

By the time the fourth study season started, I was thirty-eight years old and needed a real job. Wrapping up the third year of the study, I was receiving what amounted to an annual salary of $4,000, which came from project funds. Wilbur made $3,000 for his six to eight months of work, and the rest of the study funding went to expenses.

Shirley, the girls, and I were on a strict budget. Living on Payette Lake in picturesque McCall, we were wealthy in many ways. But we had no savings, no nest egg, and no health insurance. If I'd had my druthers, I would have pursued a solo biologist career, earning my way toward financial security through visionary research and the work ethic embedded in me as a Depression-era Iowa farm kid. But my dad's words underscored reality: "You've got a family to support."

Enter more timing and luck.

Paul Dalke, the leader of the University of Idaho Cooperative Wildlife Research Unit who'd mentioned Idaho's proposed mountain lion study on the train four years earlier, had announced his retirement. I likened his departure to an old tom leaving his territory. Competition would be stiff. Long before the cougar study started, I was aware of the unit position. I'd worked hard. I'd made the right contacts. I moved to Idaho, became part of the culture, and learned the political terrain.

But first, some perspective.

Thanks to J. N. "Ding" Darling, a renowned political cartoonist and pioneering conservationist born and raised in Iowa, there were seventeen cooperative wildlife research units across the country in 1967. Darling, who'd won two Pulitzer Prizes for his nationally syndicated witticisms and cutting-edge cartoons, also had an intense appreciation of nature. He recognized a need for scientifically trained specialists to oversee the research, management, and administration of wildlife resources.

So Darling channeled his fame and some of his own money into the creation of a prototype: the first cooperative wildlife research unit at Iowa State College (now Iowa State University) in the town of Ames. Later, after being named head of the U.S. Bureau of Biological Survey (which would eventually become the U.S. Fish and Wildlife Service), he nationalized his concept, replicating his prototype by 1936 into nine wildlife research units at universities from Maine to Oregon. Today, there are forty-one units at thirty-eight institutions of higher learning.

Simple formula: combine state fish and game departments, land grant universities, the Wildlife Management Institute, and the Department of the Interior's Fish and Wildlife Service into "cooperative units."

Simple mission: instill more science and less politics into wildlife research and management, with a high priority placed on training professional biologists.

Before Darling died in 1962, Congress passed the Cooperative Units Act, ensuring funding and stability for a scientific approach to managing fish and wildlife in the United States. In essence, unit leaders had the independence to create projects from ground zero, pursue their interests, train graduate students, and contribute important research findings—not quite solo work but my stellar second choice. Dalke, who was hired as Idaho's first cooperative unit leader in 1947, was departing twenty years later as a distinguished leader.

I solicited support from Dick Woodworth, director of the Idaho Fish and Game Department, and Ernie Wohletz, dean of the College of Forestry, Wildlife, and Range Sciences at the University of Idaho—both members of the cooperative unit coordinating committee. Another member of the committee was Clinton R. "Pink" Gutermuth, vice president of the Wildlife Management Institute, and I felt confident he would support me for the position.

"You need to update your application . . . right away," the voice on the phone urged. "It has to be here in two days to beat the deadline." I was at home in McCall, and the voice belonged to Lee E. Yeager, former leader of the Colorado cooperative unit and now overall leader of units nationwide. Of course, my pulse quickened.

"But I sent it in long ago," I responded.

"You need to include that you just received your PhD and some other necessary background information. It's got nothing to do with me but everything to do with civil service rules." I knew Lee. And while he didn't come right out and say that I had the job, I sensed an inside track. But he made it abundantly clear that I had to jump through some bureaucratic hoops. After hanging up the phone, I called my typist on the farm south of town and offered her triple pay to help meet the tight deadline.

"There's no need for you to do that," she said of the money.

"Please, don't argue. Just take it. I'll write up the additional information and be at your place soon."

"I'll have the coffee ready."

We worked through the night. Just before daybreak, I drove two hours to Boise, dropped off the revised application at the post office, and was assured it would be on a plane in time to meet the deadline.

Less than twenty-four hours later, Lee called. "I got it," he said. "It arrived just in time."

I was hired! My first official day on the job was January 1, 1968.

## CHAPTER THIRTY

# It's Hard to Be Joyous

MOST OF US HOPE OUR LIFE'S WORK ENDS UP ON THE RIGHT SIDE OF history. With that and my ninety-one years of age in mind, I hesitated to write this chapter. Lots of the clichés rattled around in my head: Let sleeping dogs lie. Water under the bridge. Don't cry over spilled milk. Sour grapes. Let bygones be bygones.

But the painfulness of the controversy surrounding mountain lions—and our study in particular—couldn't be denied more than half a century ago and shouldn't be forgotten. As Winston Churchill famously said, "Those who fail to learn from history are doomed to repeat it."

By the time I settled into my new office at the University of Idaho's Cooperative Wildlife Research Unit in January 1968, outfitter George Dovel and cougar hunter Rob Donley were preparing to enter our Big Creek study area on a mission. The two men, along with ardent critics, were systematically mounting a challenge to our research.

Dovel published a new newspaper called *The Outdoorsman*. In an early issue, he wrote,

*"We planned the hunt for the winter of 1967–68. Most of our time would be spent in the Idaho Primitive Area, including the area utilized by Dr. Hornocker for his study. Donley and I began the hunt in January of 1968. He is a veteran woodsman with twenty-six seasons of chasing big cats behind him."*

I knew these men as hunters, self-proclaimed Idaho Department of Fish and Game watchdogs, and more recently as critics of my work. Ironically, Donley was one of several houndsmen I'd initially queried by letter to see if he'd like to join the project. I don't remember if he responded. Then again, it doesn't matter because I picked Wilbur Wiles.

Dovel had been an outfitter for Jess Taylor. We met at Taylor Ranch on the first day I flew into the study area in December 1964, just a few days before we captured our first cougars. At the time, he voiced nothing but support. Three years later, he and Donley had teamed up to disparage me and the study.

Dovel's words from the same issue of *The Outdoorsman*:

*"During our travels, we killed four lions that Hornocker had tagged. One of these was an old male, traveling with another large untagged male. We met the pair face-to-face in a remote valley nearly seventy miles from the spot where the old tom was first tagged."*

Dovel and Donley also made news in March 1968 in the *Idaho Daily Statesman* (now the *Idaho Statesman*). Under the headline of "Archer Nails Five Cougar in Primitive Area," the two were pictured with five cougar pelts draped over a vehicle. I dismissed some of the claims in the article as bluster but realized that the study could be finished if even half the reports of tagged cougars being killed were true. My contemplation to call for a closure of mountain lion hunting in Big Creek became a conviction.

At the same time, the Idaho Department of Fish and Game was under intense scrutiny. Elk and deer numbers were purportedly declining statewide. Most of the debate (in the absence of today's social media and 24/7 news cycles) was being waged in the letters-to-the-editor columns of the *Statesman*, Idaho's biggest newspaper. State congressional hearings were held. Vitriol spewed and spawned headlines like "F&G Department Gets Criticism in 5½-Hour Hearing."

The Idaho legislature, swept up in the debate, launched an investigation, which triggered more headlines: "Report Expected on Senate Probe into Charges of Big Game Mismanagement by Idaho Agency."

Governor Don W. Samuelson, elected in 1966, tried to appease both sides: "Samuelson Concerned over Game," according to another headline.

Amid the swell of controversy, the mysterious cougar became a convenient culprit. And our study became embroiled in the tumult, especially after word of my new job hit the news.

"Authority on Cougar Takes Post," a *Statesman* headline read. "Hornocker Directs Wildlife Research at Moscow Campus."

How the hell, I could hear the critics grousing, did this college cat lover finagle his way into such a powerful post? The *Statesman* unwittingly fueled the anger by declaring, "Since Dr. Maurice G. Hornocker's study of cougar was unique, he automatically ranks as the world's foremost authority on Mountain lions."

After reading that sentence, I folded the newspaper into my lap, looked away, and thought of Wilbur's adage. "The more ya learn, the more ya learn you don't know." Nobody was an authority. I knew that better than anyone. We needed at least two more years to gather data and confirm our findings.

Since the Idaho Department of Fish and Game had called for the cougar study and provided the biggest share of initial funding, the probe was technically the agency's baby. But I preferred to label the work "independent"—not to claim it as mine but to insulate findings from critics who'd asserted we were doing the devil's work, simply fortifying whatever message the Fish and Game Department wanted delivered.

Donley, the cougar hunter, intensified his public attacks. In a *Statesman* letter to the editor, he heaped praise on Pat Reed, the government hunter who claimed in the *Lewiston Tribune* story that cougars killed out of "lust." Donley went on to write,

*"The Idaho housewives are now authorities on cougar. . . . I don't know whether the people of Boise are aware of it, but they have a man by the name of Pat Reed who has been a government hunter for many years. He has forgotten more about the knowledge of cougar than the Idaho Fish and Game Department, Dr. Hornocker, the Idaho legislators will ever know."*

Outfitter Steve Jordan upped the ante in another *Statesman* letter to the editor.

*"The cougar has been replaced by man, who now harvests the thousands of animals the cougar was intended to kill. Game herds can't hold up under the pressure of both the hunter and the predator."*

Jordan went on to say that there wasn't room for both human hunters and mountain lions, so the cats had to go. He confronted cougar advocates about "what their praised pussy cat is really like."

*"They should observe the deer and elk and wildlife killed by cougars and perhaps observe a bunch of sheep tromping on their ripped out entrails, trying to escape the savage attack of the cougar."*

George Dovel, encouraged by increasing circulation numbers, used his newspaper to castigate the study from early 1968 through its completion. In one diatribe, he wrote,

*"I have discussed Hornocker's cougar study in previous issues, along with his erroneous conclusions that deer in his study area were increasing when at least 90 percent of them have actually disappeared under the combined killing by late-season hunters and protected predators. . . . Why is this man recognized internationally as an expert on predators, and given authority to make recommendations which will protect predators and destroy our wildlife and livestock production?"*

At one point, I threatened to sue for libel, but cooler minds encouraged me to stay the course and focus on the study. Eventually, the controversy spread all the way to Washington, D.C., where The Wildlife Society, one of the study's most stalwart supporters, was headquartered. Its executive director, Fred G. Evenden, wrote to John R. (Dick) Woodworth, director of the Idaho Fish and Game Department,

*"Dear Dick,*

*I have just read briefly copies of an apparently new newspaper, The Outdoorsman, which originates in Boise, Idaho. This particular publication seems to be taking on all aspects of professional wildlife management with a vengeance!*

*I note severe criticism of Idaho Department biologists and of the coop unit at the University of Idaho.*

*Are things really this rough? I would appreciate having some background on this for it looks as if we may have some professional public relations problems in*

*Idaho and elsewhere in the west since I note subscribers are taking up subscriptions from many western states.*

*Any background material which you or those who get copies of this letter can give me, will certainly be appreciated.*

*Best wishes,*
*Fred G. Evenden"*

Woodworth wrote back,

*"Dear Fred:*

*We, too, have been reading the 'Outdoorsman' with a great deal of interest—in fact, we are one of the subscribers.*

*The publisher, Mr. George Dovel of Boise, has worked as an outfitter and guide, flying service operator, freelance photographer and writer in Idaho for some time. He began publishing his paper last spring.*

*He has a real 'thing' about the Fish and Game Department which, as near as we can deduce, stems from the fact that his views on game management do not agree with ours and his reaction seems to be an all out attempt to discredit biologists and their studies. . . . To say we do not believe his articles have been ethical or fair would be a massive understatement.*

*Dr. Hornocker, leader of the Idaho Cooperative Wildlife Research Unit, had frequent contact with Mr. Dovel during his cougar research and could give you a firsthand account of how Mr. Dovel operates, if you are interested in more details . . . we feel, based on considerable past experience in attempting to talk with Mr. Dovel, any public rebuttal would only throw more wood on the fire and play into his hands by giving his paper formal recognition.*

*Sincerely*
*John R. Woodworth"*

Ultimately, Dovel wrote a letter to Wilbur that arrived via airplane at Taylor Ranch.

*"Dear Wilbur,*

*I've been hoping to run into you on the trail for a long time but I haven't, so I'll write this letter and try to say what I feel. . . . I imagine that you and Maurice are good friends by now. If so, I respect your friendship for him. A good friend is worth an awful lot. However, I have to write this like I know it. If it offends your friendship, I'm sorry."*

Dovel went on to disparage not only me, but also U.S. Forest Service and Idaho Fish and Game Department officials.

*"The ultimate result of their efforts will be the existence of a few 'managed' so-called wild preserves for observation and study. We will have no need of guns to hunt as the remaining game will have to be protected."*

Then he leveled the crosshairs on me specifically.

*"Maurice Hornocker has studied under these men. With the help of a course in the 'psychology of the hunter,' unlimited dollars for propaganda purposes, and a disregard for all truth that does not agree with the 'current concept,' he is joining them in driving nails in the coffin of our American heritage."*

Wilbur sent me Dovel's missive, accompanied by a letter of his own.

*"Dear Maurice,*

*Received your letter yesterday, and one Honest George wrote the same day. Am sending it on to you. He sent me the newspaper also. Think he is about due for the nut house.*

*If I run in to him, you will be reading the same things about me. I am going to tell him what a low class rat I think he is."*

I'm not sure if Wilbur met up with "Honest George." As for me, I stewed for years but ultimately let Wilbur's letter be the last word. Today, I jest to friends that "sometimes it's hard to be joyous," an idiom that stems from those controversial cougar days.

The right side of history? Let the critics' written words and my life's work speak for themselves.

CHAPTER THIRTY-ONE

# Ivory Tower Edict

SHIRLEY AND OUR THREE YOUNG DAUGHTERS STAYED IN MCCALL through winter of 1968–1969 while I rented an apartment in Moscow and visited them on weekends. Paul Dalke's old cooperative unit office became my new headquarters. The billet, with a big desk, filing cabinets, multiline telephone, secretarial help, overhead lights, and flushing toilets down the hallway, was located in Morrill Hall, a four-story rectangular brick and stone building on the campus of the University of Idaho—a world apart from our rustic, wood-heated, lantern-lighted Taylor Ranch headquarters in the Idaho Primitive Area.

In my new Ivory Tower office, I became ensconced in administrative work, wrote research proposals, and initiated several new graduate student projects. Meanwhile, I eagerly awaited reports from Wilbur, who had started the fourth season of fieldwork at Big Creek. His first letter, composed on December 4, 1967, at our Cave Creek camp, arrived at my office more than a month later due to backcountry logistical challenges. He reported a tardy start to hunting but beamed about getting a new hound named Rip.

*"Dear Maurice,*

*Hope the new job is going well. Will go to Taylor R. tomorrow. Will leave dogs here to rest as no tracking snow on hills below. Think Rip is going to be a rip snorter. He won't run with Red and Ranger, but does his own trailing. A little slow at it yet. But after the second cat he knows they go up a tree and he stays to give them hell.*

*Don't have any envelopes here. Don't know if I have any at Taylor Ranch. But will try and send this out some way if I don't miss the mail plane.*

*As ever,*
*Wilbur"*

I leaned back in my leather office chair and envisioned Wilbur and his hounds pursuing cats, the new pup learning the ways of mountain lions, the Big Creek cougars holding on to so many of their secrets.

With the kids finishing the school year in McCall, Wilbur keeping the study on track in Big Creek, and my new job in Moscow, I felt emotionally and professionally triangulated—pulled between family, fieldwork, and administrative duties. So I decided to prioritize and then delegate. That's what administrators do, right? Shirley would continue to take care of family matters. Wilbur would handle the cougars. With those two fronts covered, I tackled the third: to officially bring the mountain lion study under the cooperative unit's oversight.

I planned to find a graduate student to help with the final phase of the study: radiotelemetry. I knew through the grizzly bear telemetry work I'd done with the Craighead brothers in Yellowstone that transmitter collars, with some miniaturization, could be deployed on cougars in Big Creek. Rather than chasing mountain lions with hounds, I looked forward to tracking them with technology.

On February 1, 1968, the same day the *Statesman* reported my being hired to lead the cooperative unit at the university, Wilbur was searching for his missing new pup. His notes punctuate how hopeless he felt.

*"Looks like Rip got killed in bluffs."*

A day later:

*"Went from cave Cr. Camp by trail to Coxey Creek camp. Thought there was a small chance Rip may have gotten over here."*

Two days later:

*"Went from Cave Cr. Camp to Rush Pt. Camp on chance Rip might have gotten over there."*

After that, there are no more mentions of Rip in Wilbur's notes. He later told me that the inexperienced young hound, while chasing a lion, might have charged over a cliff in the heat of the moment.

A week after receiving Wilbur's letter, I flew into Taylor Ranch with Bob Fogg in his Super Cub. Seated behind Bob in the high-performance backcountry airplane, I looked down and noticed a striking lack of snow on the south-facing slopes in Rush Creek and upstream in Big Creek to the mouth of Cabin Creek, which would not provide good cat-tracking conditions. Regardless, after more than a month in my new office job, I was eager to get back in the field. This, I thought as we landed, is where my professional heart sings.

I was also excited to reunite with Tommy and Flopsy.

*My notes: "Cats in fine shape at Taylor Ranch. Really getting big, especially Flops. Arlow Lewis has been taking good care of them. Cats real glad to see me."*

"I like the cats. They're fun to watch and pretty friendly," Arlow told me during the reunion. "And yeah, they're really growing."

Remember, we'd hired Arlow Lewis (no relation to "Cougar" Dave Lewis) to care for the two captive mountain lions as part of his caretaker duties at the ranch. Like Wilbur, I think Arlow appreciated getting paid for what he'd do gratis. He took a keen interest in the study and asked a lot of questions, and I felt confident Tommy and Flopsy were in good hands.

"So, how long are you staying in?" Arlow asked.

"I wish I could stay through the season," I replied. "But can't. Be out of here in a few days. I'll head up the creek tomorrow morning to find Wilbur."

I met up with Wilbur at our Cave Creek camp, and we hunted the area for the next three days without treeing any lions. On Valentine's Day, however, we found where a female and two new kittens had left tracks all over the lower most area of a small drainage.

237

*My notes: "Wilbur had treed No. 4 (Hazel) on Feb. 5. May have had kill in area or Hazel may be weaning kittens. Two years ago she did same— dumped kittens in Cave Cr. (two-yr.-old kittens). No other cougar sign."*

At this point, we assumed Hazel and her kittens were still alive. Wilbur, who'd become protective, called the lioness and her kittens "the bunch" and had taken care not to immobilize them when unnecessary. Here's an example:

*Wilbur's notes: "Feb. 5, 68. Treed cat south of Cave. It was Hazel. In top of a big fir. Didn't take her out. As knew if she fell she would be a dead cat. Don't know if she has left kittens or looking for a tom."*

Eleven days after he wrote that, Wilbur's caring efforts appeared all for naught.

∞

We returned to Taylor Ranch after finding some fairly fresh tracks at a spring in Lobear Flat. It appeared to be a female and two kittens but not Hazel and her clan. We turned the dogs loose. They failed to follow and came back. Then we located a kill nearby. It was a young buck deer.

"I think this is female Number Sixteen," Wilbur said while examining its tracks, "the mother of the two fifty-two-pound Rush Creek kittens."

"You mean, the female whose kittens were killed by Cannibal Tom two years ago?" I asked.

"Good chance, I think."

After a few days at Taylor Ranch, after we sedated, weighed, and measured Tommy and Flopsy, three shadowy human figures appeared from the distance.

*My notes: "Feb. 16, 1968. George Dovel, Rob Donley and someone else came down trail from Cabin Creek. Did not come over to Taylors and I didn't know who it was until Bill Dorris (a pilot) told me. Bill said they killed a cat up Cabin Creek the day before."*

Immediately, I thought of Hazel.

A day later, after flying back to Moscow from Taylor Ranch, I called George Dovel's phone number and got his wife. I told her that I saw George with Donley, at Taylor Ranch, and I asked who the third person was.

*My notes: "She was real suspicious and wouldn't tell me who it was."*

I assured her nothing was wrong with killing the cats, but I needed to know which ones were killed.

*My notes: "She assured me George would cooperate. Ha!"*

The same day I flew to Moscow, Wilbur left Taylor Ranch and hunted toward Rush Point camp and once again came on what he assumed were tracks of No. 16 and her two kittens. Knowing now that Dovel, Donley, and one other hunter were scouting the area, Wilbur held his hounds back and made a quick decision to abandon the hunt.

*Wilbur's notes: "Don't want to run this bunch unless I have a good chance of getting them, as they may line out back to Big Creek ahead of Honest George."*

A week later, Wilbur wrote me a letter that again wouldn't arrive in Moscow until nearly a month later. He lamented about poor landing strip conditions at Taylor Ranch and that planes could drop mail to him midair but not land to pick up his letters. Then Wilbur updated me about more suspicious—even ominous—activities.

*"Been planes in to Lanham's the last three days so likely more hunters. Saw a dog track as I come down today. Not over a day or two old at Cabin Cr. Saw men tracks all over Cave Cr. & up East Fork of Cave Creek. So good chance by now Donley has got Hazel and her kittens."*

I could not fathom men killing this mother and her kittens in the name of vengeance, "hunting rights," or whatever motivated them. One thing for certain: It was crucial that the cougar hunting season be closed in Big Creek. Sitting at my desk in Moscow, I put Wilbur's letter aside, picked up the phone, and began making calls to build my case. It would be another ten months before members of the Idaho Fish and Game Commission would heed my warnings. On December 16, 1968, the panel unanimously passed a motion that reads as follows:

*"Since a number of cougars in the Big Creek drainage have been marked for the purpose of evaluating the effect of predation on big game populations, and in as much as protection of these animals is necessary to successfully complete this investigation, it is here by ordered that those portions of Idaho and Valley Counties lying within the drainage of Big Creek (tributary of the*

*Middle Fork of the Salmon River) shall be closed to the hunting, trapping, or killing of cougar effective midnight December 26, 1968, until further notice of the Commission."*

Unfortunately, this significant gain would amount to a short-lived victory.

# CHAPTER THIRTY-TWO

# Tragic Mistake

AFTER HAZEL, HER KITTENS, AND PERHAPS FOUR OTHER MARKED mountain lions were shot in our study area, the fourth season progressed almost in spite of the killings. I settled into the cooperative unit job and pretty much completed plans to bring a graduate student aboard for the proposed radiotelemetry phase of the project that would start within two years. I also made contact with Albert Johnson of Moscow, a ham radio operator and expert in electronics who agreed to work on designing transmitter collars that would fit cougars.

"Shouldn't be a problem," Albert assured me. "Simple doorbell technology."

Shirley and our daughters remained in McCall, taking advantage of the skiing and wintertime activities while I shopped around for a home to rent in Moscow. I managed to fly into Big Creek several more times. After Rip's disappearance, Wilbur got another hound to join Ranger and Red.

"Tiger," he said of the new pup's name. "When I try to tend his sore feet, he fights like a tiger."

"A tiger chasing cougars," I mused. "Sounds exciting."

As the fourth season progressed, Tiger, Ranger, and Red—along with Rex, the big tom—played leading roles. We recaptured and treed Rex several more times into the spring of 1968, always within the defined boundaries of his territory. On Christmas Eve, four years after he and I locked eyeballs high in the tree, Rex reminded us of his apex status by making a noteworthy kill. He'd been traveling within the Cave Creek drainage at the same time a female was also on the prowl. Tracks indicated the two were hunting alone, not coming together to breed, meaning that both, especially Rex, were practicing mutual avoidance.

Fresh tom tracks led to a cow elk kill. Nearby the dogs then treed Rex. Evidence in the snow indicated he had jumped twice and delivered instant death by snapping the elk's neck. The carcass was still warm. Rex was indeed at the peak of his predatory prowess.

Sometimes "Ol' Rex," as we now called him, would take a more languid appraisal of our pursuit, simply looking down at us inquisitively and swishing his tail. Occasionally, he growled, showed his teeth, and snarled to remind us that he remained wild to the core. One day, Rex appeared especially surly, and Wilbur paid a price. After we darted him in the chest, the cat became enraged. Finally, the drug took hold—or so we thought. Wilbur climbed the tree and reached for Rex's hindfoot. Suddenly, the cat spun around and swiped, driving a claw into the bone of Wilbur's right index finger.

"I'll get some peroxide on it later," Wilbur said dismissively after bandaging the wound back on the ground.

Rex at that point weighed 147 pounds. His tags and collar were in good shape. His continuing tenure in the study area reinforced the study's initial findings on the importance of home range, territoriality, and mutual avoidance.

Cannibal Tom was another story. On his first recapture in season four, Tom weighed only 106 pounds, down nearly forty pounds from when we first caught and released him two years earlier. When Rex began hunting in his territory, we assumed Cannibal Tom had died. We later learned that Rex eventually let another tom assume the vacancy left by Cannibal Tom and returned to his original Cave Creek proprietorship.

The fate of female No. 11 during season four epitomized the raw reality of predator–prey ecology. The dogs first treed her in early December. She looked beleaguered but had retained her collar and tags. We saw no reason to immobilize her. Two days later, however, she was treed again, and we saw bloody froth seeping from her mouth. Backtracks showed where she had attacked one of several cow elk, and the two of them slid downhill and smacked into a fir tree. The elk got up, made several long leaps to escape, and left no blood on the trail she left behind. Most telling, No. 11 didn't follow the elk and instead walked about fifty yards to lie down. It was there that the hounds eventually found her and forced her up the tree. Looking down at us, she appeared to have sustained a head injury during the downhill fracas. We left her alone in the tree.

Three weeks later, after the hounds treed her in a different location, the severity of her injuries were a macabre vision staring down at us from above. "Looks like a saber-tooth cat," Wilbur said.

Again, No. 11 had retained all her tags and collar while exhibiting a horrendous wound that rendered her helpless. Her two lower canines and part of her jaw were broken off and hanging loose. We speculated that the earlier attack she'd made on the cow elk resulted in the initial injury, and perhaps during subsequent attacks the jaw finally broke, dooming her to the slow death she was suffering. I decided to intervene with a lethal overdose of drug, and on inspection, we found holes in No. 11's shoulder and hip, perhaps inflicted by an elk's antlers. She weighed only seventy pounds.

I continued to make flights back and forth between Moscow and Big Creek as season four wound down. By this time, I'd adjusted to the mixture of office and fieldwork and continued to prepare for the radio-collar phase of the study.

In mid-April 1968, I landed at Taylor Ranch to fly big game trend counts and check vegetation plots throughout the study area. I also planned to fly out with Tommy and Flopsy, now mature two-year-olds, to a large enclosure outside of Moscow owned by the University of Idaho. There, the cougars would be located fairly close to my new office, where I could continue caring for and observing them as part of our research.

I looked forward to documenting their innate and learned behaviors, as well as continuing to follow their physical maturation. One of my new research colleagues at the university, Ken Hungerford, had built a fenced area on the university's experimental forest within the Hatter Creek drainage. On the north side of Moscow Mountain, the location was about thirty road miles (ten air miles) from the University of Idaho campus.

Technically, the deer enclosure was not an enclosure. It was designed to keep deer out, not in, so vegetation growth inside could be compared to vegetation browsed by deer on the outside. With the addition of battery-powered electric wire around the top of the fence, the enclosure became a pen and served as a great new home for Tommy and Flopsy away from the public, and it was even larger than the pen at Taylor Ranch.

"Go ahead," Hungerford told me. "If anything, mature mountain lions will help keep the deer away."

On the evening of April 22, 1968, after flying the season's last big game trend count in the upper Big Creek drainage, I lightly drugged Tommy and Flopsy, checked and found no health problems, helped them into their separate dog crates, and hefted each aboard a plane, and we flew to McCall. The next day, with Tommy and Flopsy still at their cooperative best, we drove in my pickup truck to Moscow, then made a loop around Moscow Mountain north to Potlatch, and finally south onto Hatter Creek Road. Within an hour, Tommy and Flopsy were exploring their new home.

It would turn out to be the biggest mistake I've ever made.

## CHAPTER THIRTY-THREE

# Haunting Attack

TWO MONTHS AFTER I RELOCATED TOMMY AND FLOPSY TO THEIR NEW enclosure, Tommy disappeared. For three days, I searched for him. He'd escaped from the university's enclosure, and I drove mile after mile on backcountry roads but found no sign of him. Immediately after discovering his escape, I had alerted the sheriff's office and fish and game authorities and called the local radio station and newspapers to report Tommy's disappearance. Then, on the evening of June 15, 1968, nine days after Robert F. Kennedy was assassinated, my home phone rang.

"Dr. Hornocker, this is the dispatcher at the Latah County Sheriff's Office."

"Yes."

"I think we've found your mountain lion."

"Good. Where?"

"He was treed just outside White Pine Campground, about eight miles north of Harvard. He's still in the tree."

"Thank you for calling," I responded with relief. "I'll be right there."

"And, Dr. Hornocker?"

"Yes?"

"The cat attacked a little girl."

The words seared me into silence. I didn't fully comprehend what I'd been told. I hesitated to answer, and then . . .

"She's been taken by ambulance to the hospital in Colfax."

"Is she . . . ?"

"I don't know the extent of her injuries other than she was bleeding from head wounds."

"My God!"

I had no idea how Tommy escaped. Flopsy, the other captive cougar, was secure behind the fencing when I found Tommy missing. And now, with one chilling phone call, my bafflement had been replaced by a sudden sense of anguish, remorse, and responsibility.

"I'll be there in less than an hour."

"Thank you, Dr. Hornocker. Our deputies will be waiting."

A small crowd of campers and law enforcement authorities had gathered at the campground. Tommy, wearing ear tags, peered down from high in a tree at the commotion below. Hunters with hounds, beckoned by the sheriff's office to isolate the mountain lion, ensured that he didn't try to come down. I don't remember anyone saying anything upon my arrival, except a sheriff's deputy, who asked, "What do you want us to do?"

"Kill him," I said without hesitation.

Looking back more than five decades later, I'd say the same thing today. The situation needed immediate resolution. So one of the hounds-men fired his rifle. Tommy tumbled through limbs and landed dead on the ground. I don't recall what the onlookers said or did at that point. I gathered the carcass into my arms, walked to my pickup, laid Tommy in the bed, and took him to cold storage at the university, where I'd later conduct a postmortem. (His head was promptly sent to a state lab for a rabies test, which proved to be negative.)

Fighting emotions of grief and fear, I drove thirty miles to the hospital in Colfax, Washington. I had learned from authorities that the little girl and her family lived in the small Whitman County farming community. I pulled into the hospital parking lot, entered the lobby, and was ushered by a nurse to the emergency room. There I was introduced to the child's distraught mother.

"I just want to say how sorry I am," I uttered. "I don't know what else I can say, I . . ."

"Doctors say she's going to be fine," Shirley Carlson politely interrupted. "It's okay." The mother's gracious demeanor unnerved me even more. Doctors had already tended to her daughter's injuries, she explained.

"What's her name?" I asked.

"Sally."

The child was about to turn three years old. Her mother led me into the emergency room, where Sally, her head covered in bandages, sat with her father, Terry Carlson. A total of ninety-seven stitches were needed to close the wounds. I introduced myself to the father, and we shook hands.

"Sally," her mother said, "this is Dr. Hornocker."

"Hi. How are you?" I asked, leaning down to greet the child.

"Fine."

"I'm so sorry about what happened."

Sally nodded and leaned into the comfort of her mother's arms. When she smiled, I nearly wept.

Terry Carlson, a schoolteacher in Colfax, later told me what he recalled about what happened. The family had driven from their home into Idaho to enjoy a weekend at White Pine Campground adjacent to State Highway 6 near Laird Park. It was and remains a popular getaway destination for residents of the region. Escaping three days earlier, Tommy had traveled some fifteen miles and was spotted on the periphery of the campground. While people were rightfully concerned, Tommy showed no signs of aggression.

But then, Terry said, Tommy followed the family as they began to take an afternoon walk. The cat seemed to take a special interest in Sally and approached her. In retrospect, I think Tommy may have remembered playing as a kitten with my own daughters. Or perhaps Sally's small stature triggered a predatory reaction.

At any rate, Tommy closed in, reared up onto Sally, and, with claws extended, latched onto her. Terry, who said the attack happened quickly and remained somewhat of a blur, was able to retrieve a camping shovel and strike the cat several times. Tommy ran off and was eventually treed by some hounds.

"The cuts are in the hairline," Terry told me. "Any scars will be hidden."

I couldn't believe the graciousness of these people. Here, through no one's fault but my own, a mountain lion had attacked and injured their young child. And the parents showed no animosity toward me. I was humbled then and remain so today by their kindness.

I left the hospital, contacted my insurance company, and was assured that everything would be covered. Years later, in a letter from Shirley Carlson, she confirmed that all medical bills were paid and that some of the insurance money eventually helped pay for Sally's college tuition. Always magnanimous, Shirley quipped in the letter about her daughter's tenaciousness.

*"Dear Dr. Hornocker,*

*Do you remember June, 1968, and a cougar who got out of his cage? The enclosed picture is Sally, the little girl he ran up against."*

Sally was nineteen and beautiful. I still have the portrait.

I vividly remember breaking the news to my family, especially our oldest daughter, Karen, who had claimed Tommy as her own. Younger sister Kim insisted Flopsy was hers. The girls, twelve and ten at the time, were devoted to the young cougars. They had played with the kittens in our home, helped care for Tommy and Flopsy as they grew, posed with them for countless photographs, and reminded me repeatedly that the mountain lions were "not just study animals."

When Tommy escaped, Shirley, Karen, Kim, and our youngest daughter, Lisa, were back in Iowa visiting family. I'll never forget the forlorn look on Shirley's face when she returned and I told her the news. Nor can I shed the image of Karen and Kim, who shared a bedroom, waking in the morning to hear the sad story.

"Oh, no, no!" Karen wailed as I took both daughters in my arms.

That day at White Pine Campground could have ended both the Big Creek cougar study and my career. In today's litigious world, it probably would have. The attack, of course, made big news.

Among the headlines:

*"Colfax Girl Mauled by Runaway Project Cougar"*

*"Cougar Mauls Colfax Girl, Hunted Down"*

*"Cougar Victim Is Recovering"*
Meanwhile, I still had to deal with Flopsy.

As soon as I discovered Tommy's escape and before starting my search for him, I loaded Flopsy into my pickup truck, drove back to Moscow, and put him in a secure holding pen on the agriculture college grounds. The pen was little more than a jail used for rogue bulls and other hard-to-manage livestock. Then, after Tommy attacked Sally and had to be killed, I contacted the director of the Portland Zoo to find a home for Flopsy.

"Sure, we'll take him. Bring him over," the director told me.

Much to the director's surprise, Flopsy adapted quickly. They put him on public display, and things went well until about a year later when an attendant left a gate open. Flopsy slipped through into an adjacent pen and attacked and almost killed another mountain lion.

"We have to isolate him," the director informed me. "He's too aggressive." I immediately started making plans for Flopsy's return not to the university deer enclosure, but back to the Big Creek pen at Taylor Ranch. There he could be housed and maybe even released into the wild at the end of the study. Arrangements set, I chartered a 206 Cessna from Moscow and flew to Portland.

"We're kind of afraid of him," a zoo attendant told me. "He almost killed another cat. He's back here."

Flopsy had been labeled "vicious" and relegated to a dark, damp, dungeon-like cell. No longer on display to the public, he'd been warehoused. Alone. Suspicious. Resigned to nonexistence. He lay in shadows, on a ledge of sorts, asleep as I approached.

"Flopsy," I beckoned, attempting to make my voice sound warm and engaging in the cold and detached confines. The cat awoke with a start, looked over at me, seemed to recognize a colleague (if not a friend), jumped down, and approached. Standing on his hind legs, he rose up and placed his forepaws through the bars and rested them on my shoulders. He purred and rubbed his head against the vertical bars, trying, it seemed, to hug me. I reached to unlock the cell door.

"No!" the attendant shouted.

I paid no attention. The door came open and I stepped inside with the vanquished apex predator. Flopsy lifted himself up again and nuzzled my ear. The attendant stood in wide-eyed disbelief. The director, when told of the reunion, reacted similarly.

I lightly drugged Flopsy on the spot, ushered him with a leash inside his dog travel crate, drove the rental vehicle to the Portland airport, loaded him onto the Cessna, and we flew directly to Big Creek. By the time we landed at Taylor Ranch some two hours later, he had started recovering from the drug. Within fifteen minutes, he wobbled to his legs and walked. We strolled together from the airstrip without a leash about 300 yards to the familiar pen where Pioneer Creek's cool water trickled through. Flopsy was home. He briefly explored the entry area and then sauntered to his old shelter and laid down. After a few minutes, he got back up, moseyed over to a scratching tree, and freshened his mark. He continued to tour his pen, appearing completely at ease.

Periodically, a veterinarian would fly in from Moscow to check Flopsy's health and draw blood. On one trip, I accompanied the vet. We watched as Flopsy worked out of the drug stupor and were satisfied that all was well. He went straight to his scratching tree before seeking solitude in a more remote part of the enclosure.

The veterinarian and I flew to Moscow, parted ways, and went back to our jobs. The next day, I received a radiophone message from a graduate student at Taylor Ranch.

"Flopsy is missing," he told me. "We're looking for him."

Once again, I struggled to believe what I'd been told.

"Did he escape?"

"I don't know. We're still looking for him. There doesn't seem to be a hole in the fence, and the gate is secure."

I hung up, torn between immediately flying back to Taylor Ranch and joining the search or, if he'd indeed escaped, simply letting the captive mountain lion become part of Big Creek's vast ecosystem. Despite never learning to hunt, he might know instinctively. Some three hours later, I received a call that snuffed that thought.

"We found him," the shaken student said. "He's dead, in the creek. I'm so sorry."

To this day, I don't know how Flopsy died. We flew him to Moscow for a postmortem and found no evidence that he'd drowned. The veterinarian and I discussed whether he could have suffered some unforeseen ill effect from the drugs we'd administered, but it didn't seem likely. His death remains a mystery.

Reflecting on the lives of Tommy and Flopsy as research animals, we learned a lot about innate and learned behaviors of mountain lions. I, of course, learned that such animals, if they are to be held captive in the name of science, must be secured in fail-safe enclosures. No way around it. In the decades since, there's been an international campaign to discourage, if not make illegal, the private ownership and keeping of any of the world's great cats. I fully endorse this movement.

My sorrowful memories about the deaths of Tommy and Flopsy are eased by the fact that an ultimate tragedy—the loss of a child—was averted not by me but by a protective dad wielding a shovel.

## Chapter Thirty-Four

# The Fight for Closure

THE NEED FOR LESS POLITICAL INVOLVEMENT AND MORE FUNDING HAS always hamstrung wildlife research. And by the fall of 1968, despite our scientific progress in the field, my dream of studying cougars free of outside influence had become a nightmare.

News stories earlier that summer about Tommy attacking a child emboldened already harsh critics. They used the incident to demonstrate my ill-conceived quest to save heartless monsters. The finger-pointing came mostly from within hunting and livestock ranks. Hunters clung to the notion that mountain lions were prolific killers of deer, elk, bighorn sheep, and mountain goats. Livestock owners piled on with claims of ravenous cougars sneaking out of the backcountry to devour their sheep and cattle, robbing them of their profits. And now the cats were attacking young children at family campgrounds.

I was dubbed as an uppity intellectual who, after skirting through college on a taxpayer-funded doctorate, had the gall to demand that Big Creek cougar hunting be temporarily halted. Amid the growing furor, members of the Idaho Fish and Game Commission, who continued to support the study, exercised their apolitical power by convening in mid-December 1968 to discuss and take action on the escalating debate.

A month earlier, as November snow began to fall in higher elevations, hunters with dogs, pack strings of horses and mules, and even a snow-mobile showed up in the study area. At one point, Wilbur confronted a hunter who, judging from tracks he'd left in the snow, appeared to be following one of Wilbur's hounds. The hunter denied it. But from that time on, Wilbur called him "The Nut" and suspected him of being up to no good, including slipping into one of our camp tents, staying several nights, and using Wilbur's sleeping bag.

"I burned it," Wilbur said of his long-used polyester bag. We had a new one flown in.

All the while, more human tracks appeared, and plane traffic increased. We feared a pending onslaught. Even the mountain lions seemed bent on fueling the craziness. Wilbur discovered tracks in the Cave Creek drainage, suggesting that No. 3, Ol' Rex, the dominant tom, now had a carnivorous rival in addition to human hunters within his territory. The hounds ultimately treed lion No. 2-C, the 181-pound tom captured two years earlier by Dave Wedum and Floyd Partney in the ill-fated Chamberlain Basin expansion.

Next Wilbur and the hounds treed Bessie and two small kittens in the Cave Creek drainage. This was mystifying. Why were so many cats entering an already established territory? Population dynamics screamed for answers. Yet humans, from inside and outside the study area, threatened to block our ability to figure it out.

Fish and Game Commission members finally convened on December 16, 1968. Minutes from the meeting describe their dilemma: *"The study of cougar in the Big Creek area is being jeopardized by hunters killing animals involved in the study . . . a closure is necessary to protect the investment that has been made toward the study."*

Quickly, they unanimously passed a motion to close mountain lion hunting in Big Creek. The shutdown was set to begin on the day after Christmas and run until the study concluded. Commission chairman William B. Durban underscored the urgency by casting an unnecessary affirmative vote and asked that it be reflected in the minutes.

It turned out to be a fleeting victory.

Enter Idaho Representative Walter E. Little of New Plymouth, the Republican president of the Idaho Wool Growers Association, and his cadre of attorneys. Within days, they appealed the closure on grounds that the commission lacked authority to regulate the hunting of predators. Assistant Idaho attorney general Warren Felton agreed and issued a supporting opinion, effectively voiding the closure.

Among the headlines:

*"Big Creek Cougar Study Hampered by Decision."*

*"Idaho Official Kills Exemption For Tagged Cats."*

A *Statesman* story carried the headline *"Attorney General Vetoes Exempting Study Cougar from Predator Controls."* I was quoted as saying the action was "asinine." Maybe a bit inflammatory, but I no longer cared about politeness. "International recognition is focused on this research because it's a study that has never been done before," I said. "It is 4½ years of work that could well go down the drain."

Critics countered by accusing me of fleecing taxpayers with funding shenanigans.

I wasn't about to let that one go. Already prepared to argue for more study findings, I pivoted to gather financial numbers and funneled them to John R. (Dick) Woodworth, director of the Idaho Fish and Game Department. He reviewed the ledgers and made them public.

In a nutshell, the five years of the cougar study had cost the department a mere $33,097.88—roughly $6,600 annually. In addition, none of it came from taxpayer dollars. All Fish and Game Department money, Woodworth noted, came from the sale of hunting and fishing licenses, augmented by federal sales taxes on guns, ammunition, and fishing gear.

But even that wasn't enough to quiet the noisy critics, who demanded more accounting. So I disclosed the study's private sector funding, which had doubled our budget. Those dollars came from the Boone and Crockett Club, the American Museum of Natural History, the New York Zoological Society, the National Wildlife Federation, and the Carnegie Museum.

All told, we'd spent about $66,600 over five years.

"A good investment," I countered the naysayers. "One worth protecting." I estimated that we'd need another $30,000 to complete the study by July 1972.

"These funds covering a 2½-year period, are for support of a graduate student, radio equipment, operating expenses, and a part-time employee," I wrote in a note to legislative committee members. It was my first public mention of plans to put radio transmitters on the Big Creek mountain lions.

"These are not state funds," I reminded them. "A proposal has been submitted to the National Science Foundation, and it appears it will be approved. If not, other private organizations have indicated they will provide the funds." Despite Idaho being touted, thanks to our study, as a bellwether mountain lion research state, anti-cougar factions remained dedicated to stopping the research and destroying my credibility.

By January 1969, every western state but Idaho had either declared or was in the process of designating the mountain lion as a game animal worthy of management. By invitation, I had visited each of the other states, shared my research findings, and discussed the concept of reclassifying cougars as game animals.

How ironic, I lamented, that the state promoting mountain lion research still listed the cats as vermin.

On January 28, 1969, a public hearing was held in a big conference room at the Idaho state capitol. Rather than feeling intimidated, I looked forward to testifying. I had solid data supporting a Big Creek closure. Members of both the senate's Fish, Game, and Recreation Committee and the house's Resources and Conservation Committee listened intently.

The next day, the *Statesman* published a story with the headline *"Panels in Senate, House Hear Testimony on Close of Cougar Hunting Area."*

Outdoors editor Keith Wood wrote, *"Tuesday's hearing was in connection with proposed new legislation to close cougar hunting in the area until June 1, 1972, when the study will be completed."*

On the day that article appeared, members of the Fish and Game Commission, faced with the assistant attorney general's opposing opinion, voted 3–2 to officially rescind the Big Creek closure. The court of public opinion and politics, not science and necessity, had prevailed.

Eight days later and still smarting from the defeat, I left McCall, flew into Taylor Ranch, and met Wilbur. We hunted the next day, hiking thirteen miles to the forks of Cave Creek. The following day, we treed two kittens. One of the dogs chased after the mother. Wilbur followed while I tended the kittens. I fired a dart and missed, and one kitten jumped from the tree.

*My notes: "I ran chasing it down into timber, managed to catch kitten by tail and carry back up hill to equipment. Tied him up and gave him 10 mg Sernylan. Marked him No. 38. 21 lb, male, beautiful little kitten, soft kitten fur, spotted."*

I was back in my element. Away from the politics. Back in the wilderness. Away from controversy. Back with the cougars, which, despite their enigmatic ways, I seemed to understand better than humans.

Six weeks later, Fish and Game Commission members were ready to take action a second time on the much-needed closure. Leading up to that day, I helped draft Senate Bill 1082, which granted the commission new authority over predators. I testified twice before legislative committees, and the bill passed.

After much debate and controversy, cougar hunting in the Big Creek drainage was closed by order of the Idaho Fish and Game Commission pending completion of the study.

Armed with this new power, the commissioners convened and voted unanimously again to close all cougar hunting in the Big Creek study area—effective midnight, March 27, 1969, through June 30, 1972. This time around, no one challenged the action.

I was in my Moscow office when I got word of the victory. Wilbur, back in Big Creek at Taylor Ranch, heard a report on the radio and took two days off. We agreed: the mountain lions had been hunted enough. They were the real winners and, like us, deserved a rest.

## CHAPTER THIRTY-FIVE

# Terrestrial "Woods Hole"

"WILDERNESS IS THE PERFECT LABORATORY," WROTE AMERICAN AUTHOR and ecologist Aldo Leopold. He envisioned places like central Idaho's vast roadless areas as benchmark examples of where evolution had progressed. The Idaho Primitive Area, where our Big Creek study area had been strategically located, would in 1984 become part of the Frank Church River of No Return Wilderness Area. Abutting the already established Selway Bitterroot Wilderness Area, the more than 3.6 million contiguous acres remain, for the most part, as the 1964 Wilderness Act declared: "untrammeled" country where humans are visitors who don't remain.

Each time we dropped a plane onto a backcountry airstrip, I was struck by how irrelevant humans were to the ecosystem surrounding us. To some, land like this is a product of intelligent design, placed here by a higher power for humans to enjoy, possess, and exploit. Although I felt a spiritual connection to the wilderness, I understood that nature was in charge. Cougars, not humans, were the apex predators in this place. If anything, the rhythm of the land left me feeling a sense of humble nonimportance.

Once again, there were Wilbur's words, lending lyrics to the mountains' mystic song: "The more you learn, the more you learn you don't know."

If spirituality fuels imagination, my vision for Taylor Ranch came as a by-product of a job that, after five years of work, became a calling. Now that the cougar study was legally protected from hunters, we were gearing up for the final phase that would include radio collars. An end was in sight. Yet I wondered about the rest of the ecosystem. What about the big

Masked by snow, Taylor Ranch, located adjacent to Big Creek, served as head-quarters throughout the cougar study and was later purchased by the University of Idaho as a wilderness research center.

game populations, the vegetation, the soils, the water, the fish, the other mammals, the birds, the snakes, the insects, and the microorganisms? What about a holistic look at the mountain lion's domain right down to the geological foundation of the stony earth they traveled?

I envisioned Taylor Ranch as the nucleus of a place where understanding could happen—a headquarters for a far-reaching wilderness research program, a sixty-five-acre facility where seasoned scientists and inquisitive young minds could coalesce around learning and discovery. Perhaps Taylor Ranch could become a terrestrial version of the Woods Hole Oceanographic Institution in Massachusetts, founded in 1930 and dedicated to marine science.

On May 8, 1969, I flew into the ranch with that very concept percolating in my mind. Jess Taylor was aging and had expressed an interest in selling. I thought the place had great potential, and I longed to buy it and then strike out as a solo researcher in association with other like-minded scientists. But I didn't have the money. However, the University of Idaho, where I worked, had the financial wherewithal. Maybe its administrators would support my vision.

After landing, I talked with ranch caretaker Arlow Lewis. He unwittingly fueled the vision by providing a cougar update, even though our field season had concluded.

"I saw two small kittens, four days ago, near the upper end of the airstrip," he reported. "They were drinking from the creek, right across from me. Then they ran back into the brush after spotting me."

Near the site where Arlow had seen the kittens, I found an old deer kill.

*My notes: "Kill had been dragged down from slope above trail. This must be No. 16 and her kittens. Only other female it could possibly be is No. 24 and that isn't likely."*

About to enter the radio-tracking phase of the study, our electronics expert in Moscow was already wiring a compact transmitter collar designed to stay around a cougar's neck and not inhibit the animal's behavior, including its ability to hunt successfully.

So much potential, I thought as I stood over the remains of this latest kill and looking around—not only for the cougar study but also for sweeping ecology investigations within this vast, unspoiled country. Taylor Ranch had a colorful history. And we'd proven its utility as a research headquarters. Surely its future held untapped possibilities.

Back in Moscow, I pitched the idea to Ken Dick, the university's financial vice president.

"Sounds interesting," he said. "I'll run it past Ernie."

University of Idaho president Ernest Hartung was enthusiastic and asked me to prepare a document justifying the university's purchase of the ranch. I did so, and after reading it, he gave his approval. Ernest Wohletz, dean of the forestry college, then carried the torch, which meant defending the proposed purchase amid criticism by foes. The ranch, Wohletz told the *Statesman*, offered "unparalleled opportunities" for faculty members, scientists, and graduate students. Ultimately, the newspaper championed the purchase on its editorial page with a headline that read, "University Should Buy Taylor Ranch"—this despite Governor Don Samuelson's argument against buying on grounds it would take more private land off the tax rolls. The *Statesman* reporters did some digging and found the ranch's annual property tax to be a mere $74.16. Editors labeled the amount a "pittance" and Samuelson's argument "feeble."

The sale went through for $100,000. Jess and Dorothy Taylor retained lifelong residency rights. I agreed to oversee caretaker responsibilities. With the agreement signed, I pivoted my attention to mountain lions. Radiotelemetry was crucial to disproving or confirming the findings we had obtained so far. Year-round 24/7 surveillance promised to greatly expand our understanding of cougar ecology. I had a graduate student in waiting. The ranch was secured as our headquarters. The cougar hunting season in Big Creek would remain closed for at least three years. We were on a roll. Time to let the world know. Time to query the National Geographic Society.

To my surprise and delight, society officials were eager for me to write an article about the study for *National Geographic* magazine. To this day, I'm convinced that the end product did more to steer the future of mountain lions in the eyes of the public than all the scientific publications I wrote over the years.

"We're looking for about 2,500 to 3,000 words," an editor told me over the phone. "And photographs, do you have some good photographs of mountain lions?"

"Of course. Yes. Many good photographs."

"Well, okay then. We look forward to seeing what you produce."

I credit John and Frank Craighead for my getting the writing assignment. They had a long and good history with *National Geographic*. They'd written feature articles about birds of prey and, of course, the Yellowstone grizzly bear project. Not only were they connected, they supported my work. Naturally, I dropped their names when I made my proposal. With mountain lions entrenched in mystique, the editors had great expectations.

So I wrote longhand in my university office, essentially converting my doctoral dissertation into stylized *Geographic* prose, beginning with a catchy, stage-setting anecdote:

*Still panting from the chase through the snow of Idaho's Salmon River Mountains, I pulled the gun out of my backpack. The barrel stung my hands in the cold, and my breath frosted the breech as I sighted into a fir tree 30 feet away.*

*"Careful!" gasped my companion, Wilbur Wiles. "Don't rush!"*

*Poised on a branch, staring down at her pursuers, was our target— a hundred-pound mountain lion.*

The article, all seventeen pages accompanied by eighteen full-color photographs and two maps, appeared in the November 1969 edition of *National Geographic* with the headline "Stalking the Mountain Lion—to Save Him."

"Glorious!" raved the cougar supporters.

"Garbage!" carped the critics.

"Figures," Wilbur deadpanned. "Ya can't please everyone."

By the time the article came out, we'd captured and released forty-six different mountain lions in the Big Creek drainage. We'd traveled more than 8,000 up-and-down miles, much of it on snowshoes. Wilbur and I had gotten to know each other like brothers. We knew the cats, dare I say, like no one else. And while some of my peers in wildlife research circles scoffed at popularizing scientific research, I knew that we'd turned a corner and that suddenly, from San Francisco to Houston to Boston, mountain lions were cool! That I was actually studying them in the wild with Wilbur was recognized as groundbreaking. In growing circles, saving them from extinction became a mission. Research, conducted by myself and many others, would swell exponentially over the coming decades.

As the winter of 1969–1970 and our sixth field season approached, we remained the only show in town. The first to study mountain lions, we were also first to document their territoriality, mutual avoidance, and innate population controls. Now, within a couple months, we'd be the first to place radio collars on cougars, listen with earphones for a telltale "beep beep beep" signal, and follow the cat in real time back into its enigmatic way of life.

Increasingly, I found myself thinking about a grizzly bear named Marian.

# CHAPTER THIRTY-SIX

# The Thrill of Being First

BEAR NO. 40, MARIAN, WAS THE FIRST GRIZZLY BEAR IN THE WORLD TO wear a radio collar. I remember hearing the metallic beeping in the receiver as brothers John and Frank Craighead celebrated like kids dancing among trees in a backcountry playground.

"Loud and clear!" Frank shouted as Marian, weighing an even 300 pounds, lumbered away across Yellowstone National Park's Hayden Valley. As a graduate student under John Craighead, I was there to witness it all. It was September 22, 1961, a Friday shrouded in early season snow at the park. As John liked to say, "the thrill of being first" on the road to discovery never gets old. Over the next decade, the Craigheads would put radio collars on twenty-four different grizzly bears. But that first bear, Marian, remained the most memorable, even more so after finding her again the next day by following the signal from her collar. In his book *Track of the Grizzly*, Frank wrote,

*"'There she is!' we all exclaimed in unison. John said that he could see the colored collar, and Maurice confirmed his observation as he followed the bear's movements with the scope."*

Seven years later, I hoped to collar the first-ever mountain lion with a radio transmitter. But for a cougar, a Marian-size collar would be like wearing a Buick. We needed something akin to a Volkswagen. Dick Davies of Philco Corporation, Joel Varney of Aeronutronic Ford Corporation, and Hoke Franciscus, a ham radio operator, designed the transmitters, receivers, antennas, and grizzly collars. For our study, I turned to Albert Johnson, who worked out of a garage in Moscow. Downsizing would be his mission.

"Light planes have long had locator beacons, and this is no more complex than that technology," said Johnson, who got around in a wheelchair and worked mostly out of a shop in his garage. "It's the same electrical setup. All you have to do is encase a beacon in a smaller capsule and attach it to an animal. It's as simple as that."

And yet, it turned out to be bit more complicated. The biggest hurdle, besides collar size, was battery life, which improved as batteries improved. Antennas, for gathering the beeping signals, had to be made from scratch, and the prototypes looked like metal hula hoops. We carried them while hunting on the ground or manipulated the antennas under the belly of an airplane.

"From inside a plane," Johnson explained, "all ya need is a conduit down through the fuselage attached to the antenna and a handle on the conduit up above to rotate." We wore headsets connected to the receivers and either walked while holding the directional antennas or rotated them from helicopters or fixed-wing airplanes.

"Every cat will have a different signal sequence," Johnson explained, "beeps per minute. You'll know which animal you're coming in contact with." So he busied himself paring down the collar size and refining the electronics. By late 1969, we had the first prototypes ready to be fitted around the necks of Big Creek mountain lions. Over the next three years, Johnson would make new collars as we needed them, each one an improvement over the previous.

Graduate student Jack Seidensticker checks for signals from radio-collared cougars.

To help with this new radio-collar phase of the study, I brought graduate student Jack Seidensticker aboard to pursue his doctoral degree. I'd met Jack in Montana when he was an undergraduate student working with the Craigheads. He had an outdoors orientation and a real talent for bringing data together. I saw a critical need for an analytical mind to decode the volumes of data we'd gather through radio tracking. Jack and Wilbur were from different worlds—Jack from a wealthy Montana ranching family and Wilbur the product of a Depression-era Iowa farm. Nonetheless, with occasional refereeing from me, they made a solid team.

As we readied our first collars, receivers, and antennas to be flown into Big Creek, the mountain lions seemed bent on confounding what we thought we'd learned. Rex, for example, left his Cave Creek territory to reside in Cannibal Tom's Rush Creek territory. Twice we captured Rex where we expected to find Cannibal Tom.

Even the 181-pound Chamberlain Basin tom (No. 2-C) visited the vacated area for a short time. Cougar No. 41, a new tom weighing 150 pounds, was captured in a fringe of Cannibal Tom's territory. We also failed to find two females, Nos. 16 and 35, in their territories.

*My notes: "This is strange. It has been an extremely mild winter with poor tracking conditions—possible they have just been missed."*

In addition, a young male, No. 28, first captured in the Coxey Creek drainage two years earlier, was now several miles away in Cave Creek.

*My notes: "This is Rex's territory. It may be that Cannibal Tom died, Rex shifted his territory to that vacated territory, and this cat has moved into the area left vacant by Rex."*

Wilbur also reported that Cannibal Tom had not returned to the scrape sites he routinely visited in previous years—more evidence that he died and the population was in a state of flux.

*My notes: "Radios, hopefully, will tell us."*

On January 30, 1970, before I could fly into Big Creek because of weather conditions and job duties, Wilbur and Jack loaded up the radiotelemetry gear and left Taylor Ranch with the hounds. They hiked up Cave Creek, cut a tom track going east, and followed before letting the dogs loose.

*Wilbur's notes: "Treed cougar in big bluff on East Fork. It was No. 28. He had lost his tags, but still had collar. 142 pounds now."*

As I write today, the only mention I can find in my records about history being made is one sentence written by Wilbur Wiles.

*Wilbur's notes: "Jack put a transmitter on cat & we come to Cave Cr. Camp."*

With no more recorded fanfare than that, the first cougar in the world to wear a radio collar was released back into the wild. By February 10, 1970, we had three mountain lions equipped with transmitters— No. 28, unnamed; Bessie; and Rex. To me, this was big news—so much so that I invited a renowned wildlife documentarian into Big Creek to film it.

Morley Nelson, a respected raptor expert who would become an Idaho conservationist legend and have the Morley Nelson Snake River Birds of Prey National Conservation Area south of Boise named in his honor, arrived via Cessna at Taylor Ranch on February 15, 1970. He extracted himself and his film gear from the plane, shook my hand, and said, "Let's get started."

In preparation for his arrival, Jack and I had erected an antenna above the airstrip, then tried to work some kinks out of a receiver.

*My notes: "Climbed to ridge up Cliff Creek and checked with radio receiver. Checked Cliff Cr. & Cougar Creek drainages, got no signal."*

Bessie had been treed and radio-collared by Wilbur and Jack a week earlier on a warm, clear afternoon with snow melting off the south-facing slopes. She was accompanied by one or possibly two kittens that were not treed.

Also, No. 28, the 142-pound tom who was first to wear a radio collar, couldn't be found.

*Wilbur's notes: "Radio receiver went haywire."*

While electrons and protons never fail, we were still working the bugs out of our equipment. After a day of tinkering and repairs, Wilbur, Jack, Morley, and I went on an equipment shakedown hunt along Snake Creek, circumventing bluffs toward Dunce Creek, not too far from Taylor Ranch. We turned Ranger loose on a sketchy track, which he lost. After retrieving the dog, we climbed a ridge between Dunce and Goat creeks. Jack turned on the repaired receiver and started maneuvering the directional antenna.

"Beep, beep, beep."

"It's Bessie," I told Morley.

We heard the strong signal emanating from Jack's headset and originating from the bottom of the Goat Creek drainage. We moved farther up the ridge, over and around more bluffs, stopping to listen at numerous locations. The signal remained strong. Bessie, we calculated, was holed up one-half to one mile above Goat Basin. It was getting late, so we left her alone.

The following day, with Morley filming, we picked up the signal again at the mouth of Cougar Creek and climbed to a bench overlooking the countryside.

"Beep beep beep."

The signal was coming from the west slope of Cougar Creek. We dropped down to the Big Creek trail and hiked into a basin, then to a ridge between Cougar and Cliff creeks.

Again, "Beep beep beep."

Stealthily, we closed in on the steady signal that led us toward Bessie. Although we didn't see her, we turned the dogs loose, and she treed within a quarter mile.

"Bet she's surprised how fast we closed in," Wilbur remarked as we darted the lioness and lowered her to the ground. Her new radio collar was secure, and she was in good condition. We knew Bessie had two kittens: one a seventy-eight-pound male, the other uncaptured.

*My notes: "Kittens apparently were not with her today. She moved over to Cougar Creek during the night, signal indicating she was hunting actively all day."*

The telemetry magic was back, all of it captured on Morley's film.

The following day, as Jack and Wilbur scoured a new area for more signals, Morley and I delved deeper into the art of using 16-mm film to document the ever-unfolding mysteries of mountain lions. Using almost 300 feet of Ektachrome, Morley instructed me on techniques so I could continue filming after he returned to civilization.

"I'd stay here if I could," he lamented.

We shot what Morley called "production stuff"—the Big Creek canyon from afar, the creek up close, the ranch property around us, the cliffs above, the clouds dueling with the mountain peaks, and even Jack's antenna atop the airstrip. On February 20, a writer and photographer from *Life* magazine flew in to do a story about bighorn sheep. Other media were asking to fly in. In the wake of the *National Geographic* article, Big Creek had been discovered.

Morley flew out the next day. He never did anything with the film he shot.

"I got busy with other things," he told me years later.

"I know how that is," I responded.

Morley Nelson continued to be a staunch supporter of the study, and we remained close friends until his death in 2005. I still have the reels of 16-mm film we shot that winter in 1970. Tightly spooled in metal canisters, I doubt the film has ever been run through a projector.

Ultimately, we radio-collared fifteen mountain lions. Over thirty months into May 1972, we tracked them on the ground for 669 days, covering more than 9,500 miles. We also monitored the fifteen lions ninety-seven times from light aircraft, locating them 340 times. With each location, we recorded elevation, time, and, when possible, habitat type, activity, the whereabouts of big game kills, and any interaction between other radio-collared cats. Jack, who stayed on the study through 1971, plugged the data into a computer (yes, computers were coming of age) for analysis. When Jack left after earning his PhD, graduate student John P. Messick took over until the end of the study. Our results were summarized in the December 1973 issue of *Wildlife Monographs*, a publication of The Wildlife Society.

Wilbur, it should be noted, adapted quickly to the radio-collar phase and sometimes captured cats on his own, renewed tracking equipment, and followed.

"Easier than trackin' in the snow," he said. Wilbur's dogs also enjoyed a more leisurely measure of job security. We kept them leashed as we stalked the radio signals, then turned the hounds loose to quickly tree cats if we needed to check their health or replace their radio collars. During the study's last two years, we used a total of thirty-seven transmitters on the fifteen mountain lions and tried to locate each collared cougar every time we flew. On the ground, where line of sight from receiver to transmitter was usually required, we tracked only selected cougars. Once pinpointed, we plotted their locations on a map back at the ranch.

Lest anyone think we could cheat with the radio-tracking equipment and easily observe free-roaming mountain lions, the cats' propensity to secrecy and their innate alertness usually prevailed. By following the collars' steady beeping sounds, however, we were able to interpret various behaviors. In many instances, once the cats detected us, they froze. If we further approached, they'd sneak away rapidly. Sometimes a cougar remained motionless until we moved away. Only once did we document a lion actually approaching us and coming into the open.

"I threw a stick at her," Jack said, describing how a protective lioness with kittens slowly advanced toward him after he'd honed in on the family. "The stick broke over her shoulder, and she ran to cover."

In retrospect, it seemed the mountain lions exercised a "let-by-gones-be-bygones" attitude toward us throughout the study. Obviously, we harassed them when chasing and treeing with hounds, darting and drugging them, and lowering them to the ground to equip them with collars, colored tags, and tattoos. But after recovering, they quickly returned to being cougars in the wild.

When possible, we monitored the radio-collared lions' positions or movements from our camps. Sometimes they'd come within a few hundred yards. If the hounds got wind of them and became rowdy, the cats tended to move away. We also found tracks going directly through our camps after returning from being away for an extended time. In one instance, a lioness with kittens killed a cow elk within thirty yards of a camp. Based on our findings, I suspect that the mountain lions did most of their killing during the night or around dusk and sunrise. We know from tracks and telemetry that they also prowled in broad daylight and stalked game whenever an opportunity came along.

The insights and additional data garnered through radio collars didn't change our earlier findings from the capture–recapture days.

The information confirmed that in a stable wilderness environment, mountain lions regulate their own numbers and actually help prey animals maintain or increase their population numbers.

If the big tom Rex could talk, he'd probably confirm the research findings. He was the only mountain lion that remained in the study area from beginning to end. We recaptured him twenty-six times, more than any other cougar.

"Ol' Rex," Wilbur would say when we'd run into the cat. "Wonder what sort of mood he's in today."

Besides being a superb predator, Rex was a shrewd proprietor. He patrolled his Cave Creek territory with diligence, using his claws to scratch cougar "No Trespassing" signs into tree trunks. He neatly piled pine needles and other forest debris into little warning pyramids along trails. He urinated around these locations to make sure intruders got the message. When hungry and on the prowl, Rex would probably, as author Wallace Stegner wrote, "prickle the stillness and bring every living thing to the alert."

Rex also helped corroborate my theory on mutual avoidance. After equipping him with a radio collar, we documented his leaving his Cave Creek territory for several months to occupy the late Cannibal Tom's Rush Creek territory. Rex eventually returned to his original Cave Creek drainage, and another tom settled into the Rush Creek territory once occupied by Cannibal Tom. Our telemetry data and observations indicated it was a copacetic reshuffling with no fighting necessary.

But the cougar story didn't end there. While protected in our Big Creek study area, mountain lions were still being hunted as vermin throughout the rest of Idaho.

"A state of denial," Wilbur often scoffed.

With the study's end in sight, a defining skirmish in the cougar's fight for recognition was about to be waged in Idaho's political backwaters.

## CHAPTER THIRTY-SEVEN

# A Quiet Winning Salvo

A BLACK "LAST PLACE" RIBBON HAS HUNG IN MY OFFICE FOR THE BETTER part of half a century. It reminds me of Idaho's stature in 1972 when, despite being the first state to initiate and complete an in-depth mountain lion study, it had yet to reclassify the cougar as a game animal. All the other western states had done this.

Many wildlife researchers and managers prefer to separate themselves from politics—better to stay focused on critters and not get distracted by people. But from the beginning, if the study was to survive, I couldn't afford to be apolitical. I learned early on that some level of politics figured into every big decision we made.

So with the fieldwork about to be wrapped up, I poked a finger into Idaho's conservative political winds, took a reading, and decided to become a catalyst for mountain lion reclassification, from predator to game animal. Even though we were working on bobcat, wolverine, leopard, and bird-of-prey studies out of the cooperative unit, I considered this last dash toward mountain lion reclassification worth the challenge and a capstone of our decade of study. Members of the Fish and Game Commission were already on board but lacked legal authority. They agreed that we needed more political support. We needed politicians with experience, understanding, and clout, like my landlord.

Idaho State Senator Warren H. Brown of McCall rented us our first house in McCall on Payette Lake. He and I became friends and occasionally talked about the cougar study, and he was a supporter from the beginning.

By the time the reclassification issue surfaced, he was chairman of the Idaho Senate Fish and Game Committee.

"I'll carry the bill," he offered.

Brown's counterpart in the Idaho House of Representatives was J. Vard Chatburn, a sheep rancher who was also chairman of the House Resources and Conservation Committee. His affiliation with the Idaho Wool Growers Association posed a potential problem. But after we spoke several times and I addressed his concerns, he bought in. I found him to be a gentleman with a keen understanding of Idaho politics.

Bill Siddoway, president of both the Idaho Wool Growers Association and the National Wool Growers Association, was crucial. He had a reputation for being both approachable and reasonable. But I didn't know where he stood.

Finally, there was Warren Ahlstrom, supervisor of the U.S. Fish and Wildlife Service's predator control program in Idaho. He'd been overseeing mountain lion control for decades, and I saw his support as pivotal to changing the minds of dissidents.

I met first with Ahlstrom, figuring that convincing an old bounty hunter would win half the battle.

"This proposed legislation won't keep landowners, sheep ranchers, and other livestock people from killing marauding cougars," I explained. "If a mountain lion kills your sheep, you can shoot the mountain lion. It's written in the legislation. All this bill does is allow for management of cougars rather than indiscriminate killing of them."

Ahlstrom asked a few questions, and I recited some data from the study. "Well, hell," he finally said, "I guess we can't complain about that. I'll support it."

Next, Siddoway. I decided to ask Ahlstrom to accompany me. We scheduled a breakfast meeting in Burley, Idaho, where members of the state wool growers were holding a convention. Over eggs and lamb chops, I laid it on the line.

"The legislation is win-win," I said, assuring Siddoway that wool growers would be able to protect their flocks. "If a cougar goes after your sheep, you can kill it."

Idaho Governor Cecil Andrus signs, as the author watches, a bill on March 4, 1971, granting power to the Idaho Fish and Game Commission to declare cougars game animals worthy of management. *Photo courtesy of Idaho Fish and Game Department*

Siddoway looked at Ahlstrom. "What do you think of this?" he asked.

Ahlstrom glanced at me, then back at Siddoway, and answered, "I don't see any problems."

"Well okay," Siddoway agreed, folding his breakfast napkin. "I'm in. I'll go tell the boys."

And that was the end of it. After those meetings, I heard no more criticism from sheep and livestock industry people. For the most part, the outfitters, guides, and hunters were silent as well.

Hearings were held, and I testified. By then, legislators knew my pitch, so I kept it brief. There was discussion but no dissent. A vote was taken, and the bill passed. Finally, an enlightened science-driven swing in public opinion had prevailed over decades of fear and exaggeration.

Even Representative Walt Little, the stalwart supporter of the Idaho Wool Growers Association who previously fought to reverse the Big Creek cougar hunting closure, acquiesced.

"I might not be the sharpest lawmaker in the room," Little told me after the vote, "but I'm smart enough to get off the tracks when a locomotive is coming."

I wanted to gloat but didn't. Instead, we shook hands.

"Congratulations," he conceded.

"Thank you. It's been a long, necessary battle," I replied.

Idaho's cougar war was over. The cats won.

A few days later, on March 24, 1971, I was invited to the governor's office. There I watched Governor Cecil D. Andrus sign the bill into law.

The measure granted power to the Idaho Fish and Game Commission to declare the cougar a big game animal.

Almost a year later, on January 20, 1972, after months of lawyers crafting the necessary legalese, Fish and Game Commissioner Jack Hemingway, the son of Pulitzer Prize–winning author Ernest Hemingway, made the motion.

*"The Commission does hereby amend the classification of Game Animals, as adopted May 21, 1965, to include there with the mountain lion."*

The measure passed unanimously. As of that moment, cougars in Idaho would be judiciously managed and no longer indiscriminately slaughtered.

All these years later, I'm convinced everyone, including me, was simply too worn out to keep the battle going.

One year later, on February 7, 1973, a National Geographic Society film crew landed in two airplanes at Taylor Ranch and spent the next three weeks documenting the study. Producer Dennis Kane and his staff captured the essence of our work and introduced cougars to the world.

*Tracking the North American Mountain Lion* aired on television in 1974. A condensed version is included in a four-vignette National Geographic Society special titled *The Big Cats*. The latter can still be watched on YouTube and other cable and streaming outlets.

In one of the documentary's last scenes, a passive cougar, No. 46, is shown being lowered from a tall tree to be processed while her kittens watch curiously from above.

On the ground, the lioness lies on a bed of pine boughs, and the camera slowly zooms in on her penetrative eyes, then pulls away to make a panoramic sweep of the cat's home—the vast, snow-encumbered Big Creek drainage. With my voice dubbed over the final visuals of the documentary, I spoke from what my brain had learned then and what my heart still feels today:

*"Often people ask, why are you chasing these fine animals with dogs and drugging them and all this? I tell them it's the only way we can gather the kind of information that's necessary to preserve the species. We've learned that the lion is not nearly the menace to big game herds that he was thought to be. The mountain lion is not a wanton killer, and the animals it preys upon are not threatened with extinction. We've got the information, and people are beginning to listen. This is one of the big cats that I think is going to make it."*

When I listen to those long-ago words spoken in a much younger man's voice, I appreciate that friends still grant me an audience so I can talk about the cougar study, especially when they say, "Your memory is so good. You've aged well." I've learned to appreciate such compliments after realizing how indelible some experiences become. Luck, timing, and accomplishment have left enough giddyup in my step to finally write this overdue memoir and still look ahead.

If new scientific findings are to be implemented, they must be understood. I hope we have in a small way helped to achieve this with the mountain lion—my favorite of all the great cats. The very secretiveness that worked against cougars by giving rise to myths, misunderstandings, and fear also enabled them to survive. I'd like to think that, by skirting the edges of the seemingly impossible, our work in Big Creek helped pull cougars back from the cliffs of extinction.

# Epilogue

Not long after the National Geographic Society filming, Wilbur and I reunited and treed the study's last cougar to check her health for a final time. The lioness looked good. So we didn't drug her. We admired her.

"That'll be *my* last," Wilbur declared as we walked away. He and his hounds never chased another cat. Wilbur kept Red, his favorite, as a pet and gave away Ranger and Tiger to good homes.

I returned to my family and the Cooperative Wildlife Research Unit at the University of Idaho, remaining at the unit's helm for twelve more years. There I worked with passionate and stimulating graduate students on a variety of species, including bobcats and ocelots, wolverines and river otters. We also conducted groundbreaking research on leopards in Africa and jaguars in Brazil.

Then, in 1985, I created the Hornocker Wildlife Institute. The privately funded organization became a vehicle for research on big cats such as Siberian tigers and expanded research on cougars.

In New Mexico, the institute launched a ten-year mountain lion study to investigate the lifestyle of mountain lions in the high desert. We also established a project in Glacier National Park to examine the relationships between cougars and wolves. Following that work, we began a similar study in Yellowstone National Park. The Yellowstone effort grew into a fourteen-year study of cougar–wolf relationships and became the first intensive look at these two competing carnivores. Colleagues and I expanded the study south into the more human-populated Jackson Hole area, a similar adjoining ecosystem to Yellowstone but a drastically different environment for cougars.

Each study continued to demonstrate the mountain lion's versatility and adaptability in very different environments. Meanwhile, the fundamental truths we uncovered in Big Creek—territoriality, land tenure, and predatory effect—remained scientifically established.

Eventually, the radio-collar signals in Big Creek faded away, and the project's mountain lions died. Sometimes I imagine the offspring of Rex and other "ghost cats" roaming the bluffs, cliffs, and canyons like fleeting shadows. In recent years, introduced and competing wolves have joined the mountain lions at the apex. Perhaps the cougars have retreated even farther into Big Creek's fringes. But I envision ample numbers of mountain lions—cougars, pumas, screamers, catamounts, painters, panthers, "cats of one color," whatever name you prefer—going about their predatory business in central Idaho's ancient and mostly pristine ecosystem.

I didn't oppose the legal hunting of cougars and still don't as long as populations are thriving and regulated hunting is carried out in an ethical and respectful manner. In the fifty-odd years since mountain lions were reclassified as big game animals, they have made a remarkable recovery. From dangerously low numbers throughout the western United States, populations have increased significantly and expanded into historic ranges where they had not been found for decades. When compared to problems facing big cats worldwide, cougar recovery in North America approaches miraculous.

This turnaround happened without special federal commissions or congressional action. State wildlife agencies simply regulated hunting seasons, thereby stopping the wanton killing of cougars. It's a modern-day wildlife success story that ranks up there with the equally amazing bald eagle recovery. The two narratives illustrate what can be accomplished with scientific facts and realistic policies that recognize the biological, economic, and human cultural factors involved.

Recent cougar studies have rightfully focused on unstable populations that are heavily hunted or otherwise stressed by human encroachment. As both human and cougar populations expand, conflicts arise. Individual cougars may enter suburban settings, become emboldened, and pose potential threats to people and pets. In rare incidents, cougars have attacked and killed humans, sparking justified concern. How such situations are handled is key to future management decisions and conservation.

Individual cougars who become habituated with little or no fear of humans should be removed. They can be tranquilized and relocated in appropriate wild environments or in some cases humanely euthanized with full public disclosure. One "bad apple" cougar causing one bad incident can sway public opinion and detrimentally impact cougar conservation.

Technology today has given wildlife researchers almost unlimited opportunities to obtain quantitative information not available through conventional means, especially on elusive species like cougars. Global Positioning Systems (GPS) can provide around-the-clock access to an animal's location and, to some extent, its activities. Remote sensors can transmit body temperature, heart rate, and other physiological information. Satellite imagery can locate the animal in its environment, and cameras can be attached to species as small as hummingbirds to record daily activities. Behavior never seen for some species is now routinely observed. All that remains for the investigator is proper analysis and interpretation—the art, if you will, of understanding a species and its role in the environment.

But technology has its limitations. While the computer screen can show what happens, it often won't show what *does not* happen. It might not show, for example, when a cougar attacked an elk but failed or what route the cat mistakenly took during the stalk. Failure is just as important as success in fully understanding a species and how it functions within an ecosystem.

Aldo Leopold, sitting at a computer screen, would never have witnessed the death of a wolf and beheld the "fierce green fire dying in her eyes." That moment shaped his entire career as a conservationist and punctuates all these years later the need for continued presence in the natural world.

I hope this tale I've told about Rex, Hazel, Cannibal Tom, Bessie, and the other Big Creek cougars will inspire young scientists to use the digital-age wonders available, but I also hope they'll lace up their boots, enter the world's remaining wild places, and experience the thrill of in-person discovery.

And so, as we all age along this fascinating evolutionary timeline, I've written these final sentences heeding Wilbur Wiles's paraphrase of Albert Einstein's sage axiom: "The more you learn, the more you learn you don't know."

How true!

After the *National Geographic* magazine and television movie coverage, Wilbur became somewhat of a celebrity, and numerous media outlets featured him in stories. He continued to live a humble life in Big Creek and was admired by neighbors and those fortunate enough to meet him. Later in life, Wilbur married Katie Thrall, who had her own backcountry roots, and the two spent winters in Boise and then Arizona. Katie died in 1997.

Afterward, Wilbur continued to stay at his cabin during the summer, tending his garden and fishing in local trout streams and lakes. Young friends marveled when, at age eighty-five, he walked twenty-six miles in one day on the Big Creek trail. Each fall, he drove to Arizona, where he lived in modest quarters until the greening of springtime drew him back home to Big Creek.

As he in his wisdom often intoned, "Sometimes a man just has to change his ways."

Throughout the years, Wilbur and I became even closer. Although he wanted to die in the Big Creek backcountry he loved, he spent his final days in Veterans Administration hospice care in Boise.

The author and Wilbur Wiles on one of their first hunts at the beginning of the cougar study in December 1964. *Mike Stephen photo*

I visited Wilbur often there and for the last time on April 17, 2019. He died later that evening at the age of 103. A portion of Wilbur's ashes were interred in the Boise veterans' cemetery. I buried the bulk of his ashes just outside his beloved Big Creek cabin. Friends scattered the rest at Wilbur's Monumental Creek cabin, upstream from the mouth of Cougar Creek. There, the last of Wilbur Wiles's cremains settled on the bedrock of the wilderness where he had roamed for the better part of a century.

# Acknowledgments

Thanks to the late Dick Woodworth, former director of the Idaho Fish and Game Department, for his vision and commitment.

To the late Wilbur Wiles, wilderness mentor and best friend, indispensable from start to finish in carrying out fieldwork.

To Harry Bettis for his long-term support and friendship and for making this book possible.

To the late John Craighead for introducing me to a way of life and the joy of discovery and for literally forging my career.

To the late Ian McTaggert-Cowan for guidance and inspiration.

To Prosser Mellon of the Richard King Mellon Foundation for career support and encouragement.

To Linda Weiford for her editorial expertise.

To my colleagues at the Idaho Cooperative Wildlife Research Unit—Esther Louie and the late Elwood Bizeau—for overseeing the unit's various projects during my absences in the backcountry while wrapping up the cougar study.

To Joy Tutela, of the David Black Literary Agency, for her patience and professionalism in guiding me through the publishing process.

To the Idaho fish and game commissioners during the cougar study and to those who were steadfast in supporting my work from beginning to end.

To those organizations and agencies providing financial support: Idaho Fish and Game Department, University of British Columbia, National Geographic Society, New York Zoological Society (now Wildlife Conservation Society), American Museum of Natural History, and Idaho Cooperative Wildlife Research Unit.

# Index

Note: Page numbers in *italics* refer to photographs.

109–10, 119–20, 121–24, 130, 131, 144–46, 149, 177–78; returning home after, 152, 155–59; Wilbur's notes on cat captures, 116–18. *See also* Chamberlain Basin expansion

Big Creek season 1966–1967: beginning of, 158–59, 161–63; cougar 3 (Rex), 173–75, 188–89, 192; cougar 4 (Hazel), 177–78, 202; cougar 18 (Cannibal Tom), 179–81, 183, 198–99, 201, 219; cougar 29 (Bessie), 177, 189, 192–93; mystery men prowling study area, 168, 169, 172–73; numbered but unnamed cougars, 171–75, 177, 187, 192–95, 197–98, 201, 202; state legislators' meeting, 159–60

Big Creek season 1967–1968 and beyond: Chamberlain Basin lion reappearing, 267; Cooperative Unit position, 225–27; cougar 3 (Rex), 241–42, 254, 267, 268; cougar 4 (Hazel), 221, 238; cougar 18 (Cannibal Tom), 242, 267; cougar 29 (Bessie), 254, 268–69; hunters challenging research, 229–34; last cougar being treed, 279; numbered but unnamed cougars, 238, 239, 242–43, 254, 257, 267,

268; telemetry, 267–72; wildlife documentarian's work, 268–70; Wiles's correspondence about, 235–37

black bear encounters, 90, 96
Blackburn, Joe, 167
blue grouse, 93
Boone and Crockett Club, 55, 71, 210, 255
Brigham Young University Cougars, 98, 139–41
*Bring 'Em Back Alive* (Buck), 35
Brown, Warren H., 99–100, 273–74
Buck, Frank, 35

cabins and camps, 18–19. *See also* supplies for researchers
Cannibal Tom (No. 18): in second season, 135, 146; in third season, 179–81, 183, 198–99, 201, 219; in fourth season and beyond, 242
captive cougars. *See* Tommy and Flopsy (captive cougars)
Carlson family, 246–49
"The Cat: Good Guy or Bad?," 209–10
Cave Creek drainage, 118–19
Chamberlain Basin expansion: airdrops to, 134; checking on results, 129–33; colleagues joining project, 107–13; cougar sightings/taggings, 130–31, 132, 139, 254, 267;

keeping notes, *41*, 41–42; knowledge and determination of, 51; later years, 282–83; saving author's life, 199–201; summer activities, 152. *See also* Big Creek season 1964–1965; Big Creek season 1965–1966; Big Creek season 1966–1967; Big Creek season 1967–1968 and beyond; Chamberlain Basin expansion

Wisner, Frances Zaunmiller, 208–9
Wohletz, Ernest, 69–71, 79, 226–27, 262
Wood, Kevin, 256
Woodworth, John R. (Dick), 66, 69, 71, 79, 159–60, 163, 226–27, 232–33, 255

Yeager, Lee E., 227
Yellowstone National Park study, 279

# About the Authors

**Maurice Hornocker**, PhD, is a wildlife biologist best known for advancing our knowledge of the elusive mountain lion's behavior and ecology. During his fifty-five years of research in Idaho, New Mexico, Montana, Wyoming, and Yellowstone National Park, he published numerous scientific papers about cougars, as well as books, including *Cougar: Ecology and Conservation* (edited with Sharon Negri), *Yellow-stone Cougars* (coauthored with Toni K. Ruth and Polly C. Buotte), and *Desert Puma* (foreword). His writings, research results, and mountain lion photographs have appeared in publications such as *National Geographic*, *Smithsonian*, and *National Wildlife*. He and his colleagues have also conducted pioneering research on other big cat species throughout the world. Hornocker and his wife, Leslie, live in Bellevue, Idaho, with their bird dogs and dressage horses and a domestic cat named Redd.

**David Johnson** is a retired roving regional reporter-columnist from the *Lewiston Tribune* in Lewiston, Idaho. He holds bachelor's degrees in wildlife mangament from the University of Minnesota and journalism from the University of Idaho. Johnson lives with his wife, Linda Weiford, in Moscow, Idaho.